Timeless Problems In History

Timeless Problems
in History

BY BERNARD NORLING

UNIVERSITY OF NOTRE DAME PRESS
NOTRE DAME   LONDON
1970

Library of Congress Catalog Card Number: 71–105726

Manufactured in the United States of America by
NAPCO Graphic Arts, Inc.

To Mary

Preface

Some 30,000 new titles are published every year in the United States. The author of an academic book which is not based on research in original source materials ought, therefore, to offer some justification for adding to this mountain of paper. I cannot allege that this volume contains information never before revealed or that it is replete with insights of surpassing originality and brilliance. Such subjects as the role of force in human affairs, inevitability and contingency in history, and whether human differences are innate or acquired, have been discussed exhaustively for 2500 years. Hundreds, even thousands, of volumes have been written about questions like these. Indeed, that is the heart of the matter. All the chapters in this book are the outgrowth of questions asked repeatedly by students in my classes. When a student raises his hand to inquire whether such a thing as national character exists, whether revolutions are generally helpful or harmful to humanity, or whether the strongest and wealthiest nations are also the most advanced culturally, a hopeless dilemma ensues. Such questions cannot be answered simply, briefly, and on the spot; the issues are too complex and subtle. At the same time, it avails little to tell the student that 700 books have been written on the subject and that he should read some of them.

This book attempts to grapple with this condition. Within the compass of one volume it tries to indicate the complexity of six of the most puzzling problems that have always been involved in the study of history, and to point to some of the likelier answers and conclusions. It is hoped that the reader will thereby be stimulated to think more realistically about history and will gain an appreciation of some of its "imponderables." The book is not aimed at any specific academic audience. It is hoped that both graduate students and undergraduates, history majors and non-majors, will find it profitable. Not least, it is hoped that secondary school teachers of history will find it a stimulus to their own teaching, particularly since it is in high school that so many young people first develop their lifelong interest in (or, unhappily, aversion to) history.

My thanks are due to the University of Notre Dame for financial support which enabled me to spend two summers in research and writing; to my friends Dr. Charles Poinsatte of St. Mary's College, Dr. Ralph Weber of Marquette University, and Dr. Ramon Abarca of Canisius College who read the manuscript and offered many valuable criticisms; to my friends and colleagues at Notre Dame, the late Rev. Thomas T. McAvoy, C.S.C., Professor M. A. Fitzsimons, and Professor Harvey Bender, who aided me in various ways; to my student assistants Robert Brian Cass, Kenneth Wolf, W. Marquis Anderson, Thomas Jones, Jeffrey Sobosan and Richard Wall; and to Mrs. Joan Austin who did much of the typing.

It is conventional at this point to add that "any mistakes or omissions are, of course, my own"—when the author obviously thinks there aren't any of either. In a book like this one, where many personal judgments are inevitable, it is nearer the truth to say that all the opinions expressed are my own and that not a few of them have been maintained over the demurs of those who have helped me.

My employment of footnotes, likewise, diverges from the norm. Since many of the contentions in the book cannot be "proved" by the conventional citation of sources, footnotes are included primarily as a guide to interesting books which contain a fuller discussion of many of the issues raised here.

Bernard Norling
December, 1969

Contents

*History would not be what it is, the record
of man's crimes and follies, if logic and decency
governed its events and great decisions.
(Ladislas Farago)*

I

ILLUSIONS IN HISTORY

What People Think

One cannot study any branch of history very long without becoming aware that what people *think* is true is often more important in its consequences than what actually is true. No individual can be understood without understanding the ideas (and illusions) that are in his mind. Neither can a whole society, since its character is determined heavily by the picture it has of itself and what it aspires to be.[1]

Columbus would not have sailed west in 1492 had he not underestimated the circumference of the earth by a third and believed that six-sevenths of its surface was land. Precisely *who* sank the *Maine* in 1898 was not important. What was vital was the general American belief that Spaniards sank it, for this conviction soon produced the Spanish-American War. Abraham Lincoln declared that preservation of the Union was more important than whether slavery was abolished or retained. Yet he lives in popular imagination as the emancipator of slaves and the friend of Negroes. Whether James II of England (1685–1688) strove to establish Catholic supremacy in England or whether he aimed only to secure

---

[1] For a discussion of this general principle cf. John Lukacs, *A New History of the Cold War* (N.Y.: Doubleday, 1966), especially pp. 300–301. "It is a great mistake to believe that ideas are superstructures of life. . . . This is not so. For human beings (and human beings alone) life is inseparable from the idea of life: ideas, conceptions, theories, are permanent and frequent formative factors in life and history . . . the important thing, always in the short run, and especially in democratic ages, is not so much what happened but what people think happens."

1

legal equality for his co-religionists can never be known for certain since it is impossible to read the mind of a man who died more than two and a half centuries ago. The king said he sought only equality, but the important aspect of the matter is that the majority of his Protestant subjects were convinced that he aimed at Catholic supremacy. Accordingly, they drove him off his throne in the "Glorious Revolution" of 1688 and thereby changed the whole course of British history.

At about the same time the shape of continental European history was altered dramatically by the combined delusions and greed of one man, the Hapsburg Holy Roman Emperor Leopold I (1658–1705). In 1700 the pathetic, and childless Spanish king, Charles II, was near death. He indicated a willingness to make over about 90 percent of the vast Spanish empire to his Hapsburg relatives. Louis XIV of France, far the most powerful monarch in Europe, did not welcome this arrangement but he was willing to accept it; to be content with a modest compensation for France rather than fight a major war over the inheritance. Leopold, however, shared a popular contemporary notion that Charles II was bewitched. From this he concluded that if his diplomatic agents in Madrid worked closely with various clerical exorcists there they could undo the bewitchment and persuade poor Charles II and his queen to revise their will and leave the *entire* Spanish empire to the Hapsburgs. Thus he vetoed all proposals to divide the empire. Eventually Louis XIV concluded that if France was going to have to fight to secure a small portion of the immense inheritance she might as well fight for all of it. For thirteen years the War of the Spanish Succession raged over Europe and portions of the New World. Long after the avaricious Leopold I was in his grave it was not a Hapsburg but a grandson of Louis XIV who mounted the throne of Spain and took possession of most of her European territories and her whole overseas empire.[2]

---

[2] For a fascinating discussion of the personal factors that entered into these transactions see John Langdon-Davies, *Carlos: the King Who Would Not Die* (Englewood Cliffs, N.J.: Prentice-Hall, 1963).

All modern history testifies that popular discontent is due not so much to whether or not people prosper economically but to what they *think* about their condition. According to such standard economic indicators as production and trade statistics, personal incomes, and revenues from taxation, the French nation and most French people were more prosperous in 1789 than their ancestors had been in 1715, 1740, or 1765. Yet the French Revolution did not begin in the earlier years but in 1789. The main reason was that popular attitudes had changed. Ancient grievances that had once been regarded as part of the immutable nature of things, to be endured with resignation, were now looked upon as intolerable because the avant-garde intellectuals of the age (philosophes) had declared them to be both unreasonable and unnecessary. Likewise, most Frenchmen in 1940 were better off than their fathers had been in 1914. Yet France fought with tenacity and valor in the First World War but collapsed ignominiously within a month at the beginning of World War II. One of the chief differences lay in the minds of millions of Frenchmen. Divided by a dozen political feuds, disgruntled, disillusioned, and haunted by memories of the frightful bloodletting of the first war, they simply had no stomach for a second.

In our century the myths surrounding the whole subject of race vex us constantly. Unhappily, the core of the matter is not one of trying to ascertain a fact: whether racism is scientifically sound; whether it makes sense. The crux of the matter is that innumerable millions in every part of the earth *are* racists and act on racist assumptions, thereby poisoning the relations of white with colored peoples everywhere—not to speak of exacerbating such relatively parochial animosities as those of Germans and Slavs, Hindus and Moslems, Walloons and Flemings, Catalans and Castilians.[3]

Military history is particularly replete with instances of illusions being more important than realities. In 1187 an army of Christian crusaders violated every canon of military

[3] This whole subject is discussed at length in Chapter V.

sanity by venturing into the burning Palestinian desert to do battle with the Moslem legions of the brilliant Egyptian caliph, Saladin. Outnumbered, and short of both food and water, the Christians were nonetheless confident of victory because they believed they possessed a portion of the true cross. True cross or no, they were annihilated. Within two years Saladin took Jerusalem and deprived the Christians of most of the conquests they had made in the First Crusade of the preceding century (1096–1099).

The Hundred Years' War (1337–1453) between England and France illustrates even more clearly the disasters that commonly result from cherishing unrealistic military ideas. The English longbow was the deadliest weapon of the Middle Ages, as the French discovered at Crecy in 1346 when their armored and mounted knights charged a British fixed position and were massacred by English and Welsh archers. But the French drew the wrong conclusion from the experience. They decided that their error had been to fight on horseback! Accordingly, ten years later at Poitiers they dismounted and charged the British lines on foot. Once again they were decimated by a hail of arrows. Sixty years later at Agincourt (1415) they were still unable to believe that it was really possible for social inferiors, mere peasants, to stand on the ground and defeat brave gentlemen who fought in the proper *chivalrous* fashion: mounted, encased in fine armor, wielding sword and lance. Thus there ensued another charge by feudal cavalry, another slaughter by the fearsome archers, and the conquest of most of France by the English king, Henry V.

More recent military history has been no less instructive. After suffering defeats in several wars against the Holy Roman Empire since 1680 the Turks were forced to cede many of their Balkan territories to the empire at the Treaty of Passarowitz in 1718. The lesson they drew from their set-backs was correct: their military machine had grown obsolete. Accordingly, they imported Bonneval, a French artilleryman, to refurbish it. Soon a new round of wars against the empire developed. This time the Turks were victorious, but mostly because rash European generals allowed their armies to be surrounded and cut off. The Turks, however, attributed their success to the innovations of Bonneval. Worse, they assumed that their military superiority over Europeans was now established permanently, and concluded that they need do nothing further to revamp their armies. In the next generation the Ottoman Empire remained at peace, while in those same years the Europeans were engaged in two of the greatest conflicts of the whole century, the War of the Austrian Succession (1740–1748) and the Seven Years' War (1756–1763). In the course of these conflicts they learned a great deal and modernized their armies. The next time the Turks went to war (against Russia) they were crushed and forced to sign the humiliating Treaty of Kuchuk Kainardji (1774). Never again did they catch up with the West militarily; indeed they soon stopped making any serious effort to do so.

The Character of Written History

Why do so many people grotesquely misread history in this fashion? Why do they misunderstand their own times, cherish myths and illusions, and fail to comprehend the very existence of important forces at work all about them? There are many reasons. Two of the most important relate to the character of historical sources and the interests of professional historians.

Some written history is based on coins, inscriptions, archaeological findings, and similar materials, but the bulk of it is based on written sources: annals, memoirs, charters, government records, literary works, and the like. Who produces such materials? Literate people, obviously. Yet at any time before the nineteenth century literate people were only a small minority in the whole population of any country. Moreover, they were not representative of past societies as wholes. What did they write about? What they knew most about, what interested them, what they thought most important. Above all, they wrote a great deal about people like themselves.

Peasants were a large numerical majority in every society before the Industrial Revolution, and they did most of the physical work necessary to support the whole society. Yet nearly all of them were illiterate; so they wrote almost nothing about their farms, their animals, their tools, their problems, hopes, or aspirations. Inventors, tinkerers, "practical" men who devised better ways to extract minerals, refine metals, make cloth, or color glass, profoundly influenced the character of their societies and the course of history; but they too were often illiterate, and even if not were usually of a nonliterary turn of mind and so wrote little. Much the same was true of merchants. Who, then, were the chroniclers in past societies? In the Middle Ages, to take an obvious example, most of them were ecclesiastics. Not surprisingly, they wrote disproportionately about the deeds, problems, and interests of the Church. Many of them deliberately omitted references to peasants or merchants because they did not want to bore educated or aristocratic readers by describing the prosaic doings of social inferiors. For such reasons as these, certain features of the past are known much more fully than others, and an unbalanced view of history has often been created in the popular mind.

More recently there has developed a widespread and growing realization that history has been shaped as much by the incidence of plagues and famines, the state of medical knowledge, changes in agricultural techniques, and the development of technology, as it has by the deeds of statesmen and soldiers. Yet most professional historians are still humanists in training and interest. They are much more conversant with constitutions, proclamations, treaties, and ideologies than they are with germs, soil types, tools, and industrial processes—and their works show it.

To appreciate the extent to which history is moulded by who writes it, one has only to ask himself how modern European history would appear had it been written by explorers and colonial administrators instead of academic historians. Most of the latter have lived their lives in the "mother country." They have looked at most things through the eyes of the government and from the standpoint of its European interests. Suppose their books had been written by such great French colonial administrators as Dupleix in eighteenth century India or Marshal Lyautey in twentieth century North Africa —men who gnashed their teeth in disgust as they saw opportunities thrown away to gain or hold vast overseas territories containing millions of people and fabulous wealth. And why were the opportunities missed? Because Paris was preoccupied with some squabble over a country town in the Rhineland or a few square miles of rocks and snow in the Savoyard Alps. Suppose British imperial history had been written by Robert Clive (d. 1774), or Cecil Rhodes (d. 1902), men who must have cursed and despaired at the scant support accorded them when they were trying to add half a continent to the British realm while in London the government of the day was engrossed with some wretched piece of Irish land legislation, or what Thomas Cromwell (d. 1540) once referred to derisively as "a few dog holes in France."

It is one of the ironies of our own time that in many ways historical truth has become even harder to ascertain than it used to be, and the power of myths has become more potent. In our century millions of copies of newspapers appear each day, books are published in the tens of thousands annually, information of every conceivable sort spews forth from radio and television, every organization above the level of a garden club keeps voluminous records, and everyone of even minor importance in public life keeps a diary, publishes his memoirs, or becomes the subject of a "study." The very flood of information bewilders the historian. He scarcely knows where to begin his researches: he would have to outlive Methusaleh to complete them. At the same time, *vital* information is denied him because important decisions (often the most important) in public affairs can now be made via unrecorded telephone conversations. Much information is also denied him because totalitarian and democratic governments alike suppress, destroy, or distort it. Moreover, ghost

writers and "collaborators" confuse it, journalists compete
with governments in manipulating it, and a host of propagandists, advertisers, lobbyists, and pollsters befog and debase
the whole intellectual atmosphere. Determining the truth
about the most important matters often becomes quite impossible. Who, for instance, knows the real origins of Politburo
decisions or the Eisenhower Doctrine?

In this environment the power of mythology grows immensely, for all the factors which bedevil the work of historians also profoundly shape the imaginations of hundreds
of millions of ordinary folk—and in a democratic age one
can hardly overrate the power of public opinion to form the
ideas of societies and the policies of governments. In our age,
beyond all others, what people *suppose* to be the case has become more significant than what a logician would call "realities." Contemporary "history" seems to be fast becoming not
a collection of "facts" that can be documented in archives,
but what we remember, what we believe, what we imagine.[4]

The Tyranny of the Past

Man's understanding of the present is also persistently
distorted by his attachment to the past. This attachment has
many facets.

A. *Habit*—Perhaps the most basic is sheer inertia. People
are creatures of habit, prone to think in familiar terms, act
in familiar ways, judge according to established principles
and customs. This tendency is so ingrained and obvious as to
constitute something close to instinct. Much of the time it is
a sound instinct. Human nature, after all, is constant in that
at all times and places normal men seek food, shelter, and
human companionship. It is relatively constant in that most

[4] The changing character of historical knowledge and historical awareness
is the principal theme of an exceptional book, at once illuminating and
subtle, by John Lukacs, *Historical Consciousness, or the Remembered Past*
(New York: Harper & Row, 1968), especially pp. 33–89. Though it is not
easy going, this is a most rewarding work for the serious student of history.

men habitually desire power over their fellows and seek exclusive possessions; that they normally defend their families and possessions against other men; and that they are generally hostile to men of other tribes or cultures.

Even when the *particular manifestations* of human nature vary from one culture or one historical epoch to another the fundamental sameness remains apparent. Religion was a major component of most sixteenth century European wars; those of the seventeenth and eighteenth centuries were waged mostly for territory, trade, and dynastic aggrandizement; while those since 1792 have been fought for a variety of secular ideologies, chiefly democracy, fascism, communism, and nationalism. Our ancestors of the Reformation era stabbed, shot, hanged, and burned one another because they could not bear each other's shameful theologies. Very few of their descendants any longer care enough about religion to persecute anyone: instead they shoot, gas, incinerate, and bomb one another because some have skins of a disagreeable color; others (Jews, gypsies, Slavs) belong to inferior races; others (landlords, kulaks) are members of obsolete or oppressive social classes; and still others (Fascists, Communists, plutocratic capitalists) are infected with poisonous political and economic doctrines. Thus the *excuses* men allege when they are cruel and intolerant to their fellows have changed considerably in 400 years, and so have the *particular ways* in which they choose to be cruel. But their impulse to cruelty has not.

B. *Veneration of the Past*—Men often cling to out-of-date ideas because they admire certain portions of the past and wish to preserve them. Sometimes this is a conscious, deliberate process which causes a distortion of both the present *and* the past.

. . . it helps immensely to understand why the leaders of the American and French Revolutions acted and thought as they did if we know what their idea of classical history was. They desired, to put it simply, to be virtuous republicans, and to act the part. Well, they were able to act the part of virtuous republicans much more effectively because they carried around in their heads an idea, or ideal if you prefer, of Greek republicanism and Roman virtue. But of course their own desire to be virtuous republicans had a great influence in making them think the Greeks and Romans whom they had been taught to admire by reading the classics in school, were virtuous republicans too. Their image of the present and future and their image of the classical past were inseparable, bound together—were really one and the same thing.[5]

Most often, veneration of the past is not contrived but natural. Centuries after the downfall of the Roman Empire the tradition of world empire remained firmly rooted in the imaginations of Western men. So did the belief that all Christian states should be animated by a single set of ethical and political ideals. Consequently, European kings and statesmen still talked and dreamed about "Christendom" and the "Holy Roman Empire" centuries after either concept had ceased to have any practical meaning. Germanic kings like Otto the Great (936–973) and Frederick Barbarossa (1152–1190) called themselves "Holy Roman Emperor" and posed as the heirs of the Caesars. A thousand years after the fall of Rome, dreamers like Charles the Bold of Burgundy (1467–1477) and the moronic Charles VIII of France (1483–1498) still entertained schemes to revive the ancient universal empire. Charles VIII even planned to reunite its eastern and western branches by having himself crowned emperor in Constantinople. It required that irreverent scion of the French Revolution, Napoleon Bonaparte, to finally abolish the Holy Roman Empire in 1806.[6]

The career of perhaps the most famous of all Holy Roman emperors, Charles V (1519–1556), demonstrates admirably the enormous importance of mere conservative respect for

---

[5] Carl Becker, "What Are Historical Facts?," *Western Political Quarterly*, September 1955, pp. 336–37.

[6] But even Napoleon realized that people's sentimental attachment to ancient dreams might be useful to himself. On more than one occasion he referred with studied casualness, to "my predecessor Charlemagne."

what is ancient and customary. Charles was the most influential figure in European international politics for half a century. He had some admirable qualities of character and he was not without political skill, but he was oblivious to the attractiveness—even to the meaning—of the most inflammatory conceptions of that revolutionary age. Though he was a genuine Catholic (not merely a political one) he never thought of himself as the champion of Catholic Europe against Protestantism. The reason was that his preoccupations were essentially those of Dante (1265–1321): to organize Europe under the aegis of the Holy Roman Empire and then lead Christendom in a new crusade against the infidel Turks. He viewed himself not as the leader of one Christian party against another but as the head and judge of them all. He never understood Lutheran theology and never considered this important. Why? Simply because he could not conceive that the whole Christian tradition had been wrong for 1500 years and now at last had been set right by a single monk. To him Lutheranism was only a screen behind which rebellious German princes sought to undermine imperial authority, just as other princes had long employed other pretexts in pursuit of the same unworthy object. Thus Charles V saw no incongruity in keeping Lutheran chaplains in his armies even when fighting Lutheran princes. For years he tried to compose the raging religious vendettas of the age by conventional diplomacy: by persuading the rival sectarians to meet, make some concessions to each other, and agree to accept some compromise theological formulas. Then all should renew their allegiance to the emperor and go to work on the real problem: fighting the Turks. The emperor was so serious about his grand design that he once proposed to his most persistent enemy, Francis I of France (1515–1547), that the two of them give up warring against each other and fight a personal duel. The winner would then lead the combined armies of both against the Turks. King Francis, a less romantic and less medieval type, declined.

On a lesser scale, one of the emperor's pet schemes was

to revive the old duchy of Burgundy which had been partitioned by Louis XI of France and Charles' own grandfather in 1477. This project has always looked ludicrously impractical to later generations but Charles was in earnest about it all his life. In old age he married his son Philip to the English Queen Mary Tudor (1553–1558). He hoped thereby to restore symbolically the Anglo-Burgundian alliance of the previous century and to get an English base for operations in the Low Countries that might ultimately lead to the actual resurrection of Burgundy. Not surprisingly, Charles V's policies were seldom crowned with success.

Probably no institution in the Western world has been so heavily encrusted with conservatism, so respectful of mere tradition, as the papacy. In part this has been due simply to the fact that the papacy heads a vast religious organization, and religious organizations tend to be conservative. Other factors have intensified this proclivity, however. Most popes are old men when elected and they are served by other old men in the curia. Old men seldom change their habits or ideas rapidly. Moreover since 1524 all popes have been Italians, born and raised in a country that is in a formal sense solidly Catholic. They have had difficulty appreciating the problems and attitudes that characterize religiously mixed societies. These considerations go far to account for such anomalies as papal plans for crusades against the Turks as late as 1716, and that blanket condemnation of modern libertarian ideas: Pope Pius IX's *Syllabus of Errors* (1864).

Ironically, the political Left, a "progressive" force virtually by definition, is often chained to the past as remorselessly as any pope or Holy Roman emperor. The many factions that comprise the "Left" in twentieth century France, for example, have squabbled constantly, agreeing only in their loyalty to a memory and their common opposition to "reaction." The memory is the French Revolution. "Reaction" is an amorphous mixture of monarchy, clericalism, bourgeois attitudes, aristocracy, and "the 200 families."

Diplomatic history is full of disasters and missed opportunities that derived from the inability to abandon ideas rendered inapplicable by changed circumstances. In 1870 France went to war with Prussia over an issue that would have been realistic 300 years earlier but was grotesquely out of date in the nineteenth century. Bismarck, the chancellor of Prussia, wanted to place a member of the Hohenzollern dynasty (who ruled Prussia) on the throne of Spain. If he succeeded, France would be surrounded geographically by lands ruled by members of the same family. More than three centuries earlier France had been similarly surrounded by the lands of the Holy Roman Emperor Charles V and had been forced to fight for a generation to preserve her national independence. By 1870, however, kings had far less power than in the sixteenth century and public opinion had grown vastly more important. Thus it was unrealistic to assume that two modern nations as markedly different in religion, psychology, and national tradition as Spain and Prussia would pursue a united anti-French foreign policy merely because of the accident that they happened to have kings (of different religions at that) who came from the same family. Nonetheless France declared war against Prussia. She was heavily defeated and lost two of her valuable provinces, Alsace and Lorraine.

Attachment to obsolete ideas is most tragic when it perpetuates cruelty and exploitation. Such was the case with divine right monarchy. The incredible strength of the idea itself is indicated by the doglike devotion to their kings which typified European peasants for many centuries. To be sure, some monarchs deserved the devotion. Many others were normal, moderate, reasonable men. Some, however, were insane, and many were grim tyrants who taxed without mercy and committed crimes without number. Yet the attitude of the ordinary peasant usually was that if only good King Louis, or Henry, or Wenceslas knew what his rascally advisers, governors, and tax collectors were doing he would punish them and end the injustices. The manner in which the English rebels flocked to young Richard II in 1381 and accepted his assurances and promises during the Peasants Rebellion of that year is one of the clearest examples of the depth of popular attachment to monarchy. As late as 1905 thousands of Russian peasants and city workers marched peaceably to petition Czar Nicholas II, confident that if only they could see him personally he would act as the father of his people and redress their grievances.

Tragically, scores of European kings exploited and abused this loyalty for centuries, eventually destroying it. Yet it is pointless to rebuke them on this score. Centuries ago they and their contemporaries alike considered the business of rulers to be the strengthening of the state, the defense of religion, and the pursuit of glory. Before the middle of the eighteenth century almost nobody conceived of the state as an agent to promote material prosperity and social justice for the masses.[7] Ironically, absolute monarchy began to disintegrate in popular affection at precisely the time when it *did* begin to acquire a conscience and a sharpened taste for efficiency. No rulers ever worked harder to modernize their nations and improve the lives and prosperity of their subjects than such "enlightened despots" as Frederick the Great of Prussia (1740–1786) and Joseph II (1780–1790) of Austria. Unhappily for monarchy, they lived too late. The democratic ideas enshrined in the books of Rosseau and the example of the newly created United States of America were being set before an increasingly literate and restive public. Critics no longer wanted to reform monarchy; they wanted to abolish it.

C. *Economic Thought*—Economic practice, quite as much as political and military thinking, has been burdened with the excess baggage of obsolescence. Sixteenth and seventeenth century Europeans subscribed to a set of economic beliefs and

---

[7] For a consideration of the fruitlessness of reproaching our ancestors for not sharing our preoccupations cf. *Infra.*, pp. 24–26.

Perhaps it is indicative of the extremism that characterizes so much of Russian history that exploitation of monarchical sentiment was there the most heartless, and destruction of popular faith the most sudden and violent. On "Bloody Sunday" (1905) the demonstrators were fired on by royal troops. Several hundred were killed and 3000 wounded. The monarchy itself collapsed in blood and ruins only twelve years later, soon after it had begun a serious reform program. Cf. *Infra.*, p. 144.

practices known as mercantilism. The core of mercantilism was the belief that a nation must have a favorable balance of trade, for this would assure the steady acquisition of gold and silver, metals which were regarded as the true source of national wealth and strength. By 1700 these traditional mercantilist doctrines had been modified considerably in the minds of Europe's leading economic thinkers. Many of them had become convinced that production and trade were the true sources of national power. These more sophisticated views affected the world of deeds but little, however, for those who held them were not kings and chancellors. The latter, the men who actually *ran* European governments, still believed for another century in the older, bullionist conception of mercantilism and acted according to its precepts.

D. *The History of Science*—The same condition has prevailed in the world of science. For centuries scientific advance was blocked because virtually everyone clung to certain ways of thinking about a few simple but extremely important things. Everyone assumed that the natural state of a body was to be at rest and that the only scientific problem was to explain why it assumed motion and was kept in motion. Nearly everyone took it for granted that the earth was the center of the universe. In medicine, the authority of Galen was regarded with such superstitious awe that dissectors and surgeons who saw bodily structures at variance with Galen's descriptions concluded not that Galen was wrong but that their own observation was faulty. It was not until the sixteenth and seventeenth centuries that a few geniuses dynamited these great dams in human mental processes. When Copernicus at last posited that the sun rather than the earth was the center of the universe, when Vesalius challenged the authority of Galen, and when Galileo developed the idea of inertia—then it became possible for succeeding generations to add rapidly to man's knowledge in many branches of science.[8]

[8] For an elaboration of this theme see Chaps. 1–3 in Herbert Butterfield, *The Origins of Modern Science* (London: G. Bell, 1957). This splendid little book is informative, thought-provoking, attractively written, and devoted to a fascinating subject.

E. *Old Hatreds*—Europeans are somewhat more prone than Americans to be enslaved by old ideas because their history is much longer and their societies have generally been more static. Moreover, they have suffered much more at each other's hands than have different groups of Americans. As a result Europeans notoriously have a far more vivid sense of the past than Americans, particularly when recalling their grievances or savoring some symbolic revenge on an ancient enemy. To many Irishmen the barbarities committed by Cromwell's troops in the 1650s are as real as if they had happened yesterday. Bulgarians still describe with suppressed rage how the Byzantine Greeks blinded 99 out of every 100 Bulgar war prisoners and then put out one of the eyes of each hundredth man—nearly 1000 years ago. To humiliate the defeated and despised French, the victorious Prussians in 1871 crowned William I emperor of Germany not on German soil but in the Hall of Mirrors in the Versailles palace built by Louis XIV. To achieve a symbolic revenge after World War I, the victorious Allies convened the Versailles peace conference on the forty-eighth anniversary of that humiliation and made the defeated Germans sign a peace treaty in that same room in that same palace. In 1940 Hitler forced the defeated French to sign an armistice in the same railroad car where beaten Germany had signed hers in 1918—even taking the car out of a Paris museum and hauling it back to the same spot for the occasion. Some of Hitler's predecessors in 1914 showed an even more ravenous appetite for symbolic humiliation. At that time the president of France was Raymond Poincare. Born in Lorraine, a province Germany had taken from France in 1871, Poincare had been anti-German throughout a long political life. When war broke out again between France and Germany in 1914, German troops converted into a military latrine the portion of a Lorraine cemetery occupied by deceased members of the Poincare family.

In the darkest days of World War II most of France was occupied by Germany and the rest was ruled by a German satellite state, the Vichy regime. Any chance that France might regain her independence seemed to depend entirely on whether beleaguered Britain could somehow, sometime, in some way, stop and then roll back the German juggernaut. At such a time Pierre Laval, the strongest figure in the Vichy government, proudly showed the American ambassador a battlefield where France had once won a great victory. Afterward he displayed a huge mural in his house depicting the same victory. Was it a victory over the Germans? No! It was a victory that had been gained over the detested English in the Hundred Years' War five centuries before.[9] Similar examples could be cited by the score. They all demonstrate how rational thought by entire nationalities, and therefore rational action by their governments, is often precluded merely by persistent memories of old wrongs and humiliations.

Sometimes hatreds are a good deal more personal and less important than those enumerated above, and yet still seriously distort the historical record. A case in point is that modern phenomenon, the "debunking" writer. His most obvious characteristic is an inability to endure the suggestion that a public figure might possess virtue, rectitude, or energy superior to his own. Several of the species, most notably Lytton Strachey, have severely damaged the historical reputations of Florence Nightingale, General George Gordon, and other eminent Victorians, creating myths about these figures that may never entirely die.[10]

F. *Old Fears*—Sometimes obsolete attitudes persist because something akin to mass mental paralysis has been induced by fear or by memories of a dreadful past. A curious case of this type involves the general abstention from the use of gas in warfare since 1918. Gas was used widely in World War I and rapidly acquired a "horror" reputation. This happened partly because its first employment came as a complete surprise and caused great shock, partly because many veter-

[9] Robert Murphy, *Diplomat Among Warriors* (N.Y.: Pyramid Books, 1965), pp. 73–74.

[10] Esme Wingfield-Stratford, *Truth in Masquerade* (London: Williams & Norgate, 1951) discusses this point at length. Cf. especially pp. 186–208.

ans of that war who had been gassed came home with their respiratory systems severely damaged, and partly because "Sunday Supplement" writers turned out reams of lurid prose about gas in the 1920s and 1930s. Hence gas came to be regarded as a peculiarly barbaric weapon. In fact gases of the pre-1940 variety were among the most humane weapons ever devised. Proportionately, far fewer men died from gas in the 1914–1918 war than from wounds caused by rifle, machine gun, or artillery fire. On the narrowest humanitarian grounds, the high explosives, phosphorous bombs, and napalm that were used so freely in World War II and subsequent conflicts are more frightful weapons than gas because they inflict greater suffering on those hit by them. Yet despite the fact that gas would have been extremely useful for the Allies to employ against surrounded and beleaguered Germany in 1943–1945, and by the United States against Japan on small, wet, jungle-covered Pacific islands in the same years, public sentiment was so emotionally hostile to it that it was not used.

A much more important example of this kind relates to the whole Appeasement Era of the 1930s. In that decade the English and French in particular (but most of the Western world as well, in spirit), tried to placate the Fascist dictators, Hitler and Mussolini, by making concessions to them. The effort, culminating in the infamous Munich Agreement of 1938, was a ghastly failure and a direct cause of World War II. Not everyone in Western countries was blind to the ultimate aims of these dictators, but for years the wills of the vast majority were paralyzed. On the political Right, fear and hatred of the Communist regime in Russia was so intense that many accorded Hitler and Mussolini a grudging respect as men who knew how to deal with domestic "Bolsheviks" and who formed a barrier against the spread of the Communist contagion. Many on the political Left yearned to bring Hitler down but their minds were suffused with fantasies about the "unfairness" to defeated Germany of the Treaty of Versailles; the "missed opportunities" to placate a democratic German government in the 1920s; the "necessity" to disarm in order to give good example to the dictators; the "vital need" to support the League of Nations; and assorted socialist dogmas about the untrustworthiness of capitalist governments. Thus in practice, the policies they proposed not only would not have checked Hitler but if implemented would have enabled him to conquer all Europe.[11] Paradoxically, the "lessons" of the Appeasement Era have been learned so thoroughly that in almost any international dispute since 1946 if either side proposes to negotiate or mediate, there immediately arises a chorus of denunciations of "appeasement" and warnings to avoid "another Munich." "No appeasement" has become a substitute for thought and effort, a slogan to be automatically invoked everytime somebody suggests that one should try to settle disputes with other nations by a negotiated compromise rather than holding adamantly to one's own position regardless of the risk of war.

Sometimes the fears that shape history are less blatant than the foregoing but no less real or influential. A case in point is the hardihood of "The Whig Interpretation of History." Most modern Englishmen think the noblest accomplishment of their country has been to develop and bequeath to the rest of the world free political institutions; institutions which in the twentieth century contrast sharply to the brutal totalitarianism that prevails in so many lands. Of course the civil wars between king and Parliament in seventeenth century England seem a particularly dramatic chapter in the struggle of liberty against despotism. Consequently there has been a persistent tendency to link the gradual democratization of Britain in the eighteenth, nineteenth, and twentieth centuries to the controversies of the seventeenth, and to make heroes of all who fought on the side of Parliament, and villains of all the Royalists. It has long been well known that no such clear dichotomy existed at that time; indeed that most of this

[11] This state of mind is discussed briefly and ably by Hans-Albert Walter, "Leopold Schwartzchild and the *Neue Tage Buch*," in Walter Lacquer and George L. Mosse, eds. *The Left Wing Intellectuals Between the Wars, 1919–1939* (N.Y.: Harper Torchbooks, 1966), p. 108.

standard "Whig Interpretation" of that age is myth. But there remains a great reluctance to expose and abandon it. It is vaguely feared that such action would weaken the prestige of parliamentary institutions already imperilled in the world; that it is not good to debunk the "official heroes" in a struggle for democratic liberties; and that the only beneficiaries of such a procedure would be Marxists, obscurantists, reactionaries, High Anglicans and other antiliberal types. So, despite the advance of research, the essential outlines of the old story still prevail.[12]

The Tyranny of the Present

If the past is tyrannical, the present is no less so. Indeed one of the most fertile sources of misunderstanding about the past is to read back into it the values and preoccupations of the present. The history of the Reformation is particularly rich in illustrations of this proclivity. Because nationalism is the predominant mass passion of the twentieth century, many historians have attributed far too much importance to the faint glimmerings of nationalism that can be discerned 400 years ago. Because the economic interpretation of history is in vogue in our century, economic determinists have shown remarkable ingenuity in attributing the sweeping religious changes of four centuries ago to such factors as the fortunes of certain economic classes or the location of silver mines.

Still more amazing are the discoveries that have ensued from an examination of the careers of Martin Luther and John Calvin by imaginative "modern minded" historians. These gentlemen have discovered in the creeds of both men the seeds from which have developed such modern phenomena as capitalism, individualism, personal freedom, intellectual emancipation, and secularism. With equal logic one could attribute

---

[12] This point is discussed at some length by Wingfield-Stratford, *op. cit.*, pp. 119–41.

all present-day American civilization to the pilgrim fathers.[13] Reality was more prosaic. Luther was not a modern Protestant fighting for a broader and more liberal theology than that espoused in Rome. Quite the reverse. Luther rebelled against the secularist tendencies of his own day. He was outraged not by the fanaticism of the Renaissance popes but by their laxity and worldliness. While both Luther and Calvin did attack the medieval concept of religion symbolized by the papacy, each was quite as dogmatic and authoritarian as anyone in Rome. Calvin's famous regime in Geneva was legendary for its autocracy, severity, and puritanism. Ironically, it was the revolt of reforming biblical literalists like this pair that drove the Catholic church into that very narrowness and dogmatism which modern humanists deplore and which produced the bloody wars that convulsed Europe for a century. Thus in both spirit and interests the major Reformation Protestants had more in common with their Catholic contemporaries than either have with modern secularists. If the latter want to find sixteenth and seventeenth century persons whose attitudes were somewhat like their own, they should ignore the religious leaders entirely and bestow their praise on such political figures as England's procrastinating Queen Elizabeth I; the shifty, scheming mother of three worthless French kings, Catherine d'Medici; the pragmatist William of Orange; the lazy and indifferent Holy Roman Emperor Maximilian II; his eccentric son Rudolf II; or that supreme egoist, the condottieri Wallenstein. None of these people cared much for religion of any kind. All of them tried to moderate religious passions because they saw them as dangers to the state. For their efforts they were widely execrated in their own time for their "weakness" and "lack of principle." Modern lovers of personal liberty ought, logically, to cheer *them* rather than

[13] The most famous case in point here is the thesis of Max Weber that Calvinist theology markedly stimulated the growth of capitalism. The controversial literature on this subject is immense. For a summary of the main contentions and a guide to sources cf. Robert W. Green, ed. *Protestantism and Capitalism* (Boston: D.C. Heath & Co., 1959).

Protestant zealots whose chief concern was not civil liberties but theological correctness.[14]

The tyranny of the present is even evident in what we have *forgotten* about the Reformation. Thousands of books have described vividly how in England between 1530 and 1603 some 600–700 assorted Protestants and Catholics were martyred for their religion by the various governments of that age. But how many of these books also recount that in the thirty-eight years of his reign (1509–1547), Henry VIII executed 70,000 common criminals out of a population of about 4,000,000? How many relate that in Scotland, a land of perhaps 600,000 people, 8000 were burned as witches between 1560 and 1600? Who venerates *them* as martyrs? Nobody, because neither historians nor ordinary people in our time feel any emotional attachment to the criminals and alleged witches of past ages.

A. *Interest in Winners*—Distressing though it may be, most of us are "front runners." We are preoccupied with whatever cause, idea, or nation has triumphed; and correspondingly heedless of the vanquished. A lot of history is written this way too. Pick up a book on seventeenth century European political and diplomatic history. Which one of the German states (except Austria) gets the most attention? Brandenburg-Prussia. Why? Because it was the most important state then? Not at all. Saxony, Bavaria, the Palatinate, and several others seemed quite as important then. But who in the eighteenth and nineteenth centuries bullied, conquered, and annexed the other north German states and gradually formed them into the German Empire? Prussia. And so Prussia gets her innings even in centuries when her real importance was small.

Why does the same book accord so much attention to the conquests of Louis XIV and so little to those of the Hapsburg emperors of the same era? After all, after fifty years of war which nearly bankrupted France, Louis XIV gained only a

---

[14] There is an excellent detailed discussion of this question, with particular emphasis on Luther, in Herbert Butterfield, *The Whig Interpretation of History* (N.Y.: Charles Scribners' Sons, 1951), pp. 20–85.

minuscule collection of border towns and petty country districts. Leopold I, Joseph I, and Charles VI, meanwhile, paid a far smaller price to wrest whole provinces from the Turks. There are several reasons for the anomaly. In the 1960s France is still one of the world's leading powers while the Austro-Hungarian Empire no longer exists. Louis XIV was a flamboyant figure in European history, but the Hapsburg emperors were a drab lot. French culture was far more influential in seventeenth century Europe than was Austrian. Most important, France is the home of the French Revolution, a universally fascinating phenomenon, an event which an educated twentieth century man still regards as relevant to his own age. The Hapsburgs, by contrast, are remembered mostly for their failures: they could neither solve their nationality problems nor survive World War I. Thus we find the deeds of Louis XIV more meaningful to our own age than the objectively more impressive achievements of a defunct dynasty in an extinct empire.

The history of science sometimes seems to have been written largely by "front runners." Many a "History of Science" is little more than a catalog of the inventions and discoveries of famous men. Little attention is given to ideas that were once widespread and extremely influential but have since been superseded, or to extensive experiments that failed even though the failure itself might have been instructive. Consider the treatment accorded such scientists as Copernicus and Kepler in all too many modern books. Whenever their ideas happened to foreshadow some conception which prevails in physics or astronomy in the writer's own time, they get a pat on the head. Such approval, however, is usually followed by patronizing remarks about "prejudices" and "superstitions" since they and most other early scientists clung to a variety of religious and cosmological ideas common in their own time, but since disproved or fallen out of fashion.[15]

---

[15] It must be emphasized here that the best historians of science, men like Herbert Butterfield and E. A. Burtt, treat the subject with intelligence and imagination. They are emphatically not guilty of the sins enumerated above.

B. *Our Benighted Ancestors*—Oftentimes we are so attached to the principles and passions fashionable in our own age that we can scarcely forgive our forbearers for not anticipating our enthusiasm. It is even easier to condemn them for failing to measure up to the moral standards we happen to admire. Now this is not to say that moral values are all relative or that human nature changes dramatically from one age to another. Men love power as avidly in the twentieth century as they did in the thirteenth. It was just as wrong to murder, rob, or neglect one's duty in ancient Babylonia or medieval Florence as it is in twentieth century Chicago. But we must also remember that human nature *manifests* itself in different ways in different eras, and that moral values are apprehended less clearly in one epoch than another. A particular action is regarded as a grievous fault at one time or in one society but as a mere peccadillo in another. Hence if we are to do justice to the historic dead we must try to understand past environments and measure men by the norms generally accepted in their own times. In twentieth century England, for example, standards of civic morality are extremely high compared to other societies and other eras. To use a public office for personal financial gain is regarded as a flagrant betrayal of a public trust, one of the worst offenses an elected official can commit. Two or three centuries ago, however, both in England and in continental Europe the taking of bribes was close to universal. Such prominent seventeenth and eighteenth century English statesmen as Francis Bacon (d. 1626), Robert Walpole (d. 1745), and the Duke of Newcastle (d. 1768) would be regarded as monsters of corruption had they held office in our century. A bribe taker in their age, however, was regarded as reprehensible only if he refused to "stay bought" or if he obviously betrayed the interest of his government to an enemy. Thus to judge them as we would twentieth century English statesmen would be patently unjust. It would be to expect of them far more than their contemporaries did.

Leaving aside the alleged moral failings of our ancestors,

we often distort history by rebuking them for failing to foresee and strive for causes which "had a future." Legions of modern German historians, piqued because their nation was unified centuries later than England, France, or Spain, have been profoundly dissatisfied with a score of medieval emperors and early Prussian kings. They have been prone to scold these rulers for being preoccupied with religious squabbles, Italian intrigues, or the pursuit of narrowly Prussian interests when they (supposedly) ought to have been working for the political unification of all the German people. Sometimes they have tried to read into the deeds of these monarchs some glimmer of recognition that German unification *was,* after all, the cause of the future.

British history is replete with glaring anomalies if one is always thinking about how England's rulers failed to apprehend later British interests, instead of how things looked to them *at the time.* Henry VIII (1509–1547) and his chancellor, Cardinal Wolsey, are frequently chided for neglecting to build a strong navy and for periodically going to war against France on the side of Emperor Charles V, even though the emperor was the *stronger* party. Did they not understand the fundamentals of Britain's national power, or her future destiny? Alas! They weren't thinking about what would happen two or three hundred years later: that Brittania would become mistress of the seas and sovereign of a quarter of the globe; that her primary diplomatic instinct would be to maintain the balance of power in Europe by siding with the *weaker* party in major Continental wars. Their minds were on more parochial matters: the concerns of their own rather than a later age. Henry wanted to gain the imperial crown, or perhaps the throne of France. Wolsey hoped to become pope.

Later British governments were equally infatuated with the problems of their own day; equally blind to Brittania's "historic destiny." The Stuart kings ignored the stupendous opportunities for empire building that existed on four continents because the minds of two of them, James I and Charles I, were fixed on an object more immediately attractive: the establishment of a centralized monarchy like those in so many Continental states at the same time. A century later the government of the Hanoverian George III nearly gave Canada back to France in an effort to secure all the French sugar islands in the Caribbean—places of *immediate* value.

The leaders of other nations were no more prescient than the British. French intellectuals had the same opinion as the British of the relative worth of the sugar islands and Canada, and for the same reasons. (They accorded Canada only twelve lines in the famous *Encyclopedia*.) Two centuries earlier Francis I of France was so preoccupied with his campaigns against the Hapsburgs in Italy that he ignored the whole new world overseas that lay open to exploration and colonization. As late as 1867 Russia casually sold Alaska to the United States for a paltry $7,500,000—and many in the United States did not want to buy it!

Obviously, if we are to be just we must judge past nations and governments in terms of what *they* thought important; not what later writers think *should* have inspired and motivated them.

C. *Lost Causes*—Still another mode of reading the present back into the past is to dismiss as "lost causes" past movements that failed and past ambitions that went unrealized. Of course some lost causes were genuinely "lost," and rightly so. For example, it would be hard to find a class in history more addicted to the idea of returning to the past or more hopelessly incompetent in going about it than the old French aristocracy. For centuries, whenever France was under a regency or had a weak ruler on the throne (1380–1420, 1483–1498, 1558–1589, 1610–1624, 1715–1789), the nobility exerted every effort to regain the freedom from regulation of any kind that their ancestors had enjoyed in the twelfth century. Yet, as a class, the nobles lacked education, legal training, and industriousness, not to speak of their inability to identify their own interests with those of the French nation. Consequently, they never had any real idea of how to use power or consolidate it. They regularly botched their opportunities and caused everyone but themselves to long for the day when France would again have a king strong enough to curb their excesses.

Not all lost causes, however, were as hopeless as this one. Many a one was by no means so unpromising in its time as it came to seem long afterward. Often it failed not because of any intrinsic absurdity or unsuitability but because of errors in judgment, the loss of battles that might easily have turned out otherwise, or sheer bad luck. Once more, Reformation Europe provides an excellent example. To most informed twentieth century people it seems grotesque to suggest that the forces of the Catholic or Counter-Reformation once had a good chance to overwhelm and destroy European Protestantism. It did not seem so to Protestants of the 1580s. Dread of such a development was in their minds constantly, and we cannot understand the psychology and statecraft of that age if we do not recognize it. Consider the condition of Europe in 1587–1588. By far the most powerful state on the continent was Spain. She had the best foot troops in the world, a strong navy, the gold and silver of Mexico and Peru to finance her adventures, and she was ruled by Philip II, an energetic king whose former dream of saving Europe from the Turks had been transformed to zeal to save it from the Protestants. He was known to be building a vast naval armada which would attempt an invasion of England. England was officially Protestant but nobody knew how many Catholics and Catholic sympathizers remained in the country. Certainly there were many because several Catholic plots against Elizabeth I had been discovered. (The Queen had recently executed her captive and Catholic rival, Mary Queen of Scots, for Mary's alleged complicity in one of them.) France, the main rival of Spain, had been shattered by three decades of civil and religious wars. The French Protestants were no more than about 10 percent of the nation and their prospects for eventual victory in these conflicts looked dim. The Dutch Protestants had been in rebellion against Spain for nearly twenty years but their long-term chances seemed no better than those of their French coreligionists. Sigismund III, a man with pro-

nounced Catholic sympathies, had just become king of
Sweden, and that officially Lutheran land now had Jesuits
near the throne. In an age when rulers had many times
imposed their personal creed on their subjects there seemed
a distinct possibility that Sweden might soon become Catholic
again. Such a development would raise the spectre of a
Swedish-Spanish alliance which, if concluded, would give
Spain naval bases of inestimable value for operations in the
North Sea against the Dutch, the English, and Sweden's old
enemies, the Lutheran Danes. If Catholicism scored impressive victories in any of these places it would hearten all
the Catholics in the sprawling Holy Roman Empire and
might even lead Philip II's half-mad cousin, the Emperor
Rudolf II, to heed *his* Jesuit advisers and take stronger mea-
sures for the advancement of Catholicism in his own realm.
To a knowledgeable European Protestant in 1587 the future
looked bleak.

Admittedly, a complete victory for the Counter-Reformation would have been difficult to gain, but it failed due mostly
to mistaken judgments, accidents, and developments that
could not be foreseen. To start with, Admiral Santa Cruz
died. He had been one of the great sailors of the day, and he
was to have commanded the mighty Armada. Philip II made
a poor choice in selecting the duke of Medina Sidonia to
replace him. The latter, and other Spanish sea captains, made
several serious tactical errors, and the whole expedition was
persistently hampered by bad provisioning and worse weather.
Still, even after the rout of the Armada in the North Sea,
Medina Sidonia might have saved the day. He could have
landed most of his troops in Scotland and attempted a conquest of Britain from there, with a good chance of success.
But he thought only of getting back to Spain; so he did not
try. From such accidents and errors of judgment, the design to
crush Protestant Britain failed.[16]

---

[16] For a detailed description of this whole diplomatic situation and a
brilliant account of the Armada expedition cf. Garrett Mattingly, *The
Armada* (Boston: Houghton Mifflin Co., 1959). This book is an example of

Things went no better elsewhere. In France a series of natural deaths and political assassinations brought to the throne the able Henry IV who not only cared nothing for religious crusades but made many concessions to his own Protestant subjects. In the Netherlands the duke of Parma, Philip II's ablest diplomat and soldier, died in 1592. This greatly diminished any chance of crushing the Dutch rebels in the foreseeable future. In Sweden there was a reaction against Sigismund III and he was driven out of the country. Philip II himself died in 1598 and was succeeded by the incompetent Philip III. Thus by 1600 the threat to international Protestantism had clearly passed, but informed contemporaries had recognized its reality and seriousness thirteen years before.

D. *Lost Causes Unrecognized*—Ironically, a cause which *is* truly lost is sometimes not recognized to be so because of the zeal and energy (and oftentimes blindness) of its adherents. Every society contains many people, by no means its worst members, who believe on principle that one should fight for what he thinks right; not what he thinks inevitable. Especially if both their emotions and interests become involved, they simply fight on doggedly for what they love and against what they hate, regardless of the probable outcome. Revolutionary eras provide many examples of such conduct. Whether the persons be French aristocrats fleeing from the revolutionary regimes of the 1790s, "White" Russian emigres scattered about Europe after the revolution of 1917, Chinese who fled to Formosa before the mainland Communist armies in 1948–1949, anti-Castro Cuban exiles of the 1960s, or any of a dozen similar groups, they exhibit certain common characteristics. They invariably overrate the degree of sympathy for themselves and their cause that still exists in their homeland. They insist that the new regime which they have fled or which has cast them out is much weaker than it appears. They spend many years trying to persuade their friends abroad to

history at its best: a blend of first-rate scholarship and fine writing. Any serious student of history should read it and make it a model for his own endeavors.

invade their homeland, help them destroy the hated new regime, and restore everything as it once was. Thus, for a time, by sheer fervor they breathe life into what a later age recognizes to have been a political corpse.[17]

Grandiose Historical Theories

Many people have distorted conceptions of reality because they are irresistibly attracted by grand designs and sweeping syntheses. They are charmed by men more accurately described as metaphysicians or seers than historians. The latter, often fabulously learned and imaginative, proclaim that the whole course of history is a record of class struggle, or a chronicle of the "decline of the West," or the record of man's ceaseless quest for liberty, or some other. Because the total quantity of historical facts is so enormous they are able to pick and choose judiciously and thereby amass an impressive array of evidence for virtually any interpretation of history. The crucial point is that they never lack for followers because their splendid intellectual constructions provide the rationale for the deepest cravings and fears of their admirers.[18]

More specifically, people create their heroes in the image of what they themselves would like to be. They love to imagine that great deeds must have been motivated by equally great ideas; at any rate by ideas which seem great in the present. Admiration for the civilization of ancient Greece has been so general in succeeding ages that the Greeks have sometimes been referred to as "the pampered darlings of history." Not surprisingly, the Macedonian conquerer of Greece, Alexander the Great, has usually been portrayed as something of a military missionary, consciously engaged in spreading the splendors of Hellas through the rest of the known world. This interpretation of Alexander's career may be accurate, but it

---

[17] Of course many of the French emigres of the 1790s eventually returned to France, and some of them regained lands and titles. But French society as a whole never returned to the pre-1789 mode.

[18] This point is considered by Alan Bullock, "The Historian's Purposes: History and Metahistory," *History Today*, February 1951, pp. 5–11.

also may be mostly imagination. Not much is known in detail about Alexander's intentions. It is quite possible that he was motivated by sheer love of adventure and conquest.

Similarly, scholars have long debated the reasons for the coronation (800 A.D.) of the first Holy Roman emperor, Charlemagne. Many have seen in the event a deliberate effort to revive the old Roman Empire or to create a new Christian universal empire. The possibility that the entire proceeding grew out of nothing more splendid than the momentary exigencies of local Roman politics has never seemed attractive and has been championed by few historians.[19]

The same tendency can be discerned in American history. An instance, at once amusing and revealing, is related by one of America's greatest contemporary historians.

"What made the farmers fight in 1775? Judge Mellen Chamberlain in 1842, when he was twenty-one, interviewed Captain Preston, a ninety-one-year-old veteran of the Concord fight: 'Did you take up arms against intolerable oppressions?' he asked.

'Oppressions?' replied the old man. 'I didn't feel them.'

'What, were you not oppressed by the Stamp Act?'

'I never saw one of those stamps. I certainly never paid a penny for one of them.'

'Well, then what about the tea tax?'

'I never drank a drop of the stuff; the boys threw it all overboard.'

'Then I suppose you had been reading Harington or Sidney and Locke about the eternal principles of liberty?'

'Never heard of 'em. We read only the Bible, the Catechism, Watts' Psalms and Hymns, and the Almanac.'

'Well, then, what was the matter? And what did you mean in going to the fight?'

'Young man, what we meant in going for those redcoats was this: *we always* had governed ourselves, and we always meant to. They didn't mean we should.' "[20]

---

[19] One who does argue the latter case persuasively is Karl Heldmann, *Das Kaisertum Karls der Grossen* (Weimar: Hermann Bohlaus Nochfolger, 1928).

[20] S. E. Morison, *Oxford History of the American People* (N.Y.: Oxford Press, 1965), pp. 212–13.

Misunderstanding

History has been changed in many particulars because of simple misunderstanding of ideas, systems, and people unlike ourselves. For instance, the course of diplomatic history has often been altered by monarchical prejudices. To continental European kings and to most of the ministers who served them, monarchy always seemed the natural, normal, stable, predictable form of government. A look across the English Channel filled these gentlemen with puzzlement and dismay. Who ruled England anyway? There was a king on the throne, to be sure, but he seemed to be dominated by either of two political parties who were forever turning each other out of office. Worse, they persistently denounced each other, and those "out" were always threatening to abandon all the policies of those currently "in." How could such a country be stable internally? How could she possibly be a faithful and predictable ally? Due to this monarchist bias even such astute statesmen as Frederick the Great of Prussia (1740–1786) and Bismarck (1862–1890) consistently underrated the continuity of British foreign policy, the stability of British society and, consequently, the value of Great Britain as an ally. Many Europeans have since succumbed to the same illusion about the United States. They pick up their newspapers and it appears that America has at least a dozen competing foreign policies. There is of course the official one made by the president and his cabinet. But the Pentagon also appears to have one. So do the Joint Chiefs of Staff, the CIA, the chairman of the Senate Committee on Foreign Relations, all the leading presidential candidates in the party out of power, a number of maverick senators, and a varying number of influential syndicated newspaper columnists. Europeans find this bewildering and easily forget that in practice American policy is as stable and predictable as that of their own countries and that in national emergencies Americans close ranks behind their government-of-the-day quite as readily as other peoples.

Sometimes the misunderstanding of other peoples or ages is so profound that it is more properly described as blank incomprehension. Able scholars have long realized that it is extremely difficult, perhaps impossible, to accurately recapture and portray the hopes, dreams, fears, and preoccupations of people who lived centuries ago in societies unlike our own. A common reaction in such a case (though happily not among the scholars) is in effect to shrug one's shoulders and say that probably the people were really *not* so different from ourselves as historians represent them. The consequent misunderstanding is bad enough. A worse reaction, because it closes our whole mind and imagination to different cultures and historical experiences, is to say that if they *really were* so different then a study of their societies and their attitudes can have little relevance for us.

Many moderns react to the Middle Ages in this way. To citizens in twentieth century urban democratic societies medieval peasants seem puzzling creatures. Stolid, passive, tenaciously attached to the soil, incredibly narrow in their interests, they seem impossibly stupid: little better than beasts. Part of this incomprehension is, of course, due merely to the modern city man's lack of interest in agriculture. Another part derives obviously from the illiteracy and massive ignorance of medieval peasants. But there is more to it than this. There is a vital difference of *attitude*. Modern people are expected to have political and social "opinions." They are supposed to help shape the contours of public life by speaking out and voting. All this was foreign not only to the experience of the medieval peasant but to his psychology as well. He never thought it part of his station in life to have such views or exercise such privileges. Attending to public questions was the natural province of superiors: aristocrats, bishops, kings. God had created peasants for something else: to do the physical labor necessary to support Christian society in this world, and to save their individual souls for the next one. Similarly, medieval intellectuals seem strange and remote to their modern counterparts because the studies they valued most were theology and philosophy rather than the natural and social sciences which intrigue most modern secularists.

Propaganda

Many historical myths are the product of propaganda campaigns. This has long been notorious in the history of religions. The savage battles of the Reformation era gave rise to stereotypes and legends that have not vanished even four centuries later. Anti-Catholic feeling in England always owed much to Foxe's *Book of Martyrs,* a series of stirring and often fanciful accounts of the heroism of Protestants executed in the reign of the Catholic queen, "Bloody Mary" (1553–1558). Both religious and war propaganda in England and the Low Countries produced distortions of the national histories of the Netherlands and Spain that endure to this day.[21] The most lurid of these legends are related to the alleged personal villainy of Philip II of Spain and to that monstrous engine of cruelty and oppression, the Spanish Inquisition. Probably no institution in history has suffered more in reputation from impassioned propaganda than the Inquisition. Of course it must be admitted that the body was not a medieval humane society. Happily, few in our age are still enthusiasts for religious persecution. But we must retain perspective. Though falling woefully short of the ideal in practice, the Western world in our time praises a tolerant spirit, holding it to be one mark of a humane, civilized man. Not so in the age of the Reformation. A tolerant man in the sixteenth century

[21] For a discussion of the systematic distortion of Dutch history and what lay behind it cf. *Infra.,* pp. 72–73. The most *general* myth that still prevails about sixteenth century Spanish history is that rulers and ruled alike were obsessed with the extirpation of Protestantism. In fact, until about 1575 Spain was much more preoccupied with the Turkish menace. On this subject cf. such excellent works as Bohdan Chudoba, *Spain and the Empire, 1519–1643* (Chicago: University of Chicago Press, 1952); J. H. Elliott, *Imperial Spain, 1469–1716* (N.Y.: St. Martin's Press, 1964); John Lynch, *Spain Under the Hapsburgs* (Oxford: Blackwells, 1964).

was abominated as a moral weakling, one too cowardly to defend truth and resist evil. Hence the Inquisition merely typified the spirit of the age. Its procedures were, in fact, less harsh than those of European civil courts of the same era. Indeed, in the short term, it can be contended that those countries in which the Inquisition was entrenched (Italy, Spain, and Portugal), were positively fortunate! They were spared the murderous religious wars of the sixteenth and seventeenth centuries, conflicts in which robbery, torture, and death were the lot of an incomparably larger number of people than perished at the hands of Inquisitors. Finally, to consider the matter at its absolute lowest, we who live in an age of concentration camps, genocide, and world wars, where the victims are numbered in the tens of millions, ought not to be excessively moralistic about an organization that executed a few thousand people in the course of several centuries.

But to place the Inquisition in proper historical perspective, or to point out that all the impassioned polemics of the Reformation era were exaggerated and many were entirely false, is beside the point for our discussion. What counts is that for generations afterward they shaped a sizeable portion of the world view of tens of millions of Anglo-Saxons. They created the famous Black Legend: the belief that Spaniards are always cruel, faithless, superstitious, bigoted, and thus (deservedly) backward.

Political propaganda has often been quite as influential. When in power, Napoleon Bonaparte was an autocrat who posed as the protector of property and the man who brought order out of revolutionary chaos. When composing his *Memoirs* on the island of St. Helena, however, Napoleon told a different story. Then he portrayed himself as a loyal son of the French Revolution and a defender of liberty while the Bourbons stood tamely for peace, conservatism, and unimaginative orthodoxy. A generation later Napoleon's nephew exploited the legend and made himself emperor of France.

A recent exhaustive study of the famous Dreyfus Case (1894–1906) has shown that the whole affair owed much more to the ignorance, vanity, prejudices, and general muddle-headedness of most of its principal figures rather than to deliberate malevolence or plotting. Nonetheless most of the literature on the case has depicted it as a morality play, a crude struggle between heroes and villains. Since the bulk of the literature has been pro-Dreyfusard, and the anti-Dreyfusard versions, while equally distorted, have been largely forgotten, Dreyfusard propaganda has by now largely passed into official history.[22]

Taking Others' Principles Too Seriously

Oftentimes serious misunderstandings derive merely from taking the words and principles of others at face value. Few people are as logical in deed as they are in speech or in print. If Charles V never understood the appeal and power of a new religious ideology in the sixteenth century, a far more brilliant nineteenth century statesman failed to realize how much all religious ideologies had moderated in three centuries. In the 1870s Bismarck undertook a campaign to bend the Catholic church in Germany to the will of the German state. This "Kulturkampf" was waged partly because Bismarck thought that the Franco-Prussian War (1870–71) had been instigated by collusion between France and the papacy. He was further convinced that the French Empress Eugenie was a tool of the Jesuits who were, in turn, prominent protagonists of papal infallibility. This doctrine had just been officially proclaimed by the Vatican Council of 1870. Bismarck imagined that infallibility posed a threat to the unity of his newly created German Empire in that it would strengthen the tendency of German Catholics to give their primary allegiance to the papacy rather than to the fatherland. He was painfully aware that in his new empire it was the Catholic peripheral elements, Lorrainers, Alsatians, Bavarians, and Poles, who

---

[22] Guy Chapman, *The Dreyfus Case* (N.Y.: Reynal & Co., 1955), is the most interesting and perceptive account of this famous affair.

seemed the least patriotic and enthusiastic. Worse, they were the core of the Zentrum, a Catholic political party which opposed Bismarck. How antique and mistaken these notions were was shown when the Zentrum eventually came around to support Bismarck, and when German Catholics fought quite as loyally for the Reich in both world wars as German Protestants or secularists.

Interestingly, Bismarck abandoned the Kulturkampf about 1880 only to embrace a new illusion: that the Marxist and pacifist doctrines of the Social Democrats were a threat to the German Empire. For the next decade he harrassed political rather than religious sectarians. Had he lived longer he would have been amazed to see the despised socialists not only rally loyally to the fatherland and fight in 1914 but even to accept Hitler without resistance in 1933. How ironic that the ablest statesman of the nineteenth century should have made the capital error of taking his opponents' principles more seriously than they ever did themselves!

Historical Labels

An even more prolific source of misconceptions about history is the habit of taking titles and labels too literally. In the sixteenth century Francis I of France at various times allied with the Turks against the Hapsburgs and with various German princes against the papacy. A variety of national and dynastic considerations dictated the alliances. Consider, however, the formal appearance of these actions. His Most Christian Majesty (Francis), ruler of the Eldest Daughter of the Church (France), was allied with that arch-infidel (the Sultan of Turkey), against His Most Catholic Majesty (the Holy Roman Emperor); and also with German heretics against The Vicar of Christ (the Pope). Alice in Wonderland would have been unable to fathom sixteenth century diplomacy had she judged things wholly by their names and titles.

Consider also that hardy perennial from European history, "absolute monarchy." "Absolute monarchy" was never what the name means literally because it could not be. A look at the situation of that very model of seventeenth century "absolutism," Louis XIV of France, will indicate the vast gulf between name and reality. Most of the bureaucrats in his realm, at all levels, had purchased their jobs and could not normally be dislodged save by repurchase. The king lacked the money even to consider this on a meaningful scale. Most people then were illiterate, and neither radio nor television existed, so the government could shape the minds of its subjects by propaganda only very slowly. For the same reasons, and because neither railways, automobiles nor airplanes existed, information could not be transmitted quickly nor troops moved about with dispatch. The modern practice of keeping statistics about every aspect of national life was unknown. Systematic military conscription had not yet been developed. There was no national police system, public or secret, and nobody was fingerprinted. The hereditary aristocracy still had enormous influence in the country and close ties with fellow aristocrats in other countries, quite independent of the king. Thus it was technologically impossible for Louis XIV to be an "absolute monarch." Not until the French Revolution (1789–1799) was the aristocracy humbled. Not until the Industrial Revolution was well advanced (about 1850) did the necessary wealth and machines exist to make possible systematic physical control of millions of people. Not until the late nineteenth century did enough people become literate to render mass propaganda effective. Louis XIV might be styled the Sun King, and he might say "I am the state," but in fact he could not rule his subjects as efficiently as the mildest democratic government in an advanced twentieth century society. In practice, "absolute monarchy" did not mean kings ruling exactly as they chose. It meant hereditary monarchy as a *form* of government, and government conducted without any regular consultation of those ruled.

Oftentimes small differences between two situations are exaggerated inordinately because labels are plastered onto them which make them appear to be natural opposites. Eng-

lish socialists of the late 1940s proudly described their homeland as a socialist country while the United States was lauded
by Chamber of Commerce orators as the land of free enterprise. It is true that England was then governed by the Labour
party, which is officially socialist. That government enacted
much welfare legislation, established socialized medicine, and
nationalized several British industries. Yet the essential differences between "socialist" Britain and "free enterprise"
America were often hard to discover. Both had innumerable
private companies and industries of all sizes. Both also had
extensive public ownership of such things as gas, water, street
cars, and housing projects. Both had political democracy and
high progressive income taxes. Both had considerable welfare
legislation. Oddly, socialist Britain still retained a king and
hereditary titled aristocracy, institutions which have never
existed in capitalist America. Pretty clearly, the political and
economic differences between the two countries were about
20 percent substance and 80 percent phraseology.

The history of the English civil war of the 1640s has been
similarly muddied by drawing sharp distinctions where none
existed in reality. Almost any book on the subject carefully
differentiates between Presbyterians and Independents even
though the two groups overlapped in so many particulars that
their names indicate no more than somewhat divergent
tendencies.[23]

Another common type of lazy thinking about history is to
attach a label to a whole category of men and then think of
the label as describing the men fully and exactly. Thus "Fascists," "Communists," "revolutionaries," or some such, seem
a collectivity of saints or devils incarnate instead of complex,
fallible creatures of flesh and blood like the rest of us. What
person, in real life, is such a remorseless logician, such a soulless robot, such a fanatical devotee of some ideology that it
is possible to describe him satisfactorily simply by sticking on
him some label like "autocrat" or "anarchist"? If it is impos-

---

[23] See J. H. Hexter, *Reappraisals In History* (N.Y.: Harper & Row, 1963),
for a detailed consideration of this and similar cases.

sible to do this for one person, how much more impossible is it to accurately designate whole groups of people thus? How often one reads that "England did this"—as if England were a person, instead of the reference being to a government of several dozen men who represent fifty million people of all ages, types, and beliefs. How often one hears American politics discussed in terms of "the Republicans" standing for this or "the Democrats" doing that. It is as though all Republicans from the John Birch Society to eastern liberals agreed entirely; as though every Democrat from a large northern city was indistinguishable in ideas and purposes from the Democrat representatives of rural southern districts; as if each party was eternally dedicated to principles forever irreconcilable with those of the other party; as if nobody ever crossed a party line to vote with the opposition; in a word, as if "Republicans" and "Democrats" were puppets instead of men. To be sure, some general terms have to be employed in history (as in all other sectors of human affairs) to bring order into things, and they usually have some validity. But it should never be forgotten that the man never lived who perfectly typified any general characterization. It is an accurate generalization, for instance, to say that aristocrats in medieval and early modern times were sensitive about personal and family honor, devoted to a military tradition, careless about money, unwilling to do systematic work, and indifferent to intellectual attainment. One could find many individual aristocrats, however, who bore small resemblance to this description: the patient, tireless sixteenth century English statesman, Lord Burghley; the eighteenth century French political philosopher, Montesquieu; the eccentric humanitarian, social philosopher, and land speculator, Saint Simon (d. 1825); and that hard, shrewd nineteenth century Piedmontese statesman, Count Camillo Cavour.

Finally, titles and tags ought to be viewed warily because many a word that once had a specific meaning has become so mauled in the propaganda contests of our age that it no longer means anything precise. It has become merely a term

of abuse, or else it is invoked mindlessly to cast a vague aura
of benevolence over a cause somebody is promoting. Consider
"democracy." When an American businessman uses the word
he means the right of people to vote in an honest election for
political candidates of their own choice. When an English
socialist uses the term he means what the American means but
he also assumes that something approaching economic equality
exists among the people in question. When a Communist
calls something "democratic" he means any condition or
development which promises to promote Communist interests. To a Communist, "Fascist" is a smear word to be applied
to any enemy. To many Americans "socialist" serves a similar
purpose. To millions of Europeans, however, "socialism"
arouses in head and heart the same hazily benevolent sentiments that the word "democracy" does on the American shore
of the Atlantic. To a "liberal," itself a supremely imprecise
term, the words "conservative" and "reactionary" are easily
used interchangeably. To many "conservatives" such designations as "liberal," "pink," "utopian," "socialist," and "fuzzy
thinker" seem synonymous. Perhaps worst of all, in the twentieth century any idea that is disliked by more than six people
sooner or later gets an "ism" tacked onto the end of it. This
situation so disgusted a prominent economic historian (T. S.
Ashton) that he once declared his intention of writing a history
of the Industrial Revolution without mentioning a single "ism."

If the inaccurate use of words had no important practical
consequences we might safely leave the whole matter to
semanticists and logicians. But the consequences are often of
great importance, for to use a word in a context which makes
its meaning different from what the word originally connoted
is to set ourselves a problem which either does not really exist
or which is different in character from what it appears to be.
Thus in 1939 the world was astounded when the famous Hitler-
Stalin Pact was signed. How could such a thing happen? Was
not Hitler's national socialist regime an extreme "right wing"
movement: capitalist, reactionary, hyper-nationalist? Was not
this the complete antithesis of Stalinist Russia, a classless soci-

ety and the home of Marxist internationalism? Had not these two regimes exhausted the vocabularies of abuse in their respective languages when addressing each other? People would have been less surprised in 1939 (and since) had they thought more about the real character of these two regimes and less about the phraseology in which they were bedecked by friend and foe. Hitler's Third Reich was supported quite as much by the "socialist masses" as by other elements in German society, and Hitler dictated to his "capitalists" just as he did to everyone else in the country. Stalin's Russia had assumed lineaments that a resurrected Karl Marx would never have recognized. Out-maneuvering Trotsky, who wanted to concentrate on the promotion of international revolution, Stalin pressed to establish socialism in one country. His foreign policy reflected Russian national interests rather than the needs of worldwide Marxism. The leaders of foreign Communist parties were always required to be obsequious servants of Moscow, even though this weakened the appeal of communism in their own countries. Both Stalin and Hitler employed a combination of propaganda and the merciless use of force and terror to silence domestic opposition. Hence, whatever their polemical differences, Stalinist communism and German national socialism were remarkably similar in spirit and practice.[24]

[24] Lukacs, *A New History of the Cold War, op. cit.*, analyzes this point ably. A particularly keen reminder of the degree to which Russian national interests have outweighed purely Communist considerations in the making of Russian foreign policy since 1917 is contained in the following quotation. "Seldom did the rulers of Russia allow international communist interests to supersede what to them seemed the immediate national interests of the Russian Empire. The integrity and defense of that empire has remained the primary consideration in their minds from Lenin to the present day. For this purpose they collaborated on occasion with Prussian generals, African nationalists, American industrialists, Persian Shahs, Italian Fascists, British Tories, German Nazis, French conservatives, and Japanese imperialists; they made political and strategic alliances with Mustapha Kemal, General von Seeckt, Pierre Laval, Eduard Benes, Adolf Hitler, Winston Churchill, Chiang Kai Shek, Franklin Roosevelt, and Mao-Tse Tung; they discussed alliances with and proposed divisions of spheres of interests to Mussolini, Stresemann,

Probably no general political or economic designation has been more persistently and grossly misused than "capitalism." Who has not picked up a serious book and read that "capitalism" wanted this policy, opposed that one, or manipulated something or other? But try to give the word a specific and restricted meaning: e.g. apply it only to Germany. What does "German capitalism" mean? Presumably all the capitalists in Germany. But that must mean every German who runs any kind of private business, whether it be the immense Krupp industrial works or a neighborhood sauerkraut stand. Who can seriously pretend that all these men will have the same outlook and interests? Some will be generous, others selfish. Some will be intelligent, others not. Some will really understand which governmental policies will be of permanent benefit to themselves, others will not. Some will understand where the national interest differs from their own particular interest, others will not. Some will benefit from high tariffs on most industrial products, some from only a few selected tariffs, some from no tariffs at all, and some will be indifferent to the whole matter. Finally, who can pretend that even if

DeGaulle, and Nixon. Moreover, the leaders of Soviet Russia generally tended to get along much better with British Tories than with British Labourites, with American industrialists rather than American labor leaders, with resolute and conservative Finnish patriots such as Marshal Mannerheim, rather than the avowedly Communist Tito in Yugoslavia—because, far transcending all ideological or social affinities, they saw how the different interests of different nations represented by these different national leaders at certain times and occasions accorded with the national interests of Soviet Russia" p. 331. ". . . Not even Stalin would admit to himself what a typical Russian nationalist leader he had become . . ." p. 333.

How meaningless political labels often are is perhaps most vividly displayed by the official Communist stand (1968) on the population problem. In conventional parlance communism is supposed to stand on the "extreme left," to represent the most avant-garde political and social thinking. Yet communism simply ignores all aspects of the population problem; claiming that it does not exist, that its supposed existence indicates only an inability to understand the basic deficiencies of capitalism; that talk about overpopulation is defeatism before the dawn of a bright future. It would be hard to conceive a less practical, more reactionary stand.

all German capitalists *did* think and act alike, that all French, British, American, and Swedish capitalists would be just like the Germans? Merely to describe the situation exposes its absurdity. Yet much history is still written in terms of "capitalist" and "socialist" designs, as if these were invariably specific and predictable. Some of this is due to deliberate partisanship, some to mere mental laziness, and some to the fact that it is easier and superficially more impressive to write of the inexorable moulding of history by mighty abstractions than it is to try to account for what happened in specific, prosaic detail.

Interpretations

On many occasions, history has been powerfully stirred by what interested parties have read into events. The famous seventeenth century lawyer, Sir Edward Coke, read into the Magna Carta signed by King John in 1215 all sorts of meanings it did not have in the thirteenth century but which did have a polemical application to issues between King James I and Parliament in Coke's own time. Enthusiastic believers in the natural political wisdom of the Anglo-Saxon peoples have argued that the parliamentary government of modern England was a direct development from practices common among tribesmen in fifth century German forests.

A more important case concerns church-state relations through the centuries. In the Middle Ages civil rulers quarreled with the papacy over the question of where the boundary lay between civil and religious authority, and which of these authorities should take precedence in the Christian world. In an effort to settle the matter the doctrine of the two swords was invented. It was drawn from the words of the apostles on the Mount of Olives, "Lord, behold, here are two swords." To this Christ had replied, "It is enough." By itself, this would not appear to have been a particularly illuminating conversation. But human ingenuity is limitless if it is moved by a sufficiently strong interest. By the eleventh century the Holy

Roman Emperor Henry IV was proclaiming that Christ's words meant that the two swords referred to Christendom's two supreme authorities, church and state, and that these were separate and independent. St. Bernard of Clairvaux (d. 1153), however, held that what was meant was that God had bestowed both swords on the Church and entrusted her with all power in the world. Later protagonists of the papacy expanded the doctrine to mean that the Church wielded one sword directly, while the other was wielded by the secular power but only at the bidding of the Church and subject to its approval.[25]

Partisans of both civil and religious authority argued endlessly about the supposed significance of incidents surrounding the coronations of Pepin (752) and Charlemagne (800). Both men had been crowned by popes. Did that imply that some or all of their royal authority had been bestowed on them by the popes? Yes indeed, said protagonists of the papacy. But the pope who crowned Pepin had once appeared before him clad in sackcloth and ashes; and Leo III, who crowned Charlemagne, was notoriously little more than Charlemagne's chaplain. On one occasion he had even been forced to flee to his royal protector to avoid assassination. Did such considerations imply papal recognition of the superiority of royal authority? Certainly, said supporters of kings. Nobody asked whether the participants in the coronations had had any of these thoughts in their own minds on those occasions.

Centuries later, it was not so much what John Locke (d. 1704) and Sir Isaac Newton (d. 1727) said or did that changed the world. It was the public reputation they acquired, the lessons their admirers claimed were implicit in their thought, and the corresponding program of legislation and reform which the latter ceaselessly recommended to all Europe throughout the eighteenth century. Newton developed what

---

[25] This view was expounded most forcefully by Pope Boniface VIII (d. 1303). Cf. Sidney Ehler, *Twenty Centuries of Church and State* (Westminister, Md.: Newman Press, 1957). The quotation is from p. 36.

appeared to be a clear, simple, and comprehensive explanation for the operations of the physical universe. A host of European intellectuals, anxious to reform the societies in which they lived, soon proclaimed that if only Newton's intellectual procedures (to experiment, weigh, measure, observe, calculate and above all, to reason), were applied to law, government, economics, social relations, and education human society could be miraculously transformed in a short time. Thus Newton, unknown to himself, became the father of the eighteenth century intellectual revolution called the Enlightenment. John Locke's case was similar. His also demonstrates that when an idea becomes popular it becomes simplified and vulgarized. Locke believed that at birth man has no innate ideas, that all human knowledge comes through the senses, and that the senses perceive only physical objects. Now Locke was an observant and sensible man. He never supposed that human mental processes were wholly and simply mechanical. Nonetheless his French admirers and popularizers interpreted his work thus. They held that he had proved that the whole human race could be regenerated by changing man's environment. The way to do it was to improve education and pass appropriate legislation.

A century and a half later Charles Darwin confined to biology his conceptions of natural selection and survival of the fittest. It was a host of enthusiastic and uncritical disciples who insisted that these conceptions justified (variously) laissez faire capitalism, imperialism, aggressive war and, generally, unrestricted competition in all spheres of human activity. These beliefs and attitudes heavily colored the thoughts and deeds of most of the world's major nations after 1870. They intensified the aggressiveness of German foreign policy and thereby contributed to the outbreak of the First World War. They provided a rationale for American businessmen anxious to evade governmental controls. In Britain they confirmed the conviction of turn-of-the-century Englishmen that their success in acquiring a colonial empire was but a reflection of their natural preeminence among the races and nationalities of men.

Perhaps the classic case is that of the philosopher and social critic Jean Jacques Rousseau (1712–1778). Admittedly, Rousseau's writings are open to more than one interpretation, but if Rousseau could come to life now he would be dumbfounded to discover that scholars and polemicists of the last two centuries have variously proclaimed him to have been a socialist, a forerunner of communism, an embryonic fascist, an anarchist, the father of democracy, the harbinger of the Romantic Age, the founder of progressive education, and the primary cause of the French Revolution.

Faulty Analogies

Many illusions are the outgrowth of exaggerating historical analogies. To draw parallels between two different eras or developments is frequently highly instructive. But it can be misleading too, for any two given situations always have their points of difference as well as similarity.

Easily the champion among dubious analogies is the one which holds that modern American civilization is going the way of the Roman Empire. The thesis, especially favored by elderly amateur philosopher-historians, runs somewhat as follows: people are lazier and less patriotic than they used to be; they are less moral and less willing to defend their own societies; and they have so little spirit that they only want to be fed and entertained while the government runs everything. Now it must be admitted that in the very longest run our disgruntled sages will be proved correct since all civilizations have declined at *some* time. Only vanity causes us to think that ours must be an exception. Moreover, some of the shortcomings of twentieth century America are embarrassingly similar to those of the later Roman Empire. One thinks immediately of the endemic wars, chronically unbalanced federal budgets, inflation, multiplication of bureaucrats, and growth of demoralized city mobs. Still, in the short run, the analogy is full of holes because the differences between the two societies are basic and important. The governments of third and fourth century Rome wallowed in a morass of perpetual bankruptcy punctuated by civil war. Compared to governments in

general throughout history, that of twentieth century America
is well above average in stability, efficiency, and relative
solvency. Declining Rome was never free from the threat of
masses of barbarians who had been enlisted as mercenary
troops, a phenomenon unknown in the United States. Rome
had no industrial system to employ her urban masses and add
to her national wealth and strength. America has the most productive industrial system ever known. The ordinary American
has far more freedom, in practice, to make a career of his
choice than did the ordinary Roman. Finally, anyone who
has read much of the social history of the past will question
whether the personal and civic morality of the third, fourth,
and fifth centuries on one hand, and the twentieth century
on the other, was, and is, really so much worse than what
prevailed in the fifteen centuries in between. The whole comparison indicates how emphasis on similarities and forgetful-
ness of differences leads easily to erroneous conclusions.

The Need for Myths

Finally, since this entire discussion of illusions in history has
been undertaken in an effort to improve our grasp of reality,
we must conclude with some lame admissions: (1) for all the
confusion that myths and illusions introduce into human
affairs they still frequently serve a constructive purpose; and
(2) in any case, people have never been able to do without
them. The historian-prophet Arnold Toynbee has contended
with immense erudition that religion of some kind is the core
of any civilization.[26] Many students of politics consider that

---

[26] Arnold Toynbee, *A Study of History*, 12 vols. (London: Oxford Press,
1934–1961). In several of his many books Christopher Dawson has made
the claim, rather more narrowly, that Christianity is the heart of Western
civilization. The case is made most clearly in his *Religion and the Rise of
Western Culture* (Garden City, N.Y.: Doubleday, 1958).

The remarks above neither contend nor imply that religion and mythology
are synonymous. The point is that belief in some great ideal or unifying conception inspires a society and binds it together. The ideal itself may be religious or secular, real or mythical.

political *practice* at all times is concerned chiefly with power and money, but that successful political leaders are those who are most adept at identifying their own causes and ambitions with prevailing popular passions, be these religious or secular.[27] Perhaps it only proves the truth of the old adage that men do not live by bread alone. At all times they need some absolute in which to believe, some great cause to serve, some ideal to cherish, some movement to join which gives meaning to their existence. It is easy to demonstrate, for instance, that for all their defects the democratic governments in several twentieth century European countries were objectively superior to the various totalitarian regimes that overturned them. But they lacked the mystique of communism and fascism; and, sadly, "Men are more ready to die for an illusory good than for a real lesser evil."[28] Likewise, the "liberated" peoples of East-Central Europe or the ex-colonial peoples of Asia and Africa are worse off by most rational standards than they used to be when they lived in empires ruled by foreigners.[29] But that is only the lesser half of the story. Their desire for independence, their belief in their *right* to be independent, was a far stronger emotion in their psyche than any consideration of economic welfare. It still is.

Indeed so great is the need for myths that the leaders of these new societies deliberately create them. In Africa, particularly, where new nations often contain several disparate and often hostile tribes, and have boundaries which conform neither to geographical nor economic logic, the rulers have to strive mightily to bind their separated peoples together and to create a sense of nationhood. The usual technique is to speak movingly of "negritude" or "the African personality" and to

[27] A particularly blunt argument for this thesis is presented in James Burnham, *The Machiavellians* (N.Y.: John Day Co., 1943). One prominent modern statesman who not only acted on this principle but (rare indeed) openly avowed it was the French Emperor Napoleon III, 1852–1870.

[28] The phrase is taken from a fine, thought-provoking book: Raymond Aron, *The Century of Total War* (Boston: Beacon Press, 1955), p. 258.

[29] Cf. *Infra.*, p. 52.

combine this with nationalist bombast of the type common everywhere in the world.

Finally, it is heartening to record that quite apart from the need for myths to hold modern societies together, there have been occasions in past history when a myth served a wholesome, humanitarian purpose. In the sixteenth century, whose bloody side we have detailed in the preceding pages, a famous experiment in religious toleration derived in part from a myth. In 1594 Saint Francis de Sales went into the Protestant territory of Chablais near Geneva. While most missionaries of that time denounced opposing creeds, he discussed religion with the dignitaries of Chablais in the spirit of an earnest soul seeking the truth. Soon a number of local people turned Catholic. Then in 1596 the neighboring duke of Savoy sent in troops and forcibly converted the rest of the populace to Catholicism. For decades afterwards Protestants attributed *all* the conversions to force, and Catholics attributed them to the persuasive technique of Francis de Sales. The truth was somewhere in the middle, but the importance of the whole (rather small) matter was that it created a Catholic legend: that Protestants here had been won back to the old Church by reason and kindness. This strengthened the hope of many French Catholics in 1598 that the Huguenots might be won back by similar means and made them more willing then they otherwise would have been to acquiesce in the Edict of Nantes which granted extensive toleration to the French Calvinists.[30]

The Real Illusion

If there is one overmastering illusion that pervades all modern history in the Western world it is that utopia can be attained: that somehow, somewhere, at some time, in some way, the invention of this, the development of that, the victory

---

[30] For a longer account of the Chablais affair cf. John U. Nef, *The Cultural Foundations of Industrial Civilization* (Cambridge: University Press, 1958), pp. 141–45.

of such-and-such, will produce an unalloyed good of some kind and will, in the process, ennoble the nature of man. Both Renaissance humanists and nineteenth century liberals were sure that knowledge not only enlightened men but necessarily purified and elevated them as well. Hence such Christian humanists as Erasmus, Thomas More, John Colet, and Johan Reuchlin advocated freedom of theological research and speculation. Their liberal counterparts three centuries later urged the free circulation of all kinds of knowledge and opinion, confident that the ordinary man would be wise enough to contemplate all and then choose the true, the beautiful, and the good. The Renaissance humanists saw their dreams go down in the wars of religion. Those nineteenth century liberals who lived long enough saw many varieties of social, political, racial, and intellectual insanity claim parity with reason and demand the right to be heard. They saw the masses whom they had done so much to educate exploited by yellow journalists, advertisers, pornographers, demagogues, thought controllers of every species—and finally, by monsters like Adolf Hitler.[31]

The end of monarchy, the ideal of so many of the most hopeful spirits of the eighteenth century, did put an end to many ills; but it also ushered in the virus of hyper-nationalism and revived in an exaggerated form the Caesarian democracy of ancient times. Early nineteenth century nationalists were mostly generous, optimistic men, confident that the world would be everywhere more peaceful, happy and attractive if only all peoples could shake off the yoke of foreign domination, establish a nation and government of their own kind, and become free to pursue their national language, literature, culture, and ideals. It required only about half a century for nationalism of that spirit to be transformed into the sort with

[31] Two books which portray splendidly the disillusionment of late nineteenth century liberals with the twentieth century are Stefan Zweig, *The World of Yesterday* (Lincoln: U. of Nebraska Press, 1964), and H. G. Wells, *Experiment in Autobiography* (N.Y.: Macmillan, 1934). Zweig eventually despaired and committed suicide.

which the last hundred years has become all too familiar: the nationalism that manifests itself in big armies and navies, super-patriotic bombast, and claims that one's own country leads the world in all matters of any worth. In 1918 Woodrow Wilson was certain that the achievement of national self-determination would be an immeasurable boon to tens of millions of dissatisfied and oppressed East-Central Europeans. Thus such nations as Finland, Latvia, Esthonia, Lithuania, Poland, Czechoslovakia, Austria, Hungary, and Yugoslavia were brought into existence. In a quarter of a century all of them underwent experiences of the sort medieval theologians used to reserve for the damned. Most of the men who ruled them in the 1920s and 1930s were inferior in character and ability to the feudal aristocrats and monarchists they had succeeded. In one country after another democracy gave way to dictatorship. In the countries where "land reform" was carried out, (always a cause close to the hearts of liberal foreigners), agricultural production on small peasant plots dropped sharply from what it had been on big estates. Altogether, "Oppression, robbery, discontent, and disunity were greater throughout Eastern Europe in 1939 than they had been in 1914."[32] Finally, all these peoples passed successively under the harrow of Nazi Germany and Stalinist Russia. Dozens of Asian and African nations, formerly portions of European colonial empires, are now independent ("free"), but their peoples live more wretchedly in an economic sense than before, and they are now victimized by governments more corrupt and less efficient than those of the old colonial powers.

Most people in the Western world still unconsciously think chiefly in terms of freedom of expression and opinion, liberty to travel about at will, and the other democratic and civilized usages of Victorian times. Many fail entirely to realize that since 1914 the world has entered a grim age of violence and fanaticism in which these old and fine attitudes may be inap-

---

[32] The sad plight of the peoples in the Succession States is discussed with exceptional candor and realism by L. B. Namier, *Facing East* (N.Y.: Harper & Row, 1966), pp. 40–49. The quotation is from p. 46.

plicable; perhaps even suicidal. Of course this assertion raises the further question of the meaning of the years since 1914 in the long span of history. Will the historians of the distant future record that the two generations after World War I were a mere "lunatic interlude" in history; an age in which crime, violence, and despicable mythology flourished to an unprecedented degree, but which at length passed and was succeeded by the resumption of man's general progress towards peace, plenty, freedom, and democracy? Or will the historians record that it was the nineteenth century which was the exceptional age, the time when progress towards realization of these ideals moved fastest and when their attainment seemed most assured? Will they say that the world since 1914 merely reverted to history's norms before 1789: absolutism as the usual form of government; poverty, exploitation, and the threat of famine the normal lot of the ruled; torture as a standard part of legal procedure; judicial murder as the normal fate of obdurate political opponents of those in power? We still live in the twentieth century, so we cannot tell.

We may turn away from the world of politics but the picture is unchanged. Millions have believed the prophets who have told us since at least 1687 that science was going to transform the world incomparably for the better. Then the bounty of the Industrial Revolution was going to speed us to the millenium. To be sure, science and industry have provided cheap clothing of good quality, a great variety of nourishing and appetizing foods, innumerable products and gadgets which make our lives more comfortable and interesting, and advances in medicine and sanitation that have saved untold lives and eased human suffering. They have produced the wealth that has made it possible for modern nations to support many times the number of people who can survive in an agricultural society. They have produced cities, the home of so much that is entertaining, charming, and splendid in our civilization. But they have also produced slums and smog, traffic jams and water pollution, spoliation of the countryside and destruction of wildlife, poison gas and nuclear bombs, social and economic problems without number, and in the sheer growth of human population the threat of a return of famine and pestilence to ravage mankind as in ages past.

The foregoing gloomy reflections are not designed to induce despair. The products of education, liberty, science, industrialism, and the rest have been, clearly, of enormous value. The point is that we don't get them for nothing. Every advance in human affairs has a price. Often the price is well worth paying, but pay it somebody must: somewhere, sometime. Knowledge, science, control over the forces of nature, are neutral: in themselves they neither ennoble man nor debase him. They may be used for purposes worthy or despicable. The great illusion that surrounds them is the naive faith that they are an *absolute* good of some kind; that in them man will find his ethical, psychological, or spiritual salvation.

II

IS ANYTHING INEVITABLE?

It is a cliche that nothing is so clear as twenty-twenty hindsight. Nothing looks so inevitable as what has already happened, particularly if it happened long ago. It requires an effort to remember that for people who originally had to face a given situation all sorts of alternatives and developments seemed possible. Consequently, to understand history one must project his imagination into past times and past problems and consider how these appeared to contemporaries who could not foresee the future. To prepare for this enterprise we must first clear away several species of historical determinism.

Determinist Conceptions of History

> Possibly there is no more sense in human history than in the changes of the seasons or the movements of the stars; or if sense there be, it escapes our perception. But the historian, when watching strands interlace and entwine and their patterns intersect, seeks for the logic of situations and the rhythm of events which invest them with at least a determinist meaning.[1]

Innumerable men at all times have shared the "historian's" yearning. They have been fascinated by the idea that certain phenomena in history are "inevitable," that history necessarily follows some predetermined pattern, that it is "going somewhere."

---

[1] Lewis B. Namier, *Vanished Supremacies* (N.Y.: Harper Torchbooks, 1963), p. 165.

This proclivity owes much to the belief, ultimately religious, that all creatures have some purpose or goal; that they and their activities are part of a larger plan of some kind. For instance, St. Augustine and other medieval Christian writers viewed history as the process whereby God worked out his will for men—a thesis impossible either to prove or disprove since there is no way men can divine all God's purposes.

Cyclical theories of history also induce belief in determinism. The philosophers of pagan antiquity, the Renaissance skeptic Machiavelli, the eighteenth century speculator Vico, and the twentieth century prophet-historian Toynbee, are prominent among many who have believed that history moves through a series of cycles which tend to repeat themselves.

A. *Progressive*—A commoner and more influential kind of determinism, however, is the one connoted by the word "progress." Since the eighteenth century the belief has become widespread that history is essentially a process of steady improvement in all departments of human affairs. This has proved a gem of many facets. The nineteenth century German philosopher Hegel held that all history was moving towards the development of a greater Prussian state—a view which has never attracted non-Germans. (His pessimistic twentieth century countryman Oswald Spengler, by contrast, believed the decline of Western civilization to be the main theme in history. It is difficult to criticize Spengler's thesis since all civilizations have to decline at *some* time. The puzzle is, when and why?) The nineteenth century British historian Lord Acton saw the steady growth of human freedom as the mainspring of history. This hypothesis is open to at least two —and curiously different—objections. The main drift of history since 1914 certainly has not been in the direction of increasing human freedom, though of course we cannot tell whether our age of nationalist passion, race hatreds, ideological persecution, cruel dictatorships, concentration camps, genocide, and general atmosphere of fire and slaughter, is an accurate foretaste of the future or just a grim interlude through which the world is passing before resuming its (presumed) quest for greater individual freedom. The other, and more fundamental, objection is that modern Western man might never have thought about freedom at all had some ancient wars had a different outcome. Suppose the Persians had won the great battles of Marathon, Salamis, and Plataea in the fifth century B.C.? Given the character of Persian civilization at that time, and the way Persia customarily dealt with conquered peoples, it is likely that she would have ruthlessly crushed the Greek city states, destroyed their experiments in popular government, and altered the whole subsequent character of Western civilization.[2]

The most interesting advocates of the faith that history is essentially the record of man's upward progression are the "Whig" historians.[3] These sectarians have been extremely numerous and influential in the English-speaking world. The Whig's forte is studying the past not for its own sake but to discover how it shaped the present. Whig historians value chiefly those persons, practices, and institutions which seem to them forerunners of praiseworthy modern counterparts. They begin with certain assumptions: (1) history is the record of human progress, (2) the whole world wants democracy and is moving towards it, (3) Protestants have usually been the friends and promoters of progress and democracy, (4) Tories and Catholics have usually been against these laudable goals. Starting thus, they collect such information from the past as fits these assumptions and ignore what does not fit. Then they say their evidence proves their assumptions. If detailed research shows that some aspect of their version of history is untrue they will usually modify appropriate small portions of their works but leave the overall pattern unchanged. This procedure, long the dominant one in Anglo-Saxon histori-

[2] Sidney Hook, *The Hero in History* (N.Y.: Humanities Press, 1950) pp. 126–27. Considerable portions of this chapter are drawn from this excellent study of the importance of the individual man as a shaper of history.

[3] Herbert Butterfield, *The Whig Interpretation of History* (N.Y.: Charles Scribners' Sons, 1951) is much the best work on this subject. The following discussion is drawn heavily from its earlier sections.

ography, has been defined as "the process of reducing the complex truth to the simple lie."

The Whig approach to history embraces several other anomalies as well. One of the most glaring is that it draws straight lines from past persons, ideas, and institutions to present ones. Thus the signing of the Magna Carta in 1215 was a great advance towards human freedom. Thus the eighteenth century philosophes, enemies of absolute monarchy and established churches, were noble and praiseworthy men, the harbingers of a sparkling future, while their opponents were obscurantists and rascals. In real life nothing is this clear. No modern corporate body, common practice, or noteworthy idea ever came straight from a single mind or a single institution. All have developed out of the whole complex fabric of the historic past. Furthermore, there is no more reason to assume that our times and our interests are ideal or permanent than to assume this about any time in the past. If we say that the only important things in the past are those that led to what we approve in the present, then why study the past at all? Why not just study the present? And why should not men in the future invoke the same principle against us: treat with respect only the bits and pieces of our civilization that happen to attract them? Surely the sensible procedure is to value the whole past for its own sake and study it whole.

The multiple fallacies involved in the Whig interpretation of history are best exposed by a brief analysis of some historical subject on which Whiggish writers have expended much ink. The English Reformation and the last four centuries of English history are together a good illustration. To oversimplify, but not distort essentials, Whig historians have usually seen the Protestant leaders of the sixteenth century as the forerunners of modern Anglo-Saxon liberalism, constitutional government and freedom of thought. Measuring this act of faith against plain historical evidence is disconcerting. In England the religious sectarians most enthusiastic in asserting the supremacy of Parliament over the crown were the Puritans. They were also the most ardently Protestant and the most eager advocates of suppressing Catholicism. The parliamentary cause which they supported in the seventeenth century English revolutions triumphed mostly because its leaders were abler men than the inept Stuart kings whom they opposed and because the kings of England lacked the standing army and paid royal bureaucracy which any continental monarch had to oppose revolutionaries. The parliamentary victories in these revolutions were not followed by either religious or political tolerance. The triumphant Anglicans in 1660 and after did their best to suppress both Puritanism and Catholicism and to keep adherents of both out of public life. The victors in the "Glorious Revolution" of 1688 were only slightly more magnanimous. Throughout the eighteenth century a small oligarchy of wealthy English families controlled the government and all public bodies of any importance. Democracy came to England only in the nineteenth and twentieth centuries, and then only in slow stages. Frequently it advanced in the shadow of threatened revolution; always in an atmosphere of disintegrating religious loyalties. As for the triumph of democracy in the world at large, that is scarcely inevitable—whatever might or might not be its connection with Reformation Protestantism. What would have been the historical fate of democracy if the Central Powers had won the First World War, or if Nazi Germany and her allies had won the Second? Apart from wars, and disregarding the third of the world that is now (1968) Communist, one has only to read the newspapers to know that the prospects of democracy on much of our planet are precarious.

B. *Scientific*—The idea that great patterns can be discovered in history owes considerably to the correlation, regularity, and predictability that exists in the natural sciences. Ever since the seventeenth century a growing number of intellectuals have found it increasingly difficult to resist the alluring prospect that similar order and predictability also exists in the social sciences, and that we have only to devise the correct intellectual techniques to reveal it. The theory of evolution, most prominently associated with Charles Darwin, gave great impetus to this faith. Enthusiastic Darwinists assumed that due to the incessant competition for survival, everything develops in an orderly, logical fashion: the strongest, ablest, and most adaptable specimens eventually emerging victorious. Against this universal "law" of development the deeds or influence of an individual could hardly possess real significance. Evolutionary theory has itself evolved, however. It is now thought that changes in species do not proceed only in the grand, inexorable, and gradual patterns dictated by natural selection. They also appear to be due to mutations, recombination of genetic information, and gene migration. Some of these latter changes represent sudden and inexplicable alterations in the germ plasm. Thus the evolutionary hypothesis no longer so clearly implies some kind of historical determinism as it seemed to a generation or two ago.

C. *Marxist*—The most evangelical contemporary proponents of historical inevitability are the disciples of Karl Marx. These pugnacious dogmatists insist that history is essentially a chronicle of the struggles of competing economic classes. At any given time the class which dominates society is the one that owns the means of production. In the Middle Ages this was the feudal aristocracy; they owned most of the land in a largely agricultural society. By the nineteenth century the feudal caste had been overcome by bourgeois capitalists, the real rulers in an increasingly industrialized world. Capitalism, however, is vexed with numerous internal contradictions. These have already produced revolutions in which the bourgeoisie have been vanquished by the proletariat, a process bound to continue in the future. Eventually all classes, and government itself, will vanish and a completely egalitarian society of pure communism will prevail everywhere. This whole denouement is inevitable. It is enjoined by the iron laws of historical development, first discovered and analyzed by Marx himself. Before these laws of history the individual is essentially powerless, able to influence only the surface appearance of events from time to time.

Unquestionably, Marxist emphasis upon the importance of

economic factors in history has improved our understanding of the past. Nonetheless, insistence that there are laws of historical development which inexorably ordain the rise to preeminence of the burgeoisie, their inevitable defeat by the proletariat in revolution, and all the rest, raises numerous perplexing questions. To start with, one is taking leave of the real world when he lumps together vast numbers of quite different people, calls them all "capitalists," or "bourgeoisie," or "proletarians," and attributes to all of them the same ideas, interests, and objectives.[4]

The "inevitability" of proletarian revolution is equally fanciful. Suppose we grant, merely for the sake of argument, that the Russian Revolution of 1917 was inevitable. Would this prove that it was equally inevitable that a handful of Bolsheviks should have emerged from it in control of one seventh of the earth? In actuality, of course, the Revolution was not inevitable at all. It is true that most Russians who were politically alert before 1914 expected the Czarist regime to collapse or change drastically at *some* time; but none of them, Lenin included, expected it when it did come. It ran counter to all Marxist theory that revolution should come first in a backward, agricultural society like Russia instead of in an advanced industrial nation like Britain, Belgium, or Germany. Moreover, if revolutions are caused by "objective conditions" why weren't there revolutions in, say, Italy in 1922, Germany in 1923, England in 1926, or the U.S.A. in 1932–1933?

The plain truth of the matter is quite different. Before 1914 the Czarist government had begun to attack the fundamental problems that afflicted Russian society. Had it not been for the exceptional stresses and defeats of the First World War there would have been no Russian Revolution at all. Most significantly, the Revolution culminated in a Bolshevik victory for reasons that had nothing to do with all the Marxist pontification about inexorable historical forces. The democratic

---

[4] Cf. *Supra.*, pp. 43–44 for a fuller consideration of this.

Kerensky regime which eventually emerged from the February Revolution of 1917 made a disastrous mistake in trying to keep Russia actively engaged in World War I even though her army and people alike were beaten and dispirited. For a year after the Bolshevik seizure of power (October, 1917) all the world's Great Powers remained engrossed in the World War. After that bloody conflict finally ended Germany was prostrate and unable to intervene in Russia. England and France were too war weary to mount a serious effort against the Bolsheviks. The United States was concerned mostly that Japan should not take advantage of the Russian disorders to seize eastern Siberia. Had the white (anti-Revolutionary) generals possessed acumen and resolve or acted in concert they might have destroyed the Bolsheviks, a task beyond the capacity of any one of them alone. Finally, the Bolsheviks were incredibly fortunate in possessing two leaders of exceptional personal ability: Lenin and Trotsky. In the spring of 1917 the Germans hastily transported Lenin back to Russia from his place of exile in Switzerland. Had he died in Switzerland or on his return to Russia the other Bolsheviks likely would have joined a coalition government dominated by liberals. But Lenin did not die. Trotsky, then in New York, caught a ship for Russia and made his way through submarine-infested waters without incident. Once home he hurriedly joined the Bolshevik party, to which he had not even belonged previously. Lenin proved to be an organizer, conspirator, and propagandist of outstanding talent. Trotsky was equally competent. He scurried all over Russia for the next two years, raising armies, choosing officers, determining strategy, inspiring the troops, and leading the Bolshevik armies to victory. What was "inevitable" about all this? Marxist writers themselves obliquely acknowledge the absurdity of their "historical necessities" by according Lenin (though seldom Trotsky) a leading role in their accounts of the 1917 Revolution.

Even worse for their "historical necessities," since 1917 Russian society has not developed according to the Marxist blueprint. Still worse, in the half century since the Russian

Revolution several other countries have become Communist. In no case did "the laws of history" have anything to do with it. They were communized either by being occupied by the Russian army or else domestic Communists employed a mixture of force, subversion, and Russian aid to overthrow some existing regime. One historian sums up the whole wonderland of Marxist historical theory trenchantly: e.g. Marx wanted certain things to happen, therefore he invented theories to prove that they would happen. Like nearly everyone else, wishes and action came first; theory was devised afterward.[5] And what *did* happen bore small relation to what Marx either foresaw or would have wished.

Absurdity of Determinism

One of the knottiest difficulties in the claim that history is shaped remorselessly by "laws" which men can discover, is that there is so much disagreement about what those laws are and that there are so many different kinds of them. Whether the particular laws be the relentless decline of Western civilization, the propulsion of history by the "masses," the "inevitable" triumph of collectivism, or some other, they all bear the visage of titanic supernatural forces like the gods and demons of old. One of the most popular of them (usually expressed in the cliche "ideas make history") appears to assume that the nonintellectual masses are heavily influenced by the cerebrations of more intellectual types, and that important public acts are but reflections of the "intellectual currents" of the age. This is easier to assert than to prove. How was it possible for the English Parliament in 1571 to pass a law allowing loans at 10 percent when English intellectuals and divines were still condemning usury after the medieval fashion? What "intellectual currents" caused Charles XII of Sweden to invade Russia in 1707–1709, or Frederick the

[5] A. J. P. Taylor, *From Napoleon to Lenin* (N.Y.: Harper & Row, 1966), p. 166.

Great to seize Silesia in 1740? And what of the innumerable polls and scholarly studies which show that a large percentage of the population in the most advanced twentieth century countries have never heard of the contemporary prophets or great ideas which excite intellectuals?

Even more troublesome, determinists find it impossible to act as if they believed their own principles. They point out (justly) that advances in the natural and social sciences have shown that people are heavily conditioned by environment, geography, past experiences, and training. The more intemperate of them then claim that this shows that to praise or blame this or that public figure for what he did is as pointless as blaming animals for their acts or lecturing a stone over which one has stubbed his toe. Yet the same persons urge historians to be objective when they write of the past; to avoid reading their own interests into other societies and ages. In their own writings, they stress the importance of this person or that circumstance and they criticize historians whose biases or opinions differ from their own. They are no more inclined than anyone else to resign themselves to happenings they dislike or that are detrimental to their aspirations. (What Communist ever argued that it was pointless to criticize capitalism or work for its downfall since the iron laws of history decree that it must vanish sometime anyway?) In short, those who scoff at the idea that history is shaped by the free choices of individual men do not and cannot act in accord with their professed doctrines.[6]

The truth is that there are vast areas of human experience and history where nothing has been inevitable save the proverbial death and taxes. It is to some of those that we now turn.

A. *The Processes of Government*—Anyone with experience in government knows how often what later looks like a settled, deliberate policy was embarked upon haltingly, haphazardly, even reluctantly, and frequently under pressures

---

[6] These and other complexities involved in the belief in inevitability are explored with thoroughness and acumen by Isaiah Berlin, *Historical Inevitability* (N.Y.: Oxford Press, 1954).

which later observers have either forgotten or never knew. One of the foremost architects of American foreign policy since World War II has provided an excellent description of the uncertainties and indecision in the highest circles of government that surrounded the formulation of the Marshall Plan and the Containment Policy in 1946–1947.[7]

Oftentimes governments merely muddle into some uncomfortable situation and then have to try to find a way out of it. Long afterward, of course, those with political reputations at stake insist that the whole process was the result of careful thought and planning. They are especially zealous to do this if things happened to turn out in some way that met general public approval. In the unification of Italy, the role of Count Camillo Cavour, the nineteenth century prime minister of Sardinia, illustrates the point. Cavour did not really set out to unify Italy at all. He distrusted "radical dreamers" like Mazzini, and disliked the thought of "progressive" northern Italy becoming tied to the backward, illiterate, "African" south. His objective was more limited: to increase the holdings of Piedmont-Sardinia in the north. To use revolution as a technique for unifying all Italy on a nationalist basis was Garibaldi's policy, not Cavour's. However, Garibaldi's unexpected successes in Sicily and southern Italy (1860–1861) forced Cavour's hand. He had to take over Garibaldi's conquests to prevent that romantic but quixotic adventurer from expelling the Pope and perhaps even invading Piedmont-Sardinia itself. Thus, inadvertently, he became the architect of Italian unification. Afterward, he said this had *always* been his intention. Anglo-Saxon writers largely took him at his word and depicted him as a hero, perhaps because he outwitted Napoleon III and triumphed over Pope Pius IX, the two leading bogeymen of late nineteenth century English Protestant Whig historians.[8] Bismarck played a similarly

[7] George Kennan, *Memoirs, 1925–1950* (Boston: Little, Brown & Co., 1967), pp. 325–67.

[8] L. C. B. Seaman, *From Vienna to Versailles* (N.Y.: Harper & Row, Colophon Books, 1963), pp. 69–95.

equivocal role in the unification of Germany (1848–1871), and similarly misrepresented his intentions when he wrote his memoirs in the 1890s. A less serious example of the uncertainties that surround the making of government policies concerns the eccentric British Prime Minister Lord Melbourne (1834–1841). At the conclusion of a long and boring cabinet meeting about a subject of which he knew little, Melbourne called out after his departing colleagues, "Bye the bye, there's one thing we haven't agreed on, which is, what are we to say? Is it to make corn dearer, or cheaper, or to make the price steady? I don't care which, but we must all be in the same story."[9]

B. *The Fate of Nations*—Innumerable patriot-historians have delighted their fellow citizens by assuring them that such a talented, stalwart folk as themselves must have a "historic mission" of some kind. Thus the French are chained to the "historic mission" of restraining the Germanic barbarians, the Germans have the "historic mission" of holding back the tide of Slavic barbarism, and the Poles and Swedes used to have the mission of shielding Western civilization from the Russian barbarians. (Perhaps the Russians will one day defend the world against Mongolian barbarism.)

Likewise, people have often been told that they have a historic mission to form a great state, and that once established their state must inevitably expand its natural boundaries. In America this historic mission used to be called Manifest Destiny. The natural boundaries steadily retreated in all directions: to the Mississippi, to Florida, to the Pacific, to the Arctic, and to the western Pacific. This expansionism was justified at different times by a wide variety of appeals and arguments drawn from geography, alleged defense needs, the American mission to spread freedom, the law of nature requiring growth as the only alternative to stagnation and senescence, the white man's burden, the need to help maintain world peace, the need to set an international good example,

---

[9] Bertram Newman, *Lord Melbourne* (London: Macmillan, 1930), p. 296.

and much else.[10] In Europe one of the most familiar examples of natural boundaries concerns those that are supposed to be the birthright of France: the Rhine, the Jura, the Alps, the Pyrenees, and the sea. The English philosopher-statesman Lord Balfour once delivered an apt evaluation of this kind of disguised chauvinism by remarking that he had never heard of a state whose natural boundaries were smaller than its actual boundaries.

The whole idea that there was ever anything inevitable about the formation of the world's present political entities is nonsense. Was it inevitable that in the early Middle Ages the Lombards should have overrun Italy, that the Franks should then have crossed the Alps to oppose them, the papal states then been founded in collusion with the Franks, and the Holy Roman Empire subsequently revived in the West? Hardly. If the Byzantine Emperor Justinian (527–565) had not been obsessed with schemes to reconquer the western Roman Empire he would not have molested the Ostrogoth kingdom in Italy. In that case the Ostrogoths probably would have been able to contain the barbarous Lombards north of the Alps. If so, the other events enumerated above would not have happened, and Italy would have been unified throughout the Middle Ages.[11]

Was it inevitable that Poland, a large, populous state, should have been partitioned by her neighbors in the eighteenth century, while Prussia, a smaller and poorer nation, became a Great Power? No. The difference was that Prussia developed a strong, sound political and military system and survived in the world of carnivorous international politics. Poland failed to do so and was liquidated.

Was it inevitable that Russia should have become one of the superpowers of the twentieth century; that her vast size, large population, huge expanse of fertile farmland, abundant oil and coal, myriad of minerals, and immense timber

---

[10] A good study of this American proclivity is Albert Weinberg, *Manifest Destiny* (Baltimore: Johns Hopkins Press, 1935).

[11] The example is taken from Hook, *op. cit.*, p. 165.

resources insured that she should some day surpass such lil-liputian states as England, France, Germany, and Belgium in industrial production and political strength? Certainly, *if* she ever got a progressive, efficient government. But the "if" is crucial. The land and its wealth have always been there, but there was nothing inevitable about the development of efficient government.

Indeed, several centuries ago it was doubtful whether Russia would ever become a state at all. As late as 1708–09, Charles XII of Sweden probably would have conquered what was then European Russia had the Cossacks revolted (as they promised), against the Muscovite government. However, a Cossack chieftain whose daughter had been seduced by Mazeppa, the hetman of the Cossacks, revealed the plot to the Czar and the uprising never took place. Still, even without the Cossacks, Charles might have won the great battle of Poltava in 1709 had he been able to lead his troops in person. But he had been hit by a sniper's bullet a few days earlier and had to be carried to the battlefield on a litter. Even after his defeat at Poltava he succeeded, mostly through his influ-ence with the Sultan's mother, in persuading the Turks to fight the Russians for him. The Turkish Grand Vizier Baltaji maneu-vered the Russian army into a trap—but then let it escape in return for bribes, promises, and a peace treaty favor-able to Turkey! Russia at that time comprised only about half her present European territory, contained several different "races," had a smaller population than France, and was the most primitive state in Europe. Had the Swedish or Turkish campaigns turned out as contemporaries might reasonably have expected, it is unlikely that eastern Europe would ever have been organized into one gigantic national state at all.[12]

Only in the twentieth century did Russia finally get a government sufficiently energetic and efficient to effectively exploit her enormous potential. Even then the achievements would have been destroyed had the USSR lost World War II

[12] These uncertainties in Russian history are surveyed by Dennis J. Mc-Carthy, "The Kalabalik," *History Today*, June 1965, pp. 391–99.

to the Germans. And she would have lost it save for an exceptionally cold winter (1941–1942), a variety of German military mistakes, and Hitler's mad policy of slaughtering and enslaving the Ukranians—a monstrous blunder which turned these potential friends of Germany into fierce Russian patriots. By such slender threads have nations survived!

An examination of other rich portions of the earth indicates that the mere possession of valuable natural resources determines nothing in particular. The vast mineral wealth of the New World and the immensely fertile plains of Argentina, Canada, and the United States were all there before 1492, but they did not shape the general course of history because the Indians left them unused. The mineral wealth became important historically only because the Spaniards wanted it; the expanses of fertile land only when they were broken to the plow. To this day Brazil struggles in the toils of a dozen social and economic problems and perpetually totters on the brink of bankruptcy not because she is poor (for she is rich in resources), but because she does not exploit her wealth effectively. For seventy-five years before 1945, Japan coveted the wealth of east Asia and her chauvinist politicians claimed that her prosperity depended on acquisition of these territories. Yet contemporary Japan, lacking in natural resources and utterly defeated in 1945, became a prosperous nation in fifteen or twenty years without any of the supposedly "necessary" East Asian territories. The presence or absence of natural wealth obviously affects a nation's destiny, but more important is the attitude of its people.

Nearly 500 years ago the determination of one woman, Isabella of Castile, altered in fundamentals the whole subsequent history of the Iberian peninsula. If one looks at a map it appears logical, "inevitable" many would say, that the Iberian peninsula should eventually form one state. Surrounded on three and one-half sides by water and separated from the rest of Europe by the Pyrenees Mountains, it seems a perfect example of geography providing natural boundaries for a single state. Yet to this day Spain and Portugal are separate, independent nations. In the fifteenth century it seemed unlikely that union of any kind would ever be brought to the peninsula. It then contained five separate peoples, three major religions, and five independent states. One of the latter was the Moslem enclave of Granada, finally conquered only in 1492. The two major states were Aragon and Castile. They had different cultures, their peoples were separated by deep hostility, and their historic interests differed. Aragon looked eastward to its Mediterranean empire; Castile, like Portugal, westward and southward to the sea. They were separated even by a watershed, for the rivers of Castile flow westward to the Atlantic, most of them through Portugal, while those of Aragon flow eastward into the Mediterranean. By all tests of geography, culture, and historic tradition Castile should have united with Portugal rather than Aragon. These considerations, however, proved trifling when ranged against the will of a nineteen-year-old girl. In 1469 Isabella, heiress to the throne of Castile, ignored the opposition of her brother, King Henry IV of Castile, spurned French, English, and Portugese suitors, and even incurred papal excommunication to marry Prince Ferdinand, heir to the throne of Aragon. Under the leadership of this exceptionally able and determined couple the foundations of modern Spain were laid. Moslem power in the peninsula was broken. The scattered Spanish states and conglomerate peoples were welded, at least superficially, into one entity. The sailor-dreamer Columbus, whose schemes had been (inevitably?) ignored by every other western European court, was (inevitably?) befriended and financed by Isabella. The world's most momentous overseas exploration began, and Spain soon began to build the world's greatest colonial empire. Meantime, due to the ties with Aragon, the eyes of Castile were turning increasingly towards the affairs of the rest of Europe.

Still, most of these accomplishments would likely have been undone but for a series of historical accidents. Omitting Catherine of Aragon, who is irrelevant to this discussion since she had become queen of England, all but one of the children of Ferdinand and Isabella died young. The exception was Joanna, who went totally mad when her husband, Philip of Burgundy, also died young—and quite unexpectedly. These domestic tragedies wrought a political miracle. Joanna's son (Isabella's grandson) inherited all his ancestors' possessions, something that was possible only because the Salic Law did not apply in Spain. Had it applied, the claims of the grandson, proceeding through the female line, would not have been respected. This heir soon secured his election as the Holy Roman Emperor Charles V (1519–1556). As such he ruled a larger portion of Europe (west of Russia) than any man since the Roman emperors of antiquity. Lord of half the earth, Charles drew on the fabulous wealth newly discovered in the Spanish possessions of Mexico and Peru to battle rebellious Lutheran princes in the Germanies, Turks on the Danube, Barbary pirates in the Mediterranean, English pirates in the Atlantic, Indians in the jungles of South America, domestic rebels in Spain, and French armies all over western Europe. All the great international diplomatic combinations of his age were directed against Spain, and for a hundred years European Protestants lived in terror at the prospect of the Spanish colossus overrunning the continent and reversing the Protestant Reformation. What "iron laws of history" dictated all this on the wedding day of Ferdinand and Isabella in 1469?[13]

If logic were the primary factor in state building, the Scandinavian rather than the Spanish states should have become one unified nation at the end of the Middle Ages. Their ethnic and linguistic differences were much less marked than those of the Iberian peoples, they were as close geographically as the Iberian states, and they were as relatively isolated in northern Europe as the Iberian states were in the southwest. But Scandinavia never had a Ferdinand and Isabella. For only a

---

[13] For discussions of this cf. Myron Gilmore, *The World of Humanism* (N.Y.: Harper & Row, 1952), p. 75, and John Lynch, *Spain Under the Hapsburgs* (Oxford: Blackwells, 1964), pp. 1–2. For a consideration of the possibility of reversing the Reformation cf. *Supra.*, pp. 27–29.

brief moment in its history, the Union of Kalmar of 1397, was it ever united under a single crown.

On the other side of the coin, there have been lands that *did* become nations even though all logic was against it. Such a one was the Netherlands. The Low Countries in the sixteenth century had no natural unity of any kind. They were merely a collection of small provinces clustered around the mouths of western Europe's most extensive river system. Some of their people spoke French and others a variant of German. None regarded themselves as members of a separate or distinct nationality. Accidents of dynastic marriage and inheritance had given these territories to the Spanish crown. In the 1560s these lands, for a variety of reasons (constitutional, religious, economic, and personal), rose in rebellion against Spain. Under normal conditions the powerful Spanish army could have crushed the rebellion in short order. But conditions were not normal. Spain had commitments all over Europe and the New World and could never give her undivided attention to the obstreperous "Dutch." Moreover the northern provinces of the Low Countries were separated from the southern by a maze of swamps, creeks, canals, ditches, and estuaries, many of them below sea level. These presented logistical problems which, given the resources and means of transport then available, the Spanish generals could not solve. In these circumstances the war became a hopeless stalemate. The Spaniards were able to control the ten southern provinces but could not conduct successful military operations against the seven northern provinces. On their part, the northern rebels, even with command of the sea, were not strong enough to wrest the southern provinces from Spain. The best they could do was to prevent Spanish amphibious operations against themselves. Gradually the Calvinist rebels in the north expelled Catholics from the lands they controlled. Gradually the Spaniards in the south drove out Protestants—most of whom migrated to the north. Other European powers intervened periodically, chiefly in an effort to prevent a Spanish victory. Eventually, after eighty years of ponderous, inconclusive struggle interspersed with uneasy truces, the seven northern provinces (by now largely Protestant in religion), were recognized as an independent state and the ten southern provinces (modern Belgium) remained possessions of the Hapsburgs.

This account of the formation of an independent Netherlands will not strike the casual reader as particularly remarkable but it took the effort of a lifetime by a great Dutch scholar, Pieter Geyl, to establish these sober truths in his homeland—and among most British and American historians as well. He had to combat innumerable patriotic legends, entrenched for centuries in Dutch and English historical writing. These legends related how the Dutch won their independence because they were more sober and industrious, more sturdy and self-reliant, than the Belgians; because they were Protestant rather than Catholic, and therefore more fervent lovers of liberty. Apparently patriot-historians regard it as vaguely shameful to ascribe their nation's existence to the vagaries of dynastic inheritance and the location of river mouths, rather than to supposedly sterling personal qualities.[14]

C. *The Influence of the Individual*—History has always been heavily influenced by those occupying the seats of power. This statement will not surprise the ordinary common sense man. He knows from observation and experience that it makes a great deal of difference who operates a given business, coaches a football team, or fixes his television set. If he knows much history he has no difficulty acknowledging that while Caesar, Charlemagne, Genghis Khan, Napoleon, Lenin, and such like, were not necessarily admirable men they indubitably possessed far more than the ordinary man's abilities and did deeds which affected the world for generations—even centuries—after their deaths. He accepts that the same is true of

---

[14] Among Geyl's many books on Dutch history the following are pertinent here: *The Revolt of the Netherlands, 1555–1609* (London: Williams and Norgate, 1932); and *The Netherlands Invaded, 1609–1648* (London: Williams and Norgate, 1936). For an excellent brief summary of the matter cf. Geyl's *Debates with Historians* (The Hague: Martinus Nijhof, 1955), pp. 179–97.

the giants of history in the arts and sciences: Aristotle, da Vinci, Copernicus, Newton, Rousseau, Darwin, Freud, and many others.

The foregoing judgment is in no way weakened by the fact that some prominent historical figures *thought of themselves* as merely the servants of Higher Forces. Oliver Cromwell appears to have been convinced that he was God's Instrument and Lenin was supposedly the mere tool of Historical Necessity.

But there are more sophisticated human types than our hypothetical "common sense man." Many of them contend that the individual counts for little; that the situation produces the man; that the particular needs of an age call forth a heroic figure to deal with them. While we may grant them that many a famous statesman or soldier would have lived and died in obscurity had not a war or crisis developed at a particular time and place, still this whole view of history presents insuperable difficulties. Some of any individual man's potential is determined at birth. How could any crisis affect this? More important, who or what guarantees that the Great Man will emerge in the crisis? Divine Providence? The laws of evolution? The Historical Necessity of the Marxists? Moreover, the *need* for greatness always exists. There are crises of *some* kind in the world all the time. Yet the Great Man usually does not appear. For five centuries Balkan Europe was ground under the heel of the predatory Ottoman Empire. Why didn't a great man emerge in one of these fifteen generations and inspire his fellow Europeans to abandon their internecine feuds and use their superior collective strength to hurl the Turk out of Europe permanently? The *need* certainly existed. Sixteenth century Europe was racked with religious schism, persecution, warfare, and hatred. Why didn't some towering figure appear on the Catholic side and inspire Catholicism to reform itself and win the Protestants back to Rome? Why didn't a hero emerge on the other side to unite all the warring Protestant groups and win over Catholic Europe as well? For that matter, why didn't there appear a secular statesman of superlative talent able to impose peace on all the religious factions? The "social need" certainly existed. More fundamentally, would there have been a Protestant Reformation at all, or if so what course might it have taken, had Frederick the Wise of Saxony done the ordinary thing in 1521 and surrendered Martin Luther to imperial authorities instead of protecting him from his enemies at a crucial time in Luther's career?[15]

Furthermore, suppose some great need exists, and a man has come forth. Who guarantees that he knows what he is supposed to do or, if he does know, that he will be capable of doing it? The Great Man himself is usually far less prescient than those who later sit in libraries and spin fantasies about historical inevitability. In World War I Germany desperately needed nitrates to make munitions and fertilizer. Naturally, German scientists worked feverishly to try to find a way to produce nitrates. But was it inevitable that one of them, Franz Haber, should have succeeded—and in time to stave off imminent defeat? In the seventeenth century, if the mass of Frenchmen needed anything that was in the power of their rulers to give them, it was peace, greater honesty and regularity in government, and reduced taxation. However, the king of France, Louis XIV, the very model of absolute monarchy, had not heard that great men like himself are the servants of "social needs," so he taxed his subjects extortionately and shed their blood prodigally in half a dozen major wars. If Italy in the 1920s and 1930s had an outstanding social need it was for an extension of the domestic reforms and public works projects undertaken by Mussolini. But Mussolini himself became more interested in posing as a reincarnated Julius Caesar and led his people to ruin in war instead.

Finally, reductio ad absurdum, how does one account for the occasional superfluity of great men? Why should the city of Athens have produced within a short period Socrates, Plato, Aeschylus, Sophocles, Euripides, Aristophanes, Thucydides, and Xenophon? Why should Germany have brought

[15] Philip Hughes, *A Popular History of the Reformation* (Garden City, N.Y.: Hanover House, 1957), pp. 127–28.

forth within a century Lessing, Kant, Fichte, Hegel, Schelling, and Schopenhauer? What geographical, biological, political, or psychological imperative was responsible? Why were so many great men produced only in these particular places at those particular times? Did not equivalent social needs exist elsewhere?[16]

In the many centuries when monarchs ruled as well as reigned, the quality of the person on the throne was crucial for the welfare and future of the country. (The case of Isabella of Castile has already been considered.) There were kings like Henry IV (1589–1610) and Louis XIV of France who kept a succession of mistresses but insured that this diversion was of no political consequence by denying their women any appreciable influence in state affairs. Was it inevitable that their descendant, Louis XV (1715–1772), should have been dominated by *his* mistresses? Was it inevitable that one of them, but *only* one, Madame de Pompadour, should have been an intellectual type, fascinated by affairs of state, the friend and patroness of intellectuals who desired drastic alterations in the whole structure of French society? Was it inevitable that Frederick the Great of Prussia should have made uncomplimentary personal remarks about Pompadour, and Pompadour resented these so strongly that she helped push France into the Seven Years War (1756–1763), a conflict in which the French overseas empire was lost?

Had it not been for Thomas Jefferson's purchase of the Louisiana Territory England probably would have gotten this vast tract at the Congress of Vienna in 1815. Then the fledgling United States would have been confined to the eastern third of the present U.S.A. Was it inevitable that Jefferson should have made the purchase? Let us look at the record. In 1800 Napoleon Bonaparte, then first consul of France, forced Spain to cede him the Louisiana Territory. He then planned to conquer the island of Santo Domingo and use it as a base

[16] This point and related matters are considered by Morris R. Cohen, "Causation and Its Application to History," *Journal of the History of Ideas*, III, (1942), 25–26.

from which to occupy the Louisiana Territory and reestablish for France the North American empire she had lost to the British in 1763. Unhappily for Napoleon, 80 percent of the troops he dispatched to Santo Domingo died of yellow fever. The remainder were resisted with uncommon skill by a native military hero, Toussaint l'Overture. Moreover, bad weather prevented relief ships from bringing speedy aid. By 1803 Napoleon gave up. He offered to sell Louisiana to the United States. The new territory more than doubled the area of the young republic and was the most important single event in the evolution of the former thirteen colonies into the world's richest and mightiest nation. Who can say what a different president might have decided had the offer been made to him? Jefferson himself made the purchase reluctantly, mostly out of fear that New Orleans, the gateway to the Mississippi, might be closed to American shipping by France or might fall into the hands of England. Twenty years later Jefferson still thought so little of the momentous purchase that he directed that his tombstone bear only the legend, "Author of the Declaration of American Independence, of the Statute of Virginia for religious freedom, and Father of the University of Virginia."

What this whole discussion boils down to is what anyone knows who has not abandoned the common sense bestowed on him at birth: that public affairs are always shaped considerably by what our rulers decide to do or not to do. In all societies key decisions in politics, education, public services, science, and religion, are made by a handful of national or institutional leaders. In all cases those who decide are influenced by advisors and by popular tastes and desires, but in the last analysis it is still the premiers and presidents, the popes and chairmen of the board, who decide. In Stalinist Russia it was notorious that *one man* imposed his own ideas, tastes, and standards on everyone else. In many of the newly independent states of Asia and Africa the tiny educated and westernized ruling minority will probably have to do this for a considerable time to come.

In this connection it is sometimes objected that modern society is so complex that one man counts for less than in times past. This is true in a sense, but profoundly untrue in another. Due to the development of railroads, airplanes, telephones, radios, fingerprinting, computers, and much else, the head of state in a democratic country now has far more real control over his people than used to be exercised by the most despotic king. To be sure, he does not normally exploit this control to the fullest, but the possibility exists nonetheless.

D. *Historical Accidents*—Though it is painful for human pride to admit, a good deal of history has been altered because of some small matter or other: somebody was not brave or intelligent in a crisis; something unforeseen happened which altered something else of far greater importance. The uncertainty of Russia's fate in the seventeenth and early eighteenth centuries has already been noted. To take another example, so far as we know it was sheer accident that the brown rat emigrated from Hanover to England in the seventeenth century. Nonetheless the effects were far reaching. The brown rats were more pugnacious than black rats and beat them to most food supplies. The black rats were largely driven off the land and took to ships. While both types of rats carried fleas that bore plague germs the brown rats scattered over the countryside whereas black rats customarily congregated in towns. Thus the brown rats were in regular contact with fewer people than the black rats had been and the plague declined markedly in England.[17]

Most historians have assumed that the Byzantines could never have reconquered and revived the Roman Empire. Of course they did fail in this endeavor, but one of the greatest modern scholars in early medieval history always thought that had it not been for a totally unpredictable event, the sudden rise of the Islamic religion, a latter day Justinian eventually would have reconstituted the old empire.[18]

[17] Charles Mullett, *The Bubonic Plague and England* (Lexington, Ky.: University of Kentucky Press, 1956), p. 8.
[18] Henri Pirenne, *Mohammed and Charlemagne* (N.Y.: Norton, 1939), p. 164.

Had Catherine of Aragon agreed (1520s) to an annulment of her marriage to Henry VIII, had she even been willing to cooperate in any of a number of legal and ecclesiastical subterfuges concocted in London and Rome, the whole religious history of the British Isles would have been different. Conceivably a Catholic England might have made possible a general victory for the Counter-Reformation.

Had Louis XVI (1772–1792) been an energetic and wise man he would have made some generous concessions to the Estates general early in the French Revolution. Very likely this would have gained him the confidence of its members and enabled him to emerge from the turmoil a strong, though constitutional, monarch. This would have changed the whole course of modern French—and world—history.

On the American side of the Atlantic it is likely that our recent history was altered markedly, perhaps dramatically, in 1916 by the failure of the Republican presidential candidate, Charles Evans Hughes, to shake hands with Senator Hiram Johnson of California. During the campaign Hughes, fearful of exacerbating a feud between two different Republican factions in California, one of which was headed by Johnson, did not seek out Johnson even though the two for a time shared the same hotel. Johnson, an extremely sensitive man, was offended and did not support the national ticket with vigor. On election day Johnson carried his home state in the senatorial race by 296,815 votes but Hughes *lost* the state—and with it the presidency— by 3773! Woodrow Wilson, the incumbent president, believed that newly elected presidents should take office immediately. Consequently he had worked out an elaborate sequence of resignations and appointments which would have resulted in Hughes assuming the presidency within a few days if he (Wilson) lost the election. Five months after the election the still-President Wilson took the United States into World War I. What "President" Hughes might have done is anyone's guess.[19] Similar examples could be multiplied endlessly.

---

[19] Mark Sullivan, *Our Times,* V (N.Y.: Scribners', 1926–35), 239–44.

E. *"Inevitabilities" that did not Materialize*—History is also replete with instances where a certain development looked inevitable but nevertheless did not take place. In September of 1792 an army of Prussian veterans, heirs to the stirring military tradition of Frederick the Great and commanded by one of Frederick's most famous captains, the duke of Brunswick, marched through eastern France towards Paris. France was in the throes of revolution. The nation was divided, the revolutionary government was vexed by a thousand nagging problems, the army was wretchedly disorganized, supplies were short, and morale was low. It seemed inevitable that Brunswick would shortly occupy Paris, crush the revolution, and restore the Bourbon monarchy to its ancient authority. Yet raw French levies, on a wet, foggy morning, September 20, 1792, fought the muddled battle of Valmy against the Prussian regulars and turned them back. Then, for reasons never adequately explained, Brunswick decided to break off the campaign for the winter. By the following spring the French army had been transformed: so completely reorganized and strengthened that it was not only invincible when defending its homeland but able to take the offensive as well. The revolution was saved! So miraculous did the event seem to the revolutionaries that they took the date of Valmy as the first day of the year one in their new revolutionary calendar.

In the latter part of the nineteenth century talk was common in the chancelleries of Europe that if another major war broke out it would almost certainly be between England and Russia. In 1904 Russia did fall into a war with Japan, then allied with England. In the course of that conflict the Russian Baltic fleet, on its way to the Far East, mistakenly fired on some English fishing boats in the North Sea. Had the British replied with a general attack on the Russian fleet, a response which statesmen and diplomats everywhere would have regarded as normal in the circumstances, an Anglo-Russian war would have followed. For generations afterward, diplomatic historians would have assured their readers that the conflict was the "inevitable" outcome of long standing animosities and clashes of national interest between the two countries. The

British government of 1904, however, chose to be content with a protest and a Russian apology. Thus the "inevitable" war never happened. What *did* happen was so incredible that anyone who had predicted it in 1890 would have been thought insane: within three years of this Dogger Bank "incident" of 1904 Britain and Russia resolved their differences and became allies. Not only did they never war against each other: they fought side by side against Germany in both world wars!

F. *Historical Reputations*—The permanent reputations of many of history's outstanding figures have been heavily influenced by the accident that they died at a particular time. The assassination of Abraham Lincoln was, of course, a personal and national tragedy, but it is likely that it ensured Lincoln a higher historical reputation than he would have enjoyed had he lived to serve his second term and to battle the vindictive Congress that badgered and impeached his successor.[20]

Woodrow Wilson and Adolf Hitler, by contrast, both lived too long. Suppose Wilson had died in December, 1918 at the peak of his popularity and influence. For the next five centuries the overwhelming majority of English and American historians would have written: "If only that Providential Man had lived to attend the Versailles Peace Conference he would have overcome the opposition of the rascally Old Diplomats of Europe, secured a generous peace for Germany, and brought the United States into the League of Nations. Then the League would have been powerful and effective from its incep-

---

[20] A sharp dissent to this judgment is filed by Morris R. Cohen, *loc. cit.*, p. 19: e.g. ". . . it can hardly be questioned that if Lincoln had not been murdered, his national prestige, his influence in the Republican party, and his political tact and experience would have enabled him to guide the Reconstruction of the South more successfully in a humane direction than was possible for a southern Democrat as inadaptable to the actual situation as was Andrew Johnson."

This seems to this writer unlikely. Granted that Lincoln was a far abler man than Johnson, it was the presidential Reconstruction *policy* which outraged a majority of congressmen, and Johnson merely tried to carry out Lincoln's policy. Moreover, Lincoln was nothing like the universal hero in his lifetime that he has become since.

tion and our planet would have been spared World War II."
But of course Wilson *did* live to attend the Versailles conference! He proved unable to achieve any of the wonders his
admirers expected, and he died a few years later with his
dreams in ruins. Had Hitler died in December, 1938 he would
have gone down in history as Adolf the Great, incomparably
the most successful German statesman of all the ages: the
man who in only five and one-half years overcame the depression, provided full employment, restored the nation's self-
respect, smashed the hated Treaty of Versailles, and regained
all the "lost" German territories (and more) without war.
Alas! Adolf the Great lived six years longer: six years in which
he cast away all these gains in history's most destructive war
and left Germany in smoking ruins.[21]

G. *A Hypothetical Case*—As a final illustration of the
hollowness of historical determinism let us consider a hypothetical case. Let us suppose that Richard Nixon rather than
John Kennedy had won the extremely close election of 1960
and become president of the United States. Would Nixon have
pushed through the Bay of Pigs invasion of Cuba regardless
of risk, overturned the Castro regime, and thereby avoided
the missile crisis of 1962 which Kennedy had to face? Would
Nixon have pursued such a forceful policy at either the Bay
of Pigs (or, perhaps, in the later missile crisis) that nuclear
war between Russia and the United States would have resulted
and most of us would now be dead? Or would he have acted
much the same as Kennedy in either, or both, cases? We don't
know and we never will know. All we know is that the man
who *was* elected (Kennedy), had to make the crucial decisions
in both cases and that he had several alternatives in each one.

Inevitability and Contingency

Has the foregoing discussion of the inadequacies of historical necessity proved that history has no patterns at all?

---

[21] This fascinating aspect of Der Führer's spectacular career is discussed
by Helmut Heiber, *Adolf Hitler* (London: Oswald Wolff, 1961), p. 141.

Have we justified the cynic who defined history as "just one damned thing after another"? Hardly. Generalizations about history are easily overdone, but many of them are valid. If certain situations exist, if certain policies are pursued, there are definite consequences which almost always follow. Many major historical developments are inevitable in the broad sense that something like them was bound to happen sometime; but not inevitable in that human effort could have changed their character considerably, could have hastened or postponed their coming, could have caused them to occur elsewhere, or could have significantly altered their consequences. Thus much history consists of vague, overall inevitabilities (the advance and spread of knowledge, the conflict of rival interest groups, the recurrence of wars, the growing power of central governments); but inevitabilities always extensively shaped and modified by the ideas and deeds of individual men and human organizations.

Consider the medieval church. It fell heir to a multitude of secular duties largely abandoned by civil authority for several centuries after the fall of the Roman Empire. Then for many additional centuries it was engaged in a constant struggle with worldly powers for supremacy. Throughout the whole period it was engaged in converting whole tribes and nations of illiterate barbarians. Inevitably, it became worldly and partly barbarized itself—even to the point of employing the Inquisition against Waldensian and Albigensian heretics who stressed the Christlike poverty that was supposed to be the Church's own hallmark.

Yet all its members did not become corrupt, nor did all its leaders, nor even all of them in a given epoch. Gregory VII (1073–1085), Innocent III (1198–1216), and Boniface VIII (1294–1303) all struggled mightily against secular powers. The first two remained largely untouched by worldliness; Boniface VIII did not. Neither did the Renaissance popes. Where the medieval popes had tried to increase the secular domain and wealth of the church because they had found by experience that this was the surest way to insure her religious independence, the Renaissance popes came to pursue these objectives for themselves: to aggrandize their families and friends. Yet this was not true of *all* the Renaissance popes. Adrian VI (1522–1523) was a significant exception.

The Counter-Reformation popes were, as a group, a much better lot of churchmen than their immediate predecessors, a development probably inevitable when an institution is going through a period of successful reform. Yet not all were pious and severe. Paul III (1534–1549) was indecisive, Julius III (1550–1555) a rough nepotist, and Sixtus V (1585–1590) primarily an administrator and builder.

Or, consider the history of sixteenth century exploration. It was changed markedly in details because Columbus discovered America in 1492, but its main outlines would have been similar had Columbus never lived. Fifteenth century Europeans had better ships and maps and navigational devices than ever before, they had the wanderlust, they badly needed a cheaper sea route to the Indies, and they were regularly striking out boldly into uncharted waters. Cabot, Vespucci, da Gama, Verrazano, or someone else would have discovered the New World soon after 1492, Columbus or no.

A. *Human Nature*—Some things are inevitable in history merely because certain elements in human nature are constant. For instance, save for an occasional altruist, men will normally try to buy as cheaply as possible and sell as dear as possible. Many times in the past public authorities have tried to set fixed, legal prices. The Roman Emperor Diocletian (284–304 A.D.) tried to do it to control defense expenditures. The medieval guilds tried to do it to protect the interests of their members and those of the public alike. The French revolutionary government of 1793–1794 tried to do it to check a catastrophic decline in the value of paper money and to insure provisioning of the army. Russian Communists have tried it in an effort to destroy the profit motive. The results have always been the same: an outbreak of evasion, fraud, and black marketeering. (Of course it may be objected that U.S. price regulations during world War II worked moderately well —but the evasion, black marketeering, and the rest were still in evidence.)

Deal harshly, or at least ungenerously, with a people temporarily dependent on you, but neglect to deprive them of their means of resistance, and they will soon undertake a war of revenge against you—as the Visigoths did against the Romans in 378 A.D. and the Germans did against half of Europe, 1939–1945. Treat your subjects shamefully and they will eventually revolt, though it is impossible to predict just when they will do so. The French people rebelled only in 1789, though they had been systematically cheated and exploited by their rulers for generations. It was tragic that the king who paid with his life for their wrath was the well-intentioned Louis XVI; not Louis XIV or Louis XV, both of whom were far more responsible for the conditions that caused the revolution than the hapless Louis XVI.

B. *Modes of Government*—The way the world is governed at a particular time may not be inevitable, but it is often inevitable that it will *not* be governed in a certain way. In a religious age a figure like Joan of Arc could have an important influence on the outcome of the Hundred Years' War. But what sort of a reception would an ignorant peasant girl get in the twentieth century if she came to a Russian commissar, an American president, or a Japanese premier and asked to command an army because she was guided by voices from heaven?

The few kings and queens who still sit on thrones in the Western world in our time are, as a group, at least as able and dedicated as the much larger number of monarchs who reigned two or three centuries ago. But few people in the West any longer take seriously even the idea of monarchy. Thus conditions no longer exist whereby kings can be figures of major political importance. They still reign, but they hardly rule.

Yet if monarchy is currently out of style, authoritarian government is not. In a crisis it is a normal human trait to look for leadership, guidance, authority. Our century has had crises without end. Moreover, even in normal times every society contains multitudes who seldom think seriously about public questions, who dislike responsibility, and who habitually look to leaders to solve their problems for them. Does it follow, then, that the numerous dictators of our age are the inevitable wave of the future: that mankind is forsaking its most recent experiments with democracy and returning to the authoritarian government that has been normal throughout most of recorded history? Are new dictators merely old kings in modern dress? Nonsense. It is no more inevitable that authoritarianism shall inherit the earth than it is that democracy is destined to do so.[22] Italy, Germany, and Turkey used to be dictatorships and are now (1969) democracies. The Spanish dictator Franco has visibly relaxed his grip in recent years. Greece was formerly a democracy but is currently (1969) ruled by a collective dictatorship of army officers. France had a democratic government (1958–1969), but one dominated completely by the majestic figure of Charles deGaulle. Latin American countries have notoriously wavered between democratic and dictatorial regimes for a century and a half. No particular form of government is inevitable anywhere.

C. *Policies of Government*—The needs of states render some features of history inevitable. The chaotic personal relationships of Julius Caesar, Mark Antony, and Cleopatra led Rome to occupy Egypt at a particular time, but Roman annexation of Egypt at *some* time was surely inevitable because powerful Rome, then in agricultural decline, sorely needed the grain grown in weak Egypt.[23]

The deeds of any given government are the result of an unpredictable mixture of free initiative and response to the pressure of necessities. Sometimes a general policy is forced on a government by public demand, but the regime has much latitude in deciding when and by what means the demand shall be satisfied. The public pressure for what has come to be called the welfare state has been very general in Europe and North America for several decades. No democratically elected government has been able to ignore it. Yet there has been great variation in the particular social welfare laws enacted in

[22] Cf. *Supra.*, pp. 56–57.
[23] Hook, *op. cit.*, pp. 176–77.

Sweden, Canada, Switzerland, Germany, England, and the United States, and in the circumstances of their enactment.

A classic, and more complicated case is the collapse of the Austro-Hungarian Empire in 1918 under the strains of World War I. It has often been alleged that the old ramshackle empire could not have lasted much longer, war or no, because it embodied a hopeless contradiction. The argument goes thus: the rulers of Austria-Hungary insisted upon maintaining it intact because they claimed a *dynastic right* to continue to rule the conglomeration of territories their royal ancestors had accumulated during the preceding 700 years. Its component peoples, however, subscribed with steadily growing vehemence to the idea, spawned by the French Revolution, that every "race" or "people" has a right to be free and independent. Many things can be compromised in politics but natural opposites, adamantly held, cannot. One must eventually give way. Thus the demise of the empire, it is claimed, was inevitable.

One cannot deny the strength of this argument, yet it omits some important considerations. If men are sometimes swept away by forces beyond their control we must not forget that it was other men who originally set those forces in motion and still other men who did not combat them when their strength and appeal were limited. The Hapsburgs of 1918 could not control the forces that smashed their empire to ruins, but these forces, generated by the French Revolution and by various nineteenth century Slavic writers and agitators, might have been surmounted or turned into other channels if *other* Hapsburgs had treated them differently in 1815, 1848, or even the 1890s. Suppose Austria-Hungary had been content to become merely an enlarged Switzerland, granting all her subject peoples autonomy in a free confederation and championing all of them against the Turks? It is possible that not only might they have been content to remain in the empire: they might have drawn their conationals outside it to join them. After 1870 England and France would have welcomed such a development, and it would have spared Austria-Hungary from having to make the alliance with Germany which eventually brought her to ruin. However, all this is speculation. What happened was that nationalist agitation by the subject peoples in the empire simply intensified the determination of the two ruling nationalities, Germans and Hungarians, to prevent its realization. They oppressed the despised subject peoples and regarded every public question from the standpoint of their own interests, narrowly considered. In addition, they tried to make the unwieldly empire a Great Power. This required constant interference in the Balkans, a policy which steadily worsened all the national hatreds and rivalries within the Empire. Thus the breakup of the Dual Monarchy was inevitable *given the way it was ruled*. It was not inevitable merely in the nature of things.[24]

A look at the present Russian Empire provides a useful comparison. This sprawling state contains—in Europe alone —Poles, Lithuanians, Esthonians, Latvians, and Ukranians, all peoples who have no love for the Russians. Their position in the USSR is comparable to that of the subject nationalities in the old Austro-Hungarian Empire. This ethnic mixture has not produced the dissolution of the Russian Empire, however, since it is well known that Moscow is willing to do what old Vienna and Budapest were not: to shed as much blood as necessary to quell any serious restiveness among the "minorities."

D. *Imperialism*—"Imperialism" is a bad word in our day, one suffused with connotations of aggression and racial arrogance. Yet the strong always seek to dominate the weak in *some* way. Simple, primitive peoples must give way before well-developed societies when the latter possess high morale and superior technology. Thus Australian bushmen and American Indians gave way before European white men. They lost their lands and were forced to accommodate themselves to the civilization of their conquerors. The same fate befell

[24] For a lengthy and ill-organized but illuminating discussion of this subject cf. Oskar Jaszi, *The Dissolution of the Hapsburg Monarchy* (Chicago: University Press, Phoenix ed., 1961), especially pp. 279–383.

colored Africans and Asians for a time, though many of the
Asians were not primitive peoples at all but heirs of civilizations older than those of Europe. Latin Americans, neither
primitive nor non-Western, have long been under the economic
domination, though not the physical occupation, of first,
Britain, and then the United States. The reason is that the
Anglo-Saxon powers possess far more wealth, a much more
productive industry, a more "progressive" psychology, and incomparably greater military strength than the Latin American
states.

It is equally true, nay inevitable, that when the people with
the superior political power, technology, or culture (as the
case may be) lose their zest for domination, grow decadent,
or are distracted by severe domestic problems they will be
overcome, or at least expelled, by those whom they have
dominated. The Germanic barbarians were inferior to Romans
in all respects save animal vigor and determination, yet they
eventually overran the decaying Roman Empire. In our own
time the anticolonial revolt has followed a similar course.
Asians and Africans were introduced by their conquerors to
such Western conceptions as democracy, the rights of man,
and national independence. At the same time these people
observed that a non-European nation of colored people
(Japan) was able to win a war against one of white, European
Great Powers (Russia) in 1904–1905. Within a generation
their white conquerors decimated each others' societies in
two frightful world wars. At the same time a growing number
of white men were condemning imperialism as cruel, costly,
wasteful, undemocratic, and unjust. Inevitably, the colonial
peoples lost their awe of their white masters and demanded
realization for themselves of the ideals that had been held
before them. Within fifteen years after 1945 all the great
colonial empires, save only that of Portugal, disintegrated.

E. *Science and Technology*—The history of science and
technology indicates clearly the interplay of inevitability and
human choice. Most knowledge in politics and social relations
is noncumulative; that is, each generation must learn most of

the lessons over again. This is perhaps the main reason the modern world still has to wrestle with the same political and ethical problems as the ancient Greeks. Scientific knowledge, by contrast, tends to be cumulative.[25] What each scientist owes to his predecessors was once expressed superbly by the English genius Isaac Newton: "If I have seen farther than other men it is because I have stood on the shoulders of giants." Thus learning in the sciences is more regular and systematic than in the humanities, and progress more nearly "inevitable."

Many scientific discoveries would have been made or sweeping theories developed by someone else had the actual discoverer or developer never lived. The first elaborate formulation of the theory of evolution appeared in 1859 in Charles Darwin's *The Origin of the Species.* Had Darwin never lived some similar book would certainly have appeared within a few years, for most of the basic conceptions in evolution had been developed in the preceding three generations. They had even been written about in bits and fragments by Diderot, Monboddo, Lamarck, Darwin's own grandfather, and Alfred Russell Wallace. Similarly, Roberval, Hooke, Halley, and others came close to formulating the Newtonian laws of motion before Newton. All were stymied by certain mathematical difficulties which Newton was able to overcome by inventing calculus. The latter achievement is a perfect example of how a certain pressing need or interest has often led two or more scientists to make the same discovery simultaneously. Newton and Leibniz, working in complete independence of each other, developed calculus at about the same time.[26]

Yet the "spirit of the times" or some "need" does not always bring forth the appropriate response. Who can say with assurance that someone else would have developed the theory of relativity if Einstein had not? And what of Freud's ideas? Their wide currency owed much to Freud's personal

[25] The differences between cumulative and noncumulative knowledge are discussed by Crane Brinton, *Ideas and Men* (N.Y.: Prentice-Hall, 1950), pp. 12–15.

[26] For a fuller discussion cf. Hook, *op. cit.*, pp. 33–36.

persuasiveness and literary ability. Many colleagues of both geniuses refused for a long time to take seriously either relativity or Freudian psychology, and the latter has come under fresh fire from psychologists in recent years. This hardly suggests that the spirit of the times or an innate need produced either conception.

The same ambivalence exists in the realm of technology. Improvements in industrial processes often follow an obvious need or demand for them. Any mechanical invention builds on previous ones and gives rise to still others. Though there were many outstanding individual inventors whose names always appear in any extended description of the early Industrial Revolution (Watt, Whitney, Arkwright, Crompton, Kay, Darby, and so on), nobody has ever attempted to write a history of industrialism primarily in terms of its leading figures. At least in Europe, its main outlines would have been similar had these men never lived. Their machines would have been made by somebody else. Yet this principle cannot be applied universally. The *need* of Asia and Africa for the products of industrialism was as great as that of Europe, yet before 1900 only Japan sought to import European machines and techniques and to become industrialized on a significant scale. For a society to become industrialized requires more than machines; a certain psychology or frame of mind is essential too.[27] Technology and communications strongly influence the lives of people and the policies of nations, but they are, in turn, shaped by national policies. The Panama Canal was the result of American expansion, not the cause of it. The Trans-Siberian railway was the result of Russian expansion,

[27] It might be objected here that it was difficult for people in other parts of the world to copy early industrial techniques when England long forbade the export of either machines or emigration of those persons who possessed them. Nonetheless, many a machine was smuggled out of the country and many an Englishman made his way abroad to build industrial machines from plans imprinted in his memory. The pertinent consideration is that before the twentieth century only Europeans, Americans, and Japanese effectively exploited either the contraband machines or the refugee builders.

not the cause of it. Its building occasioned the outbreak of
the Russo-Japanese war but both the underlying causes of
that war and the desire for it had existed a long time. Communications improvements make it possible for more people
to get to know and understand other peoples better, but it
does not necessarily follow that different peoples like each
other better on that account. Due to World War I and its aftermath, Americans had many more contacts with Europeans
than ever before, yet relations between the United States and
Europe worsened rather than improved. In the Western world
in the present day, the means exist to undertake public works
and educational programs on a scale sufficiently heroic to
markedly change whole societies. The people concerned, however, are not yet willing to be taxed on an equally heroic scale
for anything except war and war preparations. Who knows
what wonders might have been worked had the application of
atomic energy to a variety of peacetime pursuits been explored
with the same sense of urgency as its application to weaponry?
Lamentable though it may be, it is still true that nothing fires
men's hearts or opens their pocketbooks like war or the threat
of it. Thus technique may influence policy, but the direction
of human sentiments determines the uses made of technique.[28]

F. *Warfare*—In any consideration of whether military
operations are "inevitable" one must immediately distinguish
between the phenomenon of war itself and the existence of
particular wars. Warfare itself will probably endure as long
as two people remain on earth. This statement will grievously
offend all those congenital optimists who are convinced that
if only men will change their economic systems, their political
practices, or their modes of education, war can be eradicated.
One can only reply that the record indicates otherwise.
Throughout recorded history, men of every race, creed, color,
and economic class in every part of the world, have fought
wars against other men for liberty, land, loot, revenge, glory,

[28] Some of these points are discussed by Lukacs, *A New History of the
Cold War* (N.Y.: Doubleday, 1966), pp. 352–53.

power, religion, or mere relief from boredom. They have employed whatever weapons were currently available, from fists and stones to napalm and atomic bombs. In 1960 a statistician studied history's wars with a computer. He found that in 5560 years of recorded history there have been 14,531 wars, including forty different wars between 1945 and 1965. This is an average of 2.6 wars per year. Only ten years in more than 5000 have been completely peaceful.[29] A famous sociologist studied the same subject and reached the more generous conclusion that Europeans have fought only 967 important wars in the history of their continent.[30] Both the ferocity with which war is waged in our own day and the ease with which governments have persuaded even well-educated people to accept wartime practices of terrifying inhumanity indicate that man's antisocial instincts are still as strong as they were in the Neanderthal age. On the evidence, warfare is one of the permanent features of existence.

This unsentimental conclusion does not mean, however, that any *individual* war was inevitable, much less that its outcome was. The dozens of wars and skirmishes between England and France since the eleventh century testify to the antagonistic interests of those two peoples and to their persistent dislike for each other. They also testify to the awesome lunacy of German foreign policy in the twentieth century. Who, in 1900, would have ventured to predict that Germany could drive these two inveterate enemies together and hold them together for fifty years while they fought two world wars against her? Significantly, with the passing of the German threat after 1945 England and France have gradually resumed their normal condition of ill-disguised hostility. Yet any *particular* Anglo-French war could have been avoided, or postponed, or minimized, had governments chosen to act differently.

[29] Reported in TIME, Sept. 24, 1965, 30–31.

[30] F. R. Cowell, *History, Civilization and Culture: An Introduction to the Historical and Social Philosophy of Pitirim Sorokin* (Boston: Beacon Press, 1952), p. 184.

After all, the clashes of interest and the hatreds were not so unrelenting that they fought *all* the time.

At least two of the Crusades would never have taken place had it not been for the exceptional piety of Louis IX of France (1228–1270). The Crusades as a whole would have turned out much more favorably for the Christian Europeans if their leaders had not quarrelled so much and if their armies had not been decimated by diseases. If Napoleon Bonaparte had not become ruler of France in 1799 all Europe would have been spared fifteen years of terribly costly and destructive wars. By all the laws of probability Napoleon should have been killed or taken prisoner in 1798 when he sailed for Egypt with a small fleet, pursued by a much larger British fleet. Instead, an incredible mixture of inaccurate information, unfavorable weather, missing scouting ships, wrong guesses, and sheer bad luck caused the English to miss the French fleet en route to Egypt. Thus Napoleon landed his troops and won several showy victories at precisely the time when other French generals were being defeated in Europe. Within a year he returned home triumphant, staged a coup d'etat, and made himself the first of the modern dictators. The wars followed.[31]

Wise, responsible statesmen have always been reluctant to commit their nations to war. The reason is not that they are humanitarians or sentimentalists (though of course they may be) but because they know it is impossible to foresee the eventual outcome of a war. Once fighting begins, any kind of accident can happen and all sorts of imponderables become relevant. Marxists and other determinists, of course, ignore this and contend that (for instance), had Napoleon never lived other generals would have won his battles because the historical necessities of his age decreed the wars and the French victories in them. This is most unlikely. Many of the wars, and consequent battles, derived primarily from Napoleon's boundless personal ambition. Moreover, his armies were frequently

[31] W. A. P. Phillips, "Chance and History: Nelson's Pursuit of Bonaparte, May–June, 1798," *History Today*, March 1965, pp. 176–82, is a lively brief description of this Alice-in-Wonderland episode.

beaten when commanded by others, most notably in Spain. Finally, the men who knew him best—his own marshals and close associates, the enemy generals who opposed him, the military scholars who have studied his campaigns—with remarkable unanimity have proclaimed him one of the foremost military geniuses of all the ages.

Probably no conflict in history better illustrates the interplay of necessity and uncertainty than World War I. It has long been commonplace to maintain that the war would not have begun in July, 1914 had Europe possessed two or three statesmen of superior ability in key positions, but that given the fears, hatreds, jealousies, and conflicting ambitions of the Great Powers, complicated by the national and social tensions that had been building in central Europe for a century, it was inevitable that the war would occur at *some* time. This thesis has recently come in for criticism on the ground that all the pre-1914 "incidents" and crises have been linked together much more in books than they were in reality—that they have been made to look more like links in a chain leading to an inevitable war than they really were.[32]

Likewise, it has often been argued that the cause of the Central Powers was doomed at the outset because in men, money, natural resources, industrial power, and naval strength, they were strikingly inferior to the collective might of France, Russia, the British Empire, and the United States. This is true, but it became relevant only when the war lasted a long time. Germany came maddeningly close to taking Paris and winning the war in September, 1914, long before British strength could be made effective and two and one-half years before the United States even entered the war. Failure to exploit an overwhelmingly (and surprisingly) successful gas attack in 1915 cost Germany a "breakthrough" on the western front and, possibly, complete victory. Concentration on the eastern front might have enabled Germany to win the war there in 1915 or

[32] These points are made in an unusually stimulating study of the coming of the First World War. Joachim Remak, *The Origins of World War I, 1871–1914* (N.Y.: Holt, Rinehart, and Winston, 1967), p. 40 in particular.

1916, after which she would have gotten nothing worse than a standoff in the West. In the spring of 1917 Britain was within a few weeks of being starved out of the war by German submarines. A year later another great German offensive just failed to take Paris.

On the Allied side, the Europeans, without reference to the United States, missed two splendid opportunities to tip the scales of the war strongly in their favor long before 1918. In the first days of the war in 1914 several powerful British ships were in the Mediterranean. Had London been capable of making daring decisions these ships could have raced to the Dardanelles, bombarded the Turkish forts, seized Constantinople, prevented Turkey from entering the war on the German side, and preserved sea communications with Russia.[33] A year later the English and French landed an expeditionary force on the Gallipoli peninsula close to the Dardanelles. Had the venture been a success Turkey would have been knocked out of the war in 1915. Germany would then have been faced with Allied atacks on a third front, and the western Allies would have been able to supply Russia by sea with the money, machinery, and weapons she needed so desperately. Quite possibly the war would then have been won in 1916 or 1917 instead of 1918. Had this transpired, the Russian Revolution would not have taken place (at least in 1917)—with consequences for the world that scarcely can be imagined. Thus the Gallipoli landing was an eminently sound strategic conception. It did not "inevitably" fail: it failed only because it was planned inadequately and executed slowly and haphazardly. In the face of this collection of uncertainties and near misses who can say that any particular outcome of the 1914–1918 war was inevitable?

Contrary to popular assumption, there really was a greater

---

[33] David Woodward, "The Escape of the *Goeben* and *Breslau*, August, 1914," *History Today*, April 1960, pp. 232–39, contrasts the decisiveness of the German government in these days with the dilatoriness of the British. Cf. also F. W. Chambers, *The War Behind the War* (N.Y.: Harcourt, Brace & Co., 1939), pp. 61–62.

measure of inevitability in the war at the tactical level rather than the strategic, particularly on the western front. For forty years after the war, agreement was general among scholars and the informed public alike that the British and French generals who served in France and Belgium were a remarkably obtuse, unimaginative, unfeeling lot who threw away the lives of millions of brave men by the brainless tactic (repeated monotonously for four years), of hurling infantrymen across seas of mud at the enemy's fixed machine gun and artillery positions. This traditional indictment has been too severe. All of the generals struggled manfully with problems that were unprecedented and means that were inadequate. Because the British liberal government of 1906–1914 had lacked either the vision or the courage to develop a complete political and military understanding with the French, the battlefield efforts of the two allies were never properly coordinated. Because the Germans always had the strategic initiative, the advantage of interior lines, physical possession of northern France, and a settled determination to exert the utmost pressure on the western front, the Allies had no choice but to make their own main effort in the same place—or see France conquered. Because neither side was able to outflank the other in 1914 the battle lines soon reached from the Swiss mountains to the North Sea. No tactic was left but frontal assault. Because the Germans were brave and able soldiers with first-rate artillery and carefully prepared defenses, every attack on them was inordinately difficult and costly. Because no attack without preliminary artillery bombardment had a chance of success (since barbed wire defenses would thereby be left intact), surprise always had to be forfeited. Because the ground was usually boggy and interspersed with streams and canals, artillery fire churned it into a sea of mud. All this made it impossible for the attackers to maintain continuity of advance. Try as they might they simply could not lug supplies and heavy, clumsy guns along after them with any rapidity even when the artillery did blast a breach in the enemy line. Consequently the Germans withdrew in good order, their own artillery intact, to construct new defenses. Because the hail of artillery and machine gun fire destroyed communications facilities as effectively as it plowed the soil and slaughtered men, harrassed officers everywhere had to make crucial decisions in the heat of battle without adequate information—often without any. By 1939–1945 powerful planes, tanks, trucks, and jeeps had restored mobility to the attackers. In 1915–1918, however, all these machines were still small, slow, weak, and few, and they had to be employed in a constricted, marshy district that gave every advantage to the defense. Thus even when a bombardment was a success and a field commander's following decision was correct, the tools to convert a break-in to a breakthrough were lacking. Everywhere on the western front things, not men, prevailed.[34]

Harmfulness of Determinism

If the writing of history in terms of "inexorable forces," "irresistible trends of the times," and similar shining abstractions reflected nothing more serious than that some historians do not try hard enough to discover the real, particular reasons why things happened, then it would hardly be worth one's time to consider the subject. Unfortunately, the practical consequences of determinist beliefs about history have been, and still are, extremely harmful. They have led to every kind of indignity and oppression. More than three centuries ago the New England Puritans excused their decimation of the Pequot Indians on the ground that the latter "were damned anyway." The common contention that revolutions are inevitable and must follow a certain course is really an effort to justify violence by making it appear unavoidable. In our own century untold millions have been enslaved, tortured, or murdered in Communist countries because they belonged to "classes" which Marxist theology proclaimed "historically obsolete"

---

[34] For an excellent account of these horrendous problems and a balanced estimate of the generals who grappled with them cf. John Terraine, *Ordeal of Victory* (N.Y.: Lippincott, 1963).

and thus barriers to the speedy achievement of the classless utopia.

Even when cruelty and persecution are not present, belief that history is shaped by vast impersonal forces or by powerful subconscious drives which even psychiatrists do not really understand leads easily to a general feeling that the particular citizen has no responsibility for what happens, could not change things if he wanted to, and so might as well not try. This attitude has devastating implications for the future of democracy. Democracy assumes that the ordinary man possesses freedom of choice and that he has sufficient good sense and public spirit to make responsible choices most of the time. It assumes that he has a sense of responsibility towards other men and about the conduct of his own nation. How is it possible to profess support for a democratic society and system of government and at the same time tell everyone that what he thinks, or says, or does, is of no account because everything important in history moves according to some predestined pattern? A contemporary social critic summarizes the matter eloquently.

People believe that the great background conditions of modern life are beyond our power to influence. The proliferation of technology is autonomous and cannot be checked. The galloping urbanization is going to gallop on. Our overcentralized administration, both of things and men, is impossibly cumbersome and costly, but we cannot cut it down to size. These are inevitable tendencies of history. More dramatic inevitabilities are the explosions, the scientific explosion and the population explosion. And there are more literal explosions, the dynamite accumulating in the slums of a thousand cities and the accumulating stockpile of nuclear bombs in nations great and small. The psychology, in brief, is that history is out of control. It is no longer something that we make but something that happens to us. Politics is not prudent steering in difficult terrain, but it is—and this is the subject of current political science—how to get power and keep power, even though the sphere of effective power is extremely limited and it makes little difference who is in power. The psychology of historical powerlessness is evident in the reporting and reading of newspapers: there is little analysis of how events are building up, but we read—with excitement, spite, or fatalism, depending on our characters—the headlines of crises for which we are unprepared. Statesmen cope with emergencies, and the climate of emergency is chronic.

I believe myself that some of these historical conditions are not inevitable . . . But of course, *historically*, if almost everybody believes the conditions are inevitable, including the policymakers who produce them, then they are inevitable.[35]

Conclusion

All parts of history are interwoven into a seamless tapestry. Free human choice is intermingled with a myriad of outside influences, and the merger produces innumerable repercussions that nobody can foresee. As for the outside influences, in one age or situation the character of two or three particular rulers is crucial, in another some constitutional question, in another economic factors, in another the evolution of a military technique which determines the outcome of a war, in another the efficiency of a certain government, and so on. The patterns in history all become apparent and explicable only when analyzed after the event.[36]

If there is any principle in history which even approaches the status of a "law" it is that the future belongs to those who care the most and try the hardest.

[35] Paul Goodman, "The Psychology of Being Powerless," *New York Review of Books*, November 3, 1966, 14.

[36] Herbert Butterfield, *Man On His Past* (Cambridge: University Press, 1955), pp. 106–107.

III

FORCE AND ITS LIMITATIONS

Force is not the only element which shapes human destiny, but ever since Cain slew Abel it has been the *decisive* one. Millions of people, of course, resolutely refuse to acknowledge this. They do not coolly demonstrate that it is untrue (for they cannot); they indignantly assert that it is unworthy. Furthermore, they suspect that one who affirms the primacy of force does so because he *wishes* force and power rather than reason and good will to be decisive.

If the reader is of this opinion, if he is interested only in how things *ought to be* instead of how they *are,* he might as well stop reading, since the rest of this chapter is an attempt to assess force a factor which has shaped the historic past and which still shapes the present world. In other branches of human knowledge it is not regarded as disreputable to begin a study by dealing with facts rather than hopes or aspirations, and it ought not to be here either. If one recognizes the paramount role of force in human affairs this neither means nor implies that he wishes it so: only that he accepts a fact.

Force in Everyday Life

Civilization is an exceedingly thin crust which barely covers the seething primitive barbarism of mankind. It has been carefully constructed over the centuries by a relatively small number of intelligent, skillful, and patient men. Bit by bit, they have managed to establish civilized principles of conduct, to develop in men a sense of responsibility, and to bring considerable order and regularity into human affairs. Complete victory has never been attained, however, and periodically elemental barbarism bursts through the crust like an erupting volcano. If one doubts the accuracy of this assessment let him look at the darker side of the world about him. Among the more disagreeable things he sees are hordes of venal politicians; prostitution; drug addiction; organized crime which touches businessmen, labor unions, politicians, policemen and judges, and which nobody seems able to do much about; millions of "workers" who work little indeed and then steal from their employers in the bargain; widespread "sharp practice" in business and advertising that approaches outright fraud; systematic tax evasion under a thousand guises; robberies; muggings; riots; murders—one could extend the list indefinitely. All these manifestations of man's willingness to cheat and abuse his fellows have existed in all societies, at all times, at all economic, social, and educational levels. They even flourish among those persons in our own age who shallowly ascribe the whole condition to bad environment. Christian theologians have had a simple explanation for this somber condition: they have charged it to Original Sin.[1] Whether or not Original Sin ever existed is not our concern here; persistent human weakness indubitably does exist, whatever name one wants to give to it.

What, then, holds human society together? What prevents potentially vicious and always fallible men from destroying one another? Force, ultimately. Not force brought directly to bear on each individual every day of his life, of course; but the knowledge that police, prisons, and armies stand behind the governments that forbid antisocial activities. What life would be like without such force to maintain "law and order" becomes evident now and then when the force happens to break down or be withdrawn for a time. The precariousness of life in the American "Wild West" was legendary. So is life in an area that has been devastated by a tornado, flood,

---

[1] To be sure, many avant-garde theologians of our century explicitly or tacitly disavow Original Sin, but belief in it has been general throughout most of the Christian era.

or some other natural catastrophe. One of the first things civil authorities have to do is summon police and troops to end looting and prevent personal crimes against those who have already lost their possessions. What happens in a war when discipline breaks down in a military unit and the troops are free for a time to do as they please? Usually an orgy of drunkenness, theft, arson, rape, and vandalism, punctuated by occasional murder. It matters little whether the army is composed of sixth century Lombards, eleventh century Turks, fifteenth century Swiss, seventeenth century Swedes, twentieth century Japanese, of any of fifty other peoples. All revolutionary situations show the same thing. When customary restraints are removed, people rapidly lapse into primitive savagery.

It is one of the fables of our age that force is less necessary to restrain men now than it used to be. The myth arose because of a historical accident. The nineteenth century happened to be an exceptionally peaceful era in Europe. It was also the age of the Industrial Revolution, of the rapid growth of all branches of human knowledge, and of maximum European domination of world affairs. All this was viewed as "progress," one manifestation of which was the decreasing necessity to resort to force in the regulation of human affairs. Many people in the present day are still intellectually and emotionally marooned in the late nineteenth century, unwilling to admit that an age of violence has returned. But returned it has, stronger than ever before. The old restraints that religion imposed on men are visibly evaporating. While sixteenth and seventeenth century men realized keenly that knowledge could be abominably misused, the tendency of "post-Christian" Western man is to strive for greater knowledge, greater production, greater understanding, greater power in all areas, intellectual and material, without regard for the psychological and ethical effects of such endeavors. Faith is strong that any advance is automatically "progress."[2] At the same time the

---

[2] This condition is ably analyzed by John U. Nef, *Western Civilization Since the Renaissance* (N.Y.: Harper & Row, Torchbook ed., 1963). For a fuller treatment of these matters cf. *Supra.*, pp. 52–54.

modern world has seen tne rise of monstrous ideologies (really secular religions) which esteem their own ultimate objectives far more than they do civilized conduct. Nazism and communism specifically rule out such "weak" and "decadent" considerations as mercy and pity because these impede "rational action" against the enemies of these movements. The fanatics who worship race and nationality are equally ready to employ any technique which promises to bring them nearer to the fulfillment of their dreams. In the twentieth century all such movements have readily resorted to conspiracy, assassination, sabotage, street rioting, and mob violence of every description.

This combination of a change in man's attitude towards knowledge and a change for the worse in his public conduct has produced a situation in which anything that is physically possible has now become morally possible. What has happened in less than one lifetime is illustrated by a remark of the German historian Hans Delbruck in 1920. Voicing his disgust with the Treaty of Versailles, he said, "Let them (the victorious Allies) do what they will with us; there is one thing they cannot do: kill us." Within twenty-five years Delbruck's own countrymen had given him the lie. They had solved many of their "problems" by the mass murder of six million Jews and as many Slavs. Farther east, the "scientific socialists" of Stalin's Russia had liquidated a comparable number of "enemies of the state."

Indifference to Atrocities

Nothing indicates more clearly the addiction of twentieth century men to force and violence than popular indifference to atrocities. The Turkish massacres of Bulgarians and Armenians in the late nineteenth century outraged humanitarian feeling in England in a way hardly comprehensible today. The Bulgarian question caused the Conservative party, which had been pro-Turkish, to lose the election of 1880. The Armenian massacres of the 1890s provoked the British government to propose the dismemberment of the Turkish Empire—despite the fact that Britain had spent the previous two centuries shoring up that decrepit state. By contrast, Hitler's more extensive slaughter of the Jews half a century later produced only perfunctory protests. Most countries even refused to accept more than nominal numbers of Jewish refugees. In the seventeenth century the French War Minister Louvois tried to break the resistance of the people of the Palatinate by burning their villages, and the Holy Roman Emperor Leopold I tried to subdue rebellious Hungarians by fire and mass executions. These were pallid performances beside the saturation bombing of World War II, employed again in an equally futile but far more destructive effort to break the will of civilians to resist. In times past, European peace settlements usually saw whole provinces and their peoples parcelled out among unemployed royalty—but at least it was the kings and princes who had to change residence. After World War II it was the people who were forced to move. Millions of Poles were unceremoniously packed into trains by the Russians, transported long distances, and then dumped out with only the clothes on their backs—to live as best they could, or die. The Poles and Czechs then repeated the process with Germans as victims. Few, save the victims themselves, cared enough to complain.

Why this dramatic change for the worse in public attitudes within two generations? One reason is sheer surfeit: a numbing of human sensitivity by constant overstimulation. By now so many tens of millions have been beaten, burned, shot, starved, frozen, gassed, crippled, and "brainwashed" in Germany, Russia, China, Poland, Hungary, Algeria, Kenya, Argentina, Santo Domingo, Nigeria, Indonesia, South Africa, and forty other places that the ordinary householder who sees an atrocity tale on the front page of his newspaper glances at it unconcernedly and turns to the baseball scores.

Another, and far more shameful, reason is the attitude of multitudes of intellectuals. Many have become so infatuated with ideologies that they are incensed only at atrocities committed by those at the political pole opposite their own. Thus the Left in the 1930s shed copious tears for Hitler's victims and for those who died fighting on the government side in the Spanish civil war (1936–1939), but were either apologetic or silent about the crimes committed in Communist Russia and revolutionary Mexico. In the latter cases they sometimes said that the victims deserved what they got: exactly what Hitler said about the Jews. The political Right, equally selective, grows indignant and vocal at Communist criminality but views with great composure the activities of the Ku Klux Klan or the deeds of Latin American tyrants.

Nineteenth century men, by contrast, thought it a mark of civilization to be outraged by atrocities of *any* kind. When General Haynau, the "Hyena of Brescia," a brute who had whipped women in the process of suppressing a revolt in 1848, visited England, a mob of dock workers attempted to lynch him. Had Yagoda, a particularly savage head of the Russian secret police in the 1930s, visited London at the height of his career there would have been a delegation of "intellectuals" on hand to fawn on such an imaginative pioneer in the field of criminal investigation.[3] Who, in 1913, would have supposed that several of the world's most "advanced" nations would soon reintroduce torture on a systematic basis, much less that large segments of the intellectual community would defend such regimes? Who, then, would have predicted that the twentieth century, so full of promise and seeming enlightenment, would soon coin a new word: genocide?

Assassination

The prevalence throughout history of political assassination is an eloquent testimonial to man's readiness to try to settle his public problems by force. The Gracchi, Julius Caesar, many Roman emperors, Louis of Orleans (1407), Giuliano d' Medici (1478), several kings of Scotland, the victims of the

---

[3] The example is taken from D. W. Brogan, *The Price of Revolution* (N.Y.: Grosset and Dunlap, 1966), p. 35.

Blood Bath of Stockholm (1520), those who fell in the Massacre of St. Bartholomew (1572), Erik XIV (1576), William of Orange (1584), Henry III (1589), Henry IV (1610), Wallenstein (1634), probably Charles XII of Sweden (1717), Gustavus III of Sweden (1792), Czars Peter III (1762) and Paul I (1801), and Prime Minister Spencer Perceval (1812), are random figures from the past who fell to the knives or bullets of assassins. The last century has been no different. Only the names are new: the American Presidents Lincoln, Garfield, McKinley, and Kennedy; the French President Sadi-Carnot, Czar Alexander II, the Austrian Archduke Franz Ferdinand, Leon Trotsky, the French Foreign Minister Louis Barthou, King Alexander of Yugoslavia, the British general Sir Henry Wilson, the Austrian Empress Elizabeth, the Congolese leader Patrice Lumumba, such German political figures as Walter Rathenau, Matthias Erzberger, Kurt Eisner, Ernst Roehm—even Count Folke Bernadotte, an international servant of the United Nations. The list could be lengthened indefinitely.

War

The most flamboyant application of force is in warfare. Man's proneness to war has already been considered.[4] Suffice it to add that without wars, written history would be far shorter and simpler, and the world a vastly different place. Whether war will be as common in the future as it has been in the past and is in the present remains to be seen. Its frequency in the past has been due to many factors, not least of which are the innate self-assertiveness of political organisms and the fact that most societies have objectives and desires impossible to attain save by force. Barring war, how could France ever hope to gain the Rhine as her eastern boundary, or Russia to secure a "buffer zone" of friendly east European states to provide defense in depth against invasion

[4] Cf. *Supra.*, pp. 92–93.

from the west? Territorial disputes have caused hundreds of wars. Scores of others have resulted from the ambitions of military leaders, from rulers of declining regimes gambling on a successful war to restore lost prestige, and from a dozen other factors.

Disillusioned people and moralists sometimes grumble that all these wars never settle anything. Since people do tend to repeat their mistakes, regardless of the outcome of wars, the complaint has substance—but only in terms of thousands of years. The way particular wars end does determine many things for generations, even centuries. The society of ancient Macedon was inferior in every way to the brilliant civilization of the Greek city states. In fact, Macedon was just a name applied to an assortment of half-wild mountain tribes. But one perceptive, determined man (King Philip) united them and mastered the most advanced military techniques of his day. He observed the political instability of his Greek neighbors and their increasing dislike of fighting. He then attacked and conquered the Greek towns one by one, always protesting his desire for peace. After the battle of Chaeronea (338 B.C.) Greece was his and the way prepared for the vastly more sweeping conquests of his son, Alexander the Great. Alexander's conquests, in turn, spread Greek civilization over most of the then known world and thereby influenced its culture for centuries. The original Greek city states never recovered their independent existence. In a similar fashion Greco-Roman civilization was spread from Mesopotamia to Scotland by victorious Roman armies. In the modern world there is no political system, no code of law, no mode of technology or science that amounts to anything that is not of European or American origin. To a small degree the rest of the world has freely adopted these systems, but for the most part they were imposed by force during the great age of European imperialism.[5] The Old Regime in France was undermined by generations of critics but it still took the violent shocks and bloodshed of 1789–1794 to destroy it.

---

[5] This is discussed by D. W. Brogan, *op. cit.*, p. 153.

Every modern Great Power has been built out of the wreckage of earlier states or societies and molded in the crucible of war. The kings of France pieced together their realm town by town, province by province in numberless wars against the Holy Roman Empire, Britain, Spain, Burgundy, the Netherlands, and domestic feudal nobles, the whole process stretching over ten centuries. The history of Russia is similar, only the opponents were different: Mongols, Turks, Swedes, Poles, and Siberian tribes. Prussia owed her existence so much to her army that an eighteenth century Prussian military writer said his was not a country with an army but an army with a country as a billeting area. A modern German historian writes that the history of Prussia is essentially the history of her army.[6] A century ago (1848–1871) the scattered German and Italian states were forged into the modern German and Italian nations in the flames of wars and revolutions. The Balkan states gained their independence not because the Turks generously extended self-government to them, but because Bulgarians, Rumanians, Serbs, and Greeks revolted time after time through the centuries and, with occasional assistance from some of the Great Powers, slowly drove the Turks out of nearly all of Europe. Even in the United States, where moral reprobation of force is widespread, history's course has been similar. How did the American nation gain its independence? By victory over England in the Revolution, and again in the War of 1812. How was slavery ended and the Union preserved? By the exhortations of intellectuals? By the moral fervor of humanitarians and persons whose religious sentiments were outraged? No. By the victory of the North in the Civil War. How were most American territories acquired after 1803? Florida and Alaska were purchased, but much of the southwest was won in the Mexican War, the rest of the continental U.S.A. was seized from the Indians, and Puerto Rico and the Philippines were gained by winning the Spanish-American War.

[6] Walter Goerlitz, *History of the German General Staff 1657–1945* (N.Y.: Praeger, 1953), p. 1.

Revolutions

The outcome of revolutions is usually determined by who has the most force or who uses it most skillfully.[7] Mobs, whether revolutionary or otherwise, notoriously respect strength and force but despise weakness. In the great French Revolution the Jacobins were, as a group, less distinguished and more brutal than the Girondins but they carried the day because the Revolutionary Assemblies were more impressed by violence than by talent. The determined Bolsheviks were similarly triumphant over more attractive and democratic, but less forceful, human types in the Russian Revolution.

Oftentimes foreign governments intervene in revolutions, either because they fear the spread of revolutionary ideas or because they hope to profit from the momentary discomfiture of an old enemy. Here again the effectiveness of the intervention depends on the quantity and quality of the force employed. Foreign intervention was too little, too late, and too uncoordinated to destroy the revolutionary regimes in France in the 1790s or in Russia (1917–1920). The German and Italian aid given General Franco in the Spanish civil war, by contrast, arrived promptly, was of good quality, and probably enabled him to win his war. Similarly, French aid to the American revolutionaries after 1778 was decisive for that conflict.

Force and Ideologies

It is sometimes said that ideas rule the world. Perhaps they do ultimately, but in the short run their importance is heavily dependent on the power and force that lie behind them. Propaganda is notoriously far more effective when accompanied by force than when used alone. The readiness of Italian Fascist and German Nazi strong-arm squads to beat up their opponents and break up their meetings before 1922 and 1933, respectively, added greatly to the popular appeal of

[7] Cf. *Infra.*, pp. 148–50, for a discussion of this point, and many examples.

both movements. The brutality conveyed the impression that the movements were youthful, vigorous, energetic, determined to "do something" instead of talk and procrastinate like the older "effete" political parties. In fact, the various Fascist movements of our century have specifically glorified force over thought and reason, have even insisted that the very process of fighting and struggling is spiritually purifying. Earlier political movements had at least kept force in the background and had been careful to invoke the grandeur of their principles as a justification for their occasional employment of force against opponents.

A particularly disturbing feature of the ideological battles of the modern world is that they have shown that educated people have quite as keen a taste for violence as the lower classes. Sometimes they use force even more avidly because they are more passionately devoted to particular political and social ideals than are the less educated. The worst slaughters of the French Revolution were directed by lawyers, professors, and other products of that classical education which is alleged to broaden the understanding of men and soften their manners. The horrendous atrocities of Communists and Nazis in the twentieth century resulted from plans carefully worked out long in advance by intellectual leaders in the movements. The French revolutionary and Napoleonic regimes deliberately employed armies to spread the gospel of "Liberty, Equality, and Fraternity" from Lisbon to Moscow. The Leninist and Maoist breeds of Communists have stressed the necessity of employing force to eliminate class enemies and speed the passage to the Marxist utopia. Suiting deed to word, they have forcibly communized a third of the population of the earth since 1917. Efforts to further extend the kingdom of Marx by a combination of propaganda, terrorism, conspiracy, threats, and guerilla war have been ceaseless.

If ideologists freely employ force to extend their doctrines, it is equally true that the character of ideologies has often been shaped by force or the conditions under which it is exercised. From the ninth to the twentieth centuries the gradual growth in the offensive power of weapons in the Western world has made it possible to compel obedience over gradually widening geographical areas. This produced the slow crumbling of the feudal system and its replacement by fewer and fewer but larger and larger political units. By the early twentieth century these had come to be roughly coterminus with the major cultural and linguistic groups of Europe. Weapons advances since 1914, however, have made possible physical control over much greater areas. Consequently, as early as the 1930s ambitious conquerors had to invent appeals broader than nationalism in an effort to persuade vast numbers of people to follow them and fight for them. The appeals were now to the idea of continental blocs (The Greater East Asia Co-Prosperity Sphere), or ideological movements (fascism, nazism), or imprecise racist designations (Aryan supremacy) which transcended national boundaries.[8]

Force has affected the history of religions quite as much as that of secular ideologies. Christianity was, of course, spread primarily by peaceful missionaries. Nonetheless, they got considerable help from the armies of the Frankish kings Clovis (481–511) and Charlemagne (768–814), the Byzantine Emperor Justinian (527–565), and from such crusading Orders of military monks as the Teutonic Knights. Europe would not have remained Christian had she not possessed the force to defend herself against invading Moslems, Vikings, Magyars, Mongols, and Turks: defeating some, checking and eventually converting the rest. Significantly, Christianity made no headway in Persia where the power of the state was brought against it. In seventeenth century Japan it was destroyed entirely when the government of that country carried out a policy of ruthless extermination of Christians; and it appears to have been destroyed by systematic governmental persecution in contemporary Communist China. In medieval

---

[8] This process is traced, along with much else, in a fascinating book by one of the most imaginative of contemporary historians. Carroll Quigley, *The World Since 1939: A History* (N.Y.: Collier Books, 1968), pp. 540–48.

Europe the Albigensian heretics remained unmoved for a century by the exhortations, preachings, and pleas of orthodox Christians, but they were suppressed in a few years by fire and massacre.

The history of Islam has been similar. The creed itself was spread largely by victorious Arab armies in the seventh and eighth centuries A.D. These hordes swept like a hurricane over the Mediterranean basin and western Asia to the borders of India. To this day these areas remain the heartland of the Moslem world. The history of Islam also illustrates one of those unpredictable quirks of the human psyche that defy all logic; e.g. some of the converts it made by force exceeded in zeal those made by persuasion. A case in point was the famous Janissary Corps of the late Middle Ages. Young boys were forcibly taken from their Christian parents in Balkan Europe by the Ottoman Turks who then raised them as Moslems and trained them to be soldiers. For generations before their decline in the seventeenth century the Janissaries were a crack body of disciplined Mohammedan fanatics, the best infantry in eastern Europe.

In the religious upheavals of sixteenth and seventeenth century Christian Europe, the particular denomination which prevailed in a given country was the one able to command the most government influence and physical force. France remained overwhelmingly Catholic because the Calvinists were unable to win the civil and religious wars of 1560–1598. England and Sweden gradually became Protestant because the English Queen Elizabeth I (1558–1603) and the Swedish King Gustavus Vasa (1523–1560) had Protestant sympathies and happened to live a long time. Thus they were able to employ all the resources of the state to reduce Catholicism and establish Protestant churches of their preference. Spain remained adamantly Catholic because the government and the Inquisition suppressed Christian heretics harshly and expelled hundreds of thousands of Moriscos (converted Moslems) and Marranos (converted Jews) from the country between 1492 and 1611. Scotland became Calvinist because the local Protestant nobles were strong enough to defeat their Catholic queen, Mary Stuart, in a civil war and drive her out of the country (1567). Bohemia became Catholic between 1619 and 1622 when the armies of the Holy Roman Emperor Ferdinand II and the Catholic League overran the country, drove out the Protestants, seized their churches and schools, turned these over to the Jesuits, and resettled much of the land with German Catholic immigrants. So it went all over the continent. In America the Massachusetts colony remained resolutely Puritan in the seventeenth century by executing some Quakers and expelling the rest. Two centuries later the Mormons settled in Utah because they had been driven out of the eastern half of the country.

What Force Has Prevented

It is easily forgotten that force, like science, is neutral. It can be used for good purposes or bad: to serve malice and unbridled passion or to forestall them. Many times in history it has been used in ways which ultimately benefitted whole societies, even the whole earth. Early medieval Europe was vexed by virtually constant warfare among hundreds of petty princelings, adventurers, and foreign invaders. The gradual unification of scores of little semi-independent enclaves into the modern European nations took place over the objections of local oligarchs and was, ultimately, forced on them, particularly after the invention of cannon capable of battering down castle walls. While this development did not eliminate or even reduce the incidence of international wars it at least pacified large areas internally. It broke the local tyranny of robber barons and brought a greater measure of order, regularity, and physical safety into the daily lives of most Europeans. The achievement of the British in India was similar. They suppressed the endless internal wars fomented by the martial peoples of India, wars directed at nothing higher than the extension of the power of some local despot. Save for the northwest frontier, British rule gave India general peace for a century and a half, a respite from war unique in her history.

Throughout modern history, England has consistently used her naval strength to prevent any of the Great Powers of Europe from controlling the Low Countries. While such action was dictated by an obvious British national interest it also served the interest of the Dutch and Belgians directly, and indirectly that of all Continental peoples who did not relish the prospect of being swallowed up in some huge multinational empire. The Monroe Doctrine performed a similar service in the New World. Though its proclamation clearly served an interest of the United States, and its tacit enforcement by the British fleet served a British commercial interest, the two combined probably also saved much of Latin America from sharing the fate of Africa in the late nineteenth century.

Many times the prompt and vigorous application of force has prevented extensive conquests. Sometimes such conquests might well have been in the best interests of the conquered, in the long run; in other instances this obviously would not have been true. In all cases, however, the potential victims *did not want to be conquered*. Thus, forestalling the conquerors pleased and relieved most of the would-be subjugated people *at the time*. Napoleon did not decide one day that his attempt to make all the states of Europe satellites of France was, after all, an unworthy or impracticable policy. Rather, he was defeated in his Spanish and Russian campaigns, he lost the battles of Leipzig and Waterloo, and he was forcibly exiled to the island of St. Helena by his conquerors. German Nazism, Italian Fascism, and Japanese imperialism in the 1930s were not overcome by speeches and resolutions in the League of Nations, by the superior attractiveness of democratic ideals, or by appeals to reason. They were beaten only by six years of the hardest and most destructive war our embattled planet has ever endured. Had Germany and her allies won that war the Nazis would have destroyed all the democratic and Communist regimes in Europe, perhaps in the whole world. Or, to take another example, would Communist ideas be as influential as they are in many parts of the world, would they arouse so much fear among tens of millions, if the Marxist colossus of Soviet Russia did not exist? Would the mission-

aries of Marxism in the Soviet Union and elsewhere have
been as relatively restrained in their efforts to evangelize the
rest of our planet in the years since 1945 had not the United
States possessed an atomic, and later a nuclear, arsenal? These
considerations point up the perennial relevance of Bismarck's
famous statement that the great questions of the day are settled not by speeches and majority votes but by blood and iron.
This bald declaration has always offended sentimentalists. Yet
in international relations it is true. Those who dislike it actually dislike reality. This is not to say that principles and ideals
are ineffective; only that they gain enormously in effectiveness
if they are translated into blood and iron; that they are frequently (though not always) ineffective as long as they remain
exclusively in the realm of speeches and majority votes.[9]

Force and the Application of Law

Civilized peoples have always striven to limit the capricious
use of force by establishing the rule of law. This laudable
endeavor has clearly enjoyed considerable success—else I
would not have written this book and you would not be here
to read it! But the victory is hardly complete. Who interprets
the law and who has the power to enforce his interpretation
has always been quite as important as the law itself. To return
briefly to the religious strife of the sixteenth century: Sigismund III of Poland (1587–1632) was required to take a
coronation oath binding him to accord equal rights to all
religious groups in the country. The king chose to interpret
this to mean that he was supposed to encourage each party
to recover what it had once owned or held. Since Sigismund
conferred honors only on Catholics, allowed the Jesuits
to control education, appointed only Catholic judges, and
allowed the clergy to encourage people to bring suits before
these judges for the recovery of previously confiscated prop-

[9] This point is discussed by A. J. P. Taylor, *From Napoleon to Lenin*
(N. Y.: Harper & Row, 1966), p. 85.

erty, it was not long before Catholicism once more dominated Poland. Interestingly, this same Sigismund was also king of Sweden for a time. He had to subscribe to a similar coronation oath there. He interpreted it as he had in Poland and soon began to favor Catholics. The result was far different! In Poland he had enjoyed strong backing and widespread popular sympathy. Sweden, however, had become largely Lutheran, and in 1599 the Swedes drove Sigismund out.

Revolutionary regimes are notorious for the chasm which separates the seeming liberality of their legislation and the harshness and partiality with which it is usually interpreted. Totalitarian regimes preserve many of the trappings of democracy and fill lawbooks with phraseology about the equality of all citizens. In practice, however, they invariably discover that their domestic opponents are "enemies of the revolution," "reactionaries," "racial inferiors," or some such, and so not entitled to be regarded as equals. The "two minute trials" which preceded executions during the French Revolution, and reports of spectators at public trials in Communist countries calling out in "righteous indignation" for the punishment of the accused—these are lurid modern reminders that he who interprets and enforces the law is at least as important as he who makes it.

Even England, where respect for the law is as thoroughly grounded as anywhere in the world, has its own unsavory examples. In 1587 when Mary Stuart stood before the court that plainly had been convened to condemn her to death, she protested that it had no legal competence to try a royal person. She was answered rudely, "Lay aside this vain claim of royal privilege, which cannot now save you, and plead your cause."[10] Sixty years later when her grandson, Charles I, made the same protest in similar circumstances, he was told, "Sir, we do not sit here to reply to your questions: plead guilty or not guilty to the accusations."[11]

[10] Albert Sorel, *Europe Under the Old Regime* (N.Y.: Harper & Row, Torchbook ed., 1964), p. 36.
[11] *Ibid.*, p. 36.

The most famous comparable example in the twentieth century has been the Nuremberg war crimes trials of 1946. Here the British, French, Russians, and Americans, who had just won World War II, tried many of the leaders of Nazi Germany for war crimes, convicted most of them, executed a few, and sentenced many others to prison terms of varying lengths. Now it cannot be contended that the accused were treated unfairly. They were unquestionably guilty of terrible deeds, and richly deserved the punishments they got. The *legal proceedings,* however, were awkward indeed. The victors acted as both prosecutors and judges, a routine practice in totalitarian Russia but a flagrant violation of French and Anglo-Saxon legal usage. Likewise, all civilized legal codes forbid the enactment of ex post facto laws. Yet the accused were tried and found guilty of offenses that were not specifically forbidden by law at the time they were committed. Worse, some of those prosecuting and judging (particularly the Russians) were known to be guilty of many of the same crimes as those standing in the dock. Not surprisingly, most Germans have regarded these trials as mere acts of revenge by winners against losers. Whether that view is justified is not our concern here. What the whole episode illustrates is the flexibility of the law when it is subject to interpretation by powerful, interested parties. It is easier for "legality" to follow in the van of force than the reverse.

The Will to Use Force

Force may be the ultimate arbiter in human affairs but it is decisive only if it is used or if it is known that those who possess it are willing to use it. Mere possession by itself means little. At any time after about 1550 the European states were, collectively, markedly superior to Ottoman Turkey in population, wealth, natural resources, industrial development, and military technology. Unquestionably, they had the *power* to expel their ancient enemy from Europe. Yet so jealous were they of each other and so immersed in their own feuds and wars that they never united against their common foe. Thus the Turks continued to control most of southeastern Europe until the latter half of the nineteenth century.

In the twentieth century the old British Empire has dissolved into a collection of states that are completely independent in all save sentiment and forms. This has happened not because Great Britain was physically incapable of holding such places as India, Burma, Pakistan, and Ghana, but because the British people were no longer willing to pay the price necessary to do this. Many Britons long ago ceased to believe that the possession of a vast empire was either just or profitable. Therefore when a dozen different peoples in the empire began to clamor for independence, and it became clear that they could be silenced only by a policy of utter ruthlessness, the British preferred to grant the dissidents their wishes. The classic case was that of the Irish rebellion and civil wars of 1920–1922. Military experts estimated that the Irish could be subdued only if England employed at least 100,000 men and fought a savage war of the type waged in South Africa in 1899–1902 in which concentration camps had been used to intern civilians. Few Englishmen so soon after the slaughters of World War I had any stomach for wars of any kind, much less for one of this sort. Many of them sympathized with the Irish, others feared that such a war would alienate the United States, still others thought that it might stimulate revolutionary sentiment in England itself. So force was used only briefly and halfheartedly, and the Irish gained their independence. A similar course was followed in Palestine. From 1919 to 1948 the English government tried to persuade native Arabs and Jewish immigrants to work and live together in peace. Both groups were persistently obstreperous, however, and the British were never willing to impose a settlement by sheer force. Eventually they withdrew from Palestine in disgust merely to be rid of the problem.

Other European imperial powers have had experiences not unlike these. At any time after World War II, for instance, the French army was strong enough to crush rebellions in Morocco and Algeria *if these were dealt with as purely military problems*. Many Frenchmen, however, either were sympathetic to the aspirations of the native Moroccans and Algerians, or simply wanted no part of wars of any kind. Moreover, France was vexed by many serious domestic problems. Thus no French government was ever willing to give the army a free hand in North Africa, and the weaker Algerians and Moroccans gradually gained their independence.

In the foregoing cases the refusal of the stronger party to employ maximum available force against the weaker has probably worked out to the ultimate benefit of all concerned—save the Palestinian Arabs. Unhappily, this is not always the case. Many times the failure of one state or people to employ its power means only that another, and worse one, prevails by default. The inhabitants of the late Roman Empire were more numerous, more civilized, and better organized than the Germanic barbarian tribes but they no longer possessed the will to make war or even to defend themselves with any vigor. Thus the whole western half of the empire was overrun by the barbarians and Europe slipped into the Dark Ages, centuries when its whole civilization was markedly inferior to that of the old Roman Empire.

While World War I did not *create* the power of the United States, it certainly revealed it. This happened so suddenly, however, that most Americans did not recognize what had taken place. They were unwilling to accept the responsibilites that are an inescapable part of being a world power, often unable even to recognize that such responsibilities existed. For years America tried to evade her unfamiliar burdens: refusing to join the League of Nations, retreating into isolation, limiting her naval construction, passing neutrality legislation, and adopting an attitude of sour disdain for much of the rest of the world. The results were ruinous. America did nothing to help stem the advance of Fascist aggression in the 1930s, and was generally unprepared for World War II when it eventually developed out of that unchecked aggression. In this case the possession of power and the refusal to use it was not idealism but catastrophic abdication of responsibility.[12]

In 1918–1920 England, France, or the United States had sufficient power to destroy the new and precariously established Bolshevik government of Russia. England and France had just suffered dreadful casualties in World War I, however, and many of their citizens were sympathetic in varying degrees to the "great experiment" taking place in Russia. Consequently, their intervention was brief, hesitant, and ineffective. Aside from a desire to prevent Japanese expansion into Siberia, the United States had no clear policy: only a melange of conflicting sentiments which cancelled each other out and prevented any effective American action. Due to such foreign inhibitions the Bolsheviks survived and the whole course of twentieth century history was changed.

As late as 1937 Britain and France were sufficiently strong to defy Nazi Germany and, if it came to war, to win the war easily. Such a war almost surely would have toppled the whole Hitler regime and thereby spared our planet World War II. But because the British and French were still war-weary, suffused with pacifism, and ruled by incompetents, they did not use their power in time. Thereby they condemned themselves to endure a far longer and more costly war. Even in 1940 France and England combined had as many soldiers and as much equipment as Germany, yet France was conquered in a month because both the leadership and the will necessary to fight effectively were lacking. While it is possible to compel men to fight, in the sense of conscripting them into armies and leading them into battle, nobody has yet discovered a way to force them to fight *well* if they do not want to. The collapse of the Russian army in 1916–1917 and the Italian army in 1941–1943 also illustrate this truth.

---

[12] For a good brief analysis of this familiar subject cf. Rene Albrecht-Carrie, *The Meaning of the First World War* (Englewood Cliffs. N.J.: Prentice-Hall, 1965), pp. 137–39.

The Nature of Force

Even when the will to employ force exists, it is still no magic talisman whose invocation automatically solves every problem. Force is, after all, only a technique. It is merely one way of exercising power, and power is far more than just soldiers, guns, and bombs. Power is also iron, steel, oil, food, money, scientific knowledge, industrial development, morale, leadership, and a dozen other things. Force is but its cutting edge.

Even Prussia, which owed its greatness primarily to its army, also required able rulers, an efficient governmental system, much hard work and, finally, a lucky accident to survive. In the Seven Years' War (1756–1763) France, Austria, and Russia (then allied) were collectively many times stronger than Prussia. Yet they lost the war because Prussia was a magnificently organized state led by a military and political genius, Frederick the Great. By contrast, their own armies were led by mediocrities, their national resources were far less efficiently employed than those of Prussia, and France and Russia had governments of extraordinary incapacity. Russia was ruled by the Czarina Elizabeth, an ignorant drunkard; France by the irresponsible Louis XV and his spiteful, narrow-minded mistress, Madame de Pompadour. Still, the trio would have eventually defeated Prussia by sheer weight of numbers and resources save for the unexpected death of the Czarina and her replacement by a madman who took Russia out of the war. This development cooled still further the tepid martial ardor of Russia's allies. Within a year they, too, opted for a negotiated peace.

The sixteenth century Spanish king and Holy Roman Emperor Charles V ruled one of the most extensive empires in all history and commanded the Spanish infantry, then western Europe's best foot troops. Yet all his wars were inconclusive because his commitments were so vast that they could not be supported by the primitive economy and rudimentary tax system of Spain, even when it was augmented by the gold and silver of Peru and Mexico. Charles V's troops were forever deserting or falling into mutiny because they were unpaid, and his campaigns often ended prematurely from mere lack of money.[13]

Problematical Character of War

The most obvious application of force is, of course, the making of war. Now history has known important figures whose appetite for war was insatiable. Such psychologically abnormal men as Alexander the Great (d. 323 B.C.), Charles XII of Sweden (1697–1717), and Adolf Hitler (1933–1945), actually preferred war to peace. The vast majority of statesmen, however, are not so irrepressibly combative. They prefer to pursue their objectives by peaceful means: by cajolery, threats, bribery, the employment of propaganda, offers of "deals"—even appeals to common sense. One reason is that they remember the cost of defeat in such cases as Serbia in 1387, Burgundy in 1477, Hungary in 1526, Denmark in 1626, France in 1871, and Germany in 1918. They also know that no matter how careful the advance preparations, war is always full of uncertainties and ugly surprises. Slaughters of unimagined magnitude took place in the First World War because nearly all soldiers and statesmen gravely underestimated the destructive power of modern weapons, especially when used defensively. In World War II so much reliance was placed on the same weapons that nobody was prepared to deal with a new *tactic:* the blitzkrieg of the Germans. In the 1930s prophets of air power predicted confidently that strategic bombing would quickly destroy civilian morale. Yet in the actual war that ensued, 1939–1945, Ger-

[13] The financial plight of Charles V has been analyzed exhaustively by H. and P. Chaunau, *Seville and the Atlantic, 1504–1650* (Paris: A. Colin, 1955–1959), and by Ramon Carande, *Carlos Quintos y Sus Banqueros,* I (Madrid, 1943), II (Madrid, 1949). Good briefer accounts can be found in John Lynch, *Spain Under the Hapsburgs* (Oxford: Blackwells, 1964); and R. Trevor-Davies, *The Golden Century of Spain* (N.Y.: Harper & Row, Harper Torchbook, 1965).

man saturation bombing strengthened British civilian morale, and incessant Allied bombing of German cities, ports, factories, and railways neither broke German civilian morale nor prevented the Germans from steadily increasing their armament production from 1942 to 1944. In our own nuclear age it is freely predicted that whole societies can be obliterated in minutes, but nobody knows this for certain since no war between nuclear powers has ever been fought and it is impossible to know the effectiveness of defenses against nuclear attack until they are actually put to the test.

One can never tell how a war will develop diplomatically either. Time after time the French King Louis XIV (1643–1715) employed all the devices of diplomacy to isolate a particular country he intended to attack, only to have all the states he had bribed or otherwise "neutralized" (on paper) take fright at French aggression, rush to the aid of the intended victim, and force France to fight a long war against a coalition instead of a short war against a single opponent. The great German Chancellor Bismarck, who built the German Empire by the victorious wars of 1864, 1866, and 1870, always strove to end his wars quickly before other nations became unduly interested in their outcome and, perhaps, tempted to intervene.

Even worse, wars often breed new problems more vexatious than the old ones they were supposed to settle. The Thirty Years' War began in 1618 as a dispute inside the Holy Roman Empire over whether the throne of Bohemia should be occupied by a Catholic or a Calvinist. By the time of the Treaty of Westphalia in 1648 not just the empire but England, France, Spain, the Netherlands, Denmark, Sweden, and several lesser states had taken part in the conflict, much of central Europe had been devastated, and the original reason for the war had been virtually forgotten. World War I began as a quarrel between Austria-Hungary and Serbia. It ended by shattering three multi-national empires, enormously exalting the place in world affairs of a non-European state (the United States), and loosing the ideologies of fascism and communism to poison our whole century. None of these developments was foreseen in 1914, but shocking experiences *like* this have happened often enough in the past that few governments wish to unsheath the sword until they have lost hope of attaining important objectives by peaceful means. One of the clearest indications that this hard lesson has been learned in at least a few portions of the modern world has been the steady growth of international arbitration in the nineteenth and twentieth centuries. To be sure, Great Powers will not submit to arbitration when a major national interest is at stake, but all of them have shown many times that if some dispute with another nation is of secondary importance and if the arbiters are careful to minimize questions of national honor, they will accept a compromise or even an adverse decision in preference to the uncertainties of war.

Undesirability of Force Without Restraint

Even when states do resort to war their leaders seldom wish to use violence indiscriminately. Only madmen regard force as an end in itself. Statesmen view it as a tool, a means of doing or getting something. When the purpose is attained, or when satisfactory progress towards it has taken place, or when it is seen or feared that further use of force will bring trouble and danger disproportionate to the value of the original objective, its employment is usually ended. In Europe before 1789 no serious attempt was ever made to conquer the whole continent because it was generally realized that existing modes of transportation, communication, tax collection, administration, and weaponry made it impossible to organize and govern vast territories efficiently. A huge empire would bring its possessor more liabilities than assets. Defense would become inordinately complex and expensive, alien peoples would be too numerous to be assimilated, and enemy states would be tempted to exploit the newly created instability. Often it seemed better to retain weak and divided states along one's frontiers than to annex them outright or partition them with another Great Power who might at the moment be friendly but who could in the future become an enemy. The partition of Poland, for instance, had been discussed extensively in European chancelleries since about 1715, but that country was not actually dismembered until the 1790s.[14]

The employment of force is also moderated by the realization that it is often undesirable to crush an enemy. It has always been suspected, for instance, that the Roman general Aetius could have overwhelmed the Huns at the battle of Chalons (451 A.D.) instead of merely checking their advance and forcing them to withdraw from the field. It is surmised, though not known for certain, that Aetius feared his Visigothic allies in that battle quite as much as his Hunnish foes, and considered that if he had two enemies of comparable strength he could play one off against the other diplomatically and preserve some freedom for himself. On the other hand, if he routed the Huns utterly he might find himself too heavily dependent on the Visigoths.

Prussia in 1866 had the sheer force necessary to conquer Austria and require her to cede lands and pay war indemnities. However, the Prussian Chancellor Bismarck did not want to crush Austria or make her an enemy: he wanted only to break her influence in north Germany. Consequently, he ended the Austro-Prussian War by making an extremely lenient peace. He demanded neither land nor indemnities. Only four years later he reaped his reward when Austria remained neutral during the Franco-Prussian War.

During the Korean War, President Truman, with much urging from British Prime Minister Clement Attlee, decided to use only sufficient force to repel Communist aggression in Korea, and not to extend the war by attacking China. With the use of atomic bombs the United States surely could have defeated China or have devastated much of it, but what Communist Russia would have done in such an event was unknown, and so was the effect such action would have had on the sympathies and opinions of the rest of the world.

---

[14] Sorel, *op. cit.*, pp. 22–24, has a good discussion of this.

Thus Truman decided that it was more prudent to be content with a limited success. Whether his judgment was wise cannot now be said for certain. We are still too close to the events themselves. History has demonstrated beyond question in other cases, however, that excessive or gratuitous use of force can be gravely damaging to the user. The famous Spanish general Alva tried for five years (1568–1573) to suppress the Dutch rebellion by a policy of calculated frightfulness. The effort was such a clear failure that Alva himself acknowledged it and asked to be relieved of his command. The reason is not hard to understand if considered in human terms. If one has a reputation for treating enemy civilians and prisoners of war humanely, enemy troops who find themselves in dire straits have an incentive to surrender and save their lives. By contrast, if one is known to starve, torture, or murder prisoners, enemy troops have every incentive to defend every position to the last man, no matter how hopeless the situation. They simply adopt the attitude, "Well, at least I'll take a few with me." Thus every victory is won slowly and at great human and material cost. When no prisoners are taken, little is learned about enemy defenses, troop dispositions, equipment, morale, or plans. Hence every battle tends to be as hard as the preceding one. Since the immediate object in war is to persuade the enemy to stop fighting on terms favorable to oneself, and since to take a man prisoner removes him from the enemy army as effectively as killing him, the excessive and cruel use of force in war defeats its own purpose. Alva's blunder was most recently repeated, on a continental scale, by the Germans in Russia (1941–1944). Hitler might have won his war in Europe in 1941 had he treated the Ukranians well and posed as their liberator, for few of them had much love for Muscovite Russians or the harsh policies of Stalin. Instead, convinced that he had the war won anyway, Hitler ordered the murder, torture, and enslavement of millions of Russian civilians and soldiers, Ukranians and non-Ukranians. Thus he drove the whole Russian people to a fanatical resistance against him.

So generally recognized is the desirability of moderation in the conduct of diplomacy and war that some states long owed their existence to the very number of their enemies. Turkey lasted for centuries because France wanted to use her as a diplomatic counterweight against the Holy Roman Empire, England wanted to shore her up to keep the Russians out of the Mediterranean, and the Russians and Austrians were each jealous that the other might gain more influence than themselves in Turkey's Balkan territories. Likewise, China would have been partitioned by the Great Powers about 1900 save that they could never agree on a peaceful division and none of them thought pieces of China worth the cost and risks of a general war.

Excessive Power Engenders Fear

Paradoxically, the mere possession of excessive power sometimes reduces its effectiveness, particularly if an effort is made to increase it still further. For five centuries the great European diplomatic coalitions have been directed against the continent's strongest power: the state which seemed to threaten the independence and interests of the others merely by its might. If its policies also appeared menacing, the strength became even more an Achilles heel. A classic example was that of Wilhelmian Germany. In 1898 Germany was already Europe's foremost land power. Then she began to build a powerful fleet, one featuring large numbers of high speed, short-range warships that seemed especially suited for offensive operations in the North Sea. Britain, the world's paramount naval power, at once took fright. Anti-German feeling grew, and the British strengthened their own fleet. Other European states began to wonder why Germany needed to be *both* a great land and sea power. What were the ultimate objectives of German policy anyway, especially when the naval program was accompanied by much boasting about German might and destiny? The denouement was ironic—and ruinous. Imperial Germany, which had scored a series of brilliant diplomatic victories in the 1870s and 1880s when she did not have a fleet, now began to suffer a series of dramatic reverses. Within a few years Britain, France, and Russia became so apprehensive that they buried a host of ancient grievances and formed the Triple Entente, really an anti-German alliance. They were eventually joined by most of the rest of the world's Great Powers in the war against Germany, 1914–1918.

Since 1945 it has been within the physical and financial capacity of the United States to build the world's strongest land, sea, and air forces simultaneously, but such a program would be unpopular at home, would drain our natural resources, and would probably defeat its own purpose by leading most of the other nations of the earth (out of fear and jealousy) to organize vast coalitions against us and to miss no opportunity to whittle away at any source of American strength. An important reason England was allowed to enjoy her global naval supremacy for two centuries was that she usually employed it moderately and unobtrusively.

Some students of the uses of power contend that the Great Powers of the nuclear age probably have already defeated their own purposes. Because nuclear weapons are of unimaginable strength and destructiveness no government really plans to use them and none really expects to have them used against it. Thus, they consider, those who understand the techniques of revolution and guerilla warfare are more apt to win the ideological battles of our age than those who merely possess huge stores of "Doomsday Bombs."[15] The weakness of this conjecture lies, of course, in its assumption that because the use of nuclear weapons would be irrational and self-destructive, they will therefore not be used. Here the past is not reassuring. History has known scores of rulers and soldiers who did absurd, ruinous, even insane things. One thinks at once of Alexander the Great's horrendous march across the Gedrosia Desert (325–324 B.C.); the suicidal expedition of

---

[15] Quigley, *op. cit.*, p. 548; Hannah Arendt, *On Revolution* (N.Y.: Viking Press, 1963), pp. 6–8.

the Roman Triumvir Crassus against the Parthians (55 B.C.);
the whole career of the mad Roman Emperor Caligula (d.
41 A.D.); the massacre of the Christian Crusaders at Hattin
(1187); the catastrophic romanticism of Charles the Bold of
Burgundy (d. 1477); the crazy projects of Charles VIII of
France (1483–1498); the bizarre campaigns of the "Madman
of the North," Charles XII of Sweden (d. 1717); the Charge
of the Light Brigade in the Crimean War (1854); Pickett's
charge at Gettysburg (1863); Paraguay's war against Argentina, Brazil, and Uruguay combined, a ghastly conflict in
which two-thirds of the people of Paraguay perished (1864–
1870); the Japanese attack on Pearl Harbor (1941)—not
to speak of the famous Last Stand of George Armstrong
Custer (1876).

Deficiencies of Terrorism

It is sometimes alleged that force is most effective when
used without restraint. This is only partly true. Any idea or
movement can be crushed, or at least its adherents silenced,
if it is well known that the head of state will not shrink from
murdering dozens—or millions—to destroy whatever seems
to threaten his position. In the twentieth century this has been
amply demonstrated on a small scale by the Duvalier dictatorship in Haiti in the 1960s and on a large scale by the Stalinist
dictatorship in Russia (1924–1953).

Eventually, however, such remorseless terrorist campaigns
fail. They cannot be maintained without a fanatical conviction
of some sort. Once this begins to moderate, the terror becomes
hesitant or haphazard. Then it no longer truly terrifies but
only makes martyrs, and steels the hearts of those persecuted.
Even when the effort to solve problems and silence critics by
sheer force is maintained for a long time the system defeats
itself because it stifles intelligence. For many years under
Stalin, nobody in Russia wanted to assume responsibility or
take risks because the penalty for failure was death or enslavement. Engineers sought jobs in offices shuffling paper rather

than work on visible projects where success or failure would be evident and responsibility plain. Commissars covered up each other's mistakes. Everyone sought to be inconspicuous, to fulfill the quota, to do the *expected* thing. Intelligent and creative people made far smaller contributions to Soviet civilization than they could have. Significantly, one of the first things done by Stalin's successors was to relax the terror system in order to bring greater imagination into every phase of Russian life and to promote the desire for improvement, inventiveness, and efficiency essential in a modern industrial society.

Calculated frightfulness fails, too, because of the memories it leaves. In 1689 Louvois, the harsh war minister of Louis XIV, wanted to terrify and humiliate the Germans. So he allowed a French army to sack the cathedral of Spires and scatter to the winds the ashes of eight Holy Roman emperors. It was a "triumph" of sorts. The Germans were chagrined by the impudent desecration, yet impotent to do anything about it. But acts like this are paid for many times over. Memories of them endure for centuries; they permanently poison the relations of peoples and nations and cause wars without number.

Finally, the habitual exercise of power and force without restraint gradually produces deterioration in the character of those who employ it. A famous nineteenth century historian, Lord Acton, summed it up in a phrase quoted a million times, "Power corrupts; absolute power corrupts absolutely." No better illustration of its truth can be found than in the conduct of the men who composed the Committee of Public Safety during the French Revolution. Divided among themselves; overworked; engaged in trying to rule France, write a new constitution, and conduct a foreign war simultaneously; desperately anxious to establish their revolutionary regime firmly; they easily fell into the habit of dealing with opposition of any kind by executing the opponents. This got rid of *some* enemies at once, permanently; and it terrified others. It was the quick solution, the easy way. Having employed it once, the second time was easier, next time easier still. By 1794 the men on the committee, and especially its dominant figure, Maximilien Robespierre, were not at all the same men they had been five years, two years, even one year, before. They had become monomaniacs whose immediate response to opposition from any quarter was "to the guillotine."

A pronounced personal deterioration of the same sort took place in Adolf Hitler between 1940 and 1945. Before 1939–1940 Hitler's fanaticism had been tempered by Machiavellian calculation, and his foreign policy had been brilliantly successful. After 1940 the unbroken successes and the possession of unbridled power overbore him completely. He accelerated the massacres of "inferior races," took wild gambles in military strategy out of the irrational conviction that a "world historical" genius like himself could achieve what had always been impossible for past conquerors, and finally in his mad last days melodramatically tried to drag Germany down in ruins with him.

Force and Conscience

Terrorism in particular, but also the use of force in general, has additional severe practical limitations simply because most men have consciences. In 1605 the architects of the Gunpowder Plot planned to kill King James I and the whole English Parliament, and to seize control of the country in the ensuing confusion. Whether they would have been successful had they remain undetected will never be known. What did happen was that one of them became conscience-stricken and sent a warning letter to a friend. Soon the plot was exposed and the plotters seized.

Oftentimes a particular national objective, which may or may not be desirable in itself, can be attained only by the extensive and prolonged use of force. The *means,* however, become so repugnant to many of the nation's people that they come to oppose the *policy.* This phenomenon is most marked in North America and the western European countries. The unwillingness of substantial sections of the British and French public to pay the price in blood and suffering necessary to hold colonial territories, and the consequent loss of those possessions, has been noted earlier. In the 1960s much American opposition to the Vietnamese war has grown out of abhorrence of the devastation wrought in a small country and the suffering inflicted on hapless civilians caught in the conflict.

Many Americans even feel guilty about winning wars. After both world wars the United States rushed to bestow on ex-allies and ex-enemies alike a variety of gifts, loans, relief missions, and advisory commissions. While one motive was the eminently "practical" one of reviving the economies of customers for American products, another was a desire to clear the national conscience by "helping the unfortunate." This is a phenomenon without parallel in recorded history. It has even given rise in small, poor nations to grim jokes about solving national problems by declaring war on the United States, accepting the inevitable quick defeat, and then awaiting the U.S. postwar aid programs.

Frequent Ineffectuality of Force

The effectiveness of force is limited further by the fact that there are many objectives which by their nature can never be achieved by force alone. If a war is waged for land, plunder, or a trading concession the object can be secured by winning the war. But when war is waged to make the world safe for democracy, to end war altogether, to extirpate fascism, or to defeat communism, "victory" is only the beginning. How does one know when he has "made the world safe for democracy"? When all states have governments that observe democratic forms? When all public opponents of democracy have been killed or jailed? When all writings hostile to democracy have been burned? When nobody hides an undemocratic sentiment in his heart? When wars are fought for ideological abstractions, as they have been in the twentieth century, military victory merely makes it possible to *begin* the longer, more complex, and incomparably more difficult process of employing education, propaganda, bribes, threats, and promises to shape the minds and hearts of the losers in a fashion that pleases the winners.

The Imponderables of History

The effectiveness of force is often strongly conditioned by what Bismarck called the imponderables of history. In 1935 the Soviet dictator Stalin was told by a foreign visitor that the Vatican would be pleased if the Russian government showed more consideration for religion. Stalin's reply has become famous: e.g. "How many divisions does the Pope have?" Napoleon put it another way, "God fights on the side with the heaviest artillery." The cynicism of such remarks is obvious, but that is irrelevant. What is important is whether or not they reflect reality. Many able men with extensive experience in public life have considered them accurate. The eighteenth century French statesman Vergennes wrote, "With the passage of time, hatred of the methods of expansion of a monarchy is dissipated, and the power remains."[16] A contemporary American diplomat of exceptional capacity and long experience concurs. Writing about the brutal Russian suppression of the Hungarian revolt of 1956, he acknowledges that Russia suffered considerably in the opinion of the world. Still, he thinks, in the long run her position as a Great Power was not damaged. If anything, the reverse was true, for force plays such a paramount role in human affairs that small nations were actually more deferential to the Soviet Union after the Hungarian uprising than before.[17]

One cannot deny the essential realism of these observations, but they still represent only part of reality. Two of the most successful statesmen of recent centuries were Cardinal

---

[16] Sorel, *op. cit.*, pp. 17–18.
[17] Robert Murphy, *Diplomat Among Warriors* (N.Y.: Pyramid Books, 1965), p. 481.

Richelieu (1624–42) and Otto von Bismarck (1862–1890). Both were unsentimental machiavellians. Yet nobody was more aware than they of the importance in statecraft of intangibles: the loyalties people have to religion, to their social or economic class, to their occupational group, to their local neighborhood; the deep attachment most people have to mere custom; the humanitarian sentiments which most of them cherish in varying degrees. Bismarck called factors like these the great "imponderables" of history. Both men considered another imponderable extremely important: that a statesman should acquire a reputation for predictability (not honesty, necessarily) in order that his peers should have confidence in him and not fear to deal with him freely. Richelieu summed it up by saying that nobody was so stupid in statecraft as one who studied it alone, for he thereby lost perspective and could no longer accurately weigh the other features of human existence.

The practical wisdom of heeding the imponderables could hardly be more clearly demonstrated than in comparing Bismarck's own career with the course of German history after his retirement. After German unification had been achieved in 1871, the Iron Chancellor strove to avoid giving the impression that the newly created Empire was a threat to the rest of Europe. He did not build a big navy to match the powerful German army. He was studiously indifferent to the acquisition of overseas colonies. For years he tried to follow the illogical but obviously peace-seeking policy of befriending both Austria and Russia, even though they were inveterate enemies in the Balkans. His public pose was always that of the "honest broker of Europe," anxious to settle disputes fairly and to be a friend to all. How long it would have been possible to follow a policy so full of inconsistencies one cannot say. What *is* clear is that the opposite policy, the consistent, aggressive Weltpolitik of Bismarck's successors, was disastrous. It made most of the rest of the world suspicious of Germany and hostile to her. In 1914 the German government took a calculated gamble that rested on rating force and speed higher than "imponderables." It decided to violate Belgian neutrality, in the belief that this would make possible a sweeping German victory over France in six weeks. It was realized in Berlin that the action would unite the currently divided British public and bring British intervention in the war on the side of France. Generals and civilian statesmen alike, however, considered that the British army was so small and Britain so likely to be faced with uprisings in Ireland, India, and Egypt, that her intervention would be too little and too late to affect the outcome of the war. It was a disastrous miscalculation. The rebellions did not materialize, and the few British troops immediately dispatched to France helped their ally survive in August and September, 1914. Worse, after the war the Germans considered that the factor most responsible for their eventual defeat had been the relentless blockade imposed on them for more than four years by the British fleet. In 1917 General Ludendorff, by then the real ruler of Germany, repeated the mistake. He was warned repeatedly by Count Bernstorff, the German ambassador in Washington, that resumption of unrestricted submarine warfare would bring the United States into the war on the side of the Allies. Ludendorff calculated, however, that it would take at least a year for American intervention to become effective. He was sure that if he could use submarines without restrictions and launch one more gigantic offensive on the western front, Germany could be victorious within a few months and thereby render the affront to American interests and sensibilities meaningless. Of course this gamble did not come off either, but still Germany's rulers failed to learn from experience. In 1941 Hitler was so contemptuous of the "negrified and judaized" civilization of the United States that he gratuitously declared war against America after Pearl Harbor even though Germany currently had her hands full with Russian armies at the onset of a dreadful Russian winter. Twentieth century Germany has paid a high price for the luxury of being governed by men who have measured everything in terms of numbers, firepower, and military timetables. The British government, by contrast, in the early stages of World War I did not interfere with American shipments of cotton to Germany even though cotton was used in the manufacture of munitions. The British knew that such action would antagonize American senators from the southern states that produced cotton. They judged that it was more important to keep the good will of the American government than to deprive the enemy of a particular war material. This respect for an "imponderable" was amply rewarded: Germany soon developed a substitute for the cotton anyway, and American entry into the war in 1917 insured eventual Allied victory.

A prominent contemporary example of an imponderable is that evanescent abstraction "world opinion." Much nonsense has been spoken and written about the calamities that supposedly await nations who flout the "moral conscience" of the world, particularly its institutional embodiment, the United Nations. It is conveniently forgotten that "world opinion" in the underdeveloped two-thirds of the globe is, after all, only the opinion of a tiny handful of educated leaders. Most of them heed their particular national interests far more readily than moral imperatives of any kind. Elsewhere, world opinion is mostly that of small groups of political activists, officials, the highly educated, and journalists. Still, the error is not total: it is merely one of proportion, of making "world opinion" seem more important than force. The groups enumerated above do have enormous influence in all major nations, and other pages in this chapter have indicated some of the disasters that have ensued in the past from failure to appreciate intangibles such as these. Likewise, ineffective though the Old League of Nations was and its sucsor, the United Nations, is, it is significant that men have twice formed such bodies after the most devastating of modern wars. Indeed, for the past three centuries the Western world has been fumbling towards the development of international law and the establishment of some scheme or organization to prevent, or at least limit, war.[18]

---

[18] A good survey of this subject is F. H. Hinsley, *Power and the Pursuit of Peace* (Cambridge: Cambridge University Press, 1963).

While international forums like the United Nations or the International Court of Justice have never been able to prevent or stop wars save between minuscule nations, they do serve the cause of peace in a way their founders never foresaw. Their very existence allows aggrieved nations to vent their indignation dramatically and the political leaders of such nations to mollify the voters back home by heroic but harmless oratory before an international tribunal. National pride is preserved thereby and the compulsion to go to war is often avoided. Finally, millions of people believe deeply in the worth of these international organizations and the principles on which they are based, and strive to make them more effective. This is *itself* a fact of international life. For a statesman to ignore it when formulating his nation's foreign policy is just as unrealistic and quite as apt to lead to difficulties as failure to consider such matters as the size of one's own and other armies or the morale of one's people.

Conclusion

Cynics used to say "Artillery is the logic of kings." While the remark encompasses much of the essence of politics and international relations at all times, it still falls short of the whole truth. Force is the most important single factor in the shaping of human affairs, but if it is not employed with calculation and prudence, if it is not tempered by a dozen intangibles, it can as easily damage, discredit, even destroy its user as those against whom it is used.

IV

ARE REVOLUTIONS
WORTH THEIR PRICE?

At any given time in our age it is a safe bet that a revolution is going on somewhere in the world. The words and deeds of revolutionaries are constantly in the newspapers. Innumerable books have been written about particular revolutions: their causes, course, and effects. Fewer efforts have been made, however, to analyze revolution, to determine whether the phenomenon itself has been a constructive force in human history. Have revolutions brought benefits to man in excess of the crimes, brutalities, and bloodletting that inevitably attend them? Would it have been possible to secure the benefits without the revolutions? Are the regimes that revolutions establish generally superior to those that they overthrow? If so, superior from whose standpoint? Is the *habit* of resorting to revolution harmful? If so, does the harm, in the long run, outweigh the specific benefits that may accrue from particular revolutions? It is to such questions that this chapter is addressed.

The discussion will be confined to what the ordinary person thinks of as revolution: e.g. political upheavals, usually with social and economic overtones, that result in the destruction of a particular government and its replacement with another. Religious revolutions like the rise of Christianity or Islam, or such phenomena as the scientific revolution of the sixteenth and seventeenth centuries, or the Industrial Revolution of the nineteenth, are deliberately excluded. These were vastly more complex than political revolutions, the transformations they worked in human society were more fundamental and sweep-

ing, and any serious consideration of their effects would
require a far more detailed analysis than is possible here.

Traditional Views

Revolutions designed to change the *form* of government or
the social structure of a country are a relatively new development in history. Slave rebellions, peasant revolts, and uprisings
directed at getting rid of some tyrannical ruler are as old as
recorded history. They were discussed with solemnity and
learning by the ancient Greeks.[1] Nonetheless these revolts
were of a different character from the revolutions of modern
centuries. Before 1640 in England, and about 1750 in continental Europe, the object of a rebellion was merely to replace
one set of persons in authority with another: to determine who
should *not* rule. The very political language of early modern
continental Europe does not contain words to describe anything so radical as subjects themselves becoming rulers,
though it has many words describing the rising of subjects
against their rulers. The "professional revolutionary" may be
a common type in the twentieth century, but he was unknown
before the French Revolution.

To this it is sometimes objected that it was the Protestant
Reformation which introduced the world to the successful
revolutionary as a historical type. This is true only in a special
sense. Luther, Calvin, and the other sixteenth century Protestant leaders loosed ideas and forces that eventually produced
sweeping changes of many kinds, but they did so uninten-
tionally. In the realm of religion they did not consider themselves revolutionaries or even innovators, but leaders of a
return to the supposedly uncorrupted religion of the early
Christian era. On social and political questions most of them
were conservatives. In a famous case, Martin Luther sided
unashamedly with princes against peasants in the German
Peasants Revolt of 1525. If Reformation Protestants some-

---

[1] Plato, *Republic*, Books 8 & 9; Aristotle, *Politics*, Book 5; Thucydides,
History of the Peloponesian War, Book 3.

times made war on contemporary governments their primary objective was to gain greater freedom or power for their churches, not to revamp the organization of the secular world.

Before the Industrial Age neither the conditions of existence nor the state of men's minds conduced to fundamental political or social upheavals. Before 1770 few Europeans believed that there was enough of everything in the world for everybody and that the whole problem was one of distribution. And they were correct. Not until the Industrial Age did it become possible for more than a minority of men to rise above poverty. A typical seventeenth or eighteenth century European of some affluence was usually more concerned to avoid losing what he already had in wealth and status than he was to grow richer or rise higher. He took it for granted that the world and its problems are always much the same. He had not yet come to believe that change is the breath of life and is nearly always for the better. On a lower social and economic level there was no real proletariat in eighteenth century Europe, much less an educated one, and thus no *mass* faith in wonders to be worked by social engineering. The idea of the state as a liberating force, a positive agent working for man's well-being, was only in its labor pains two centuries ago.[2] How dimly men then comprehended "revolution" as we think of it is shown by the fact that those involved in the early stages of the American and French revolutions had no idea how things would eventually turn out. Most Europeans who were not caught up in the French Revolution thought it was "over" in 1790 when the nobles had lost their privileges and limitations had been imposed on the authority of King Louis XVI.[3]

Modern Concepts

In dramatic contrast to the attitude of the Old Regime is the widespread modern faith that revolutions are splendid

[2] This condition is discussed briefly by R. J. White, *Europe in the 18th Century* (N.Y.: St. Martin's Press, 1965), pp. 22–23, 34.

[3] *Ibid.*, p. 24; Hannah Arendt, *On Revolution* (N.Y.: Viking Press, 1963), p. 21.

events in human history; that it is not only possible but desirable—even necessary—to employ revolution as a tool to uproot an oppressive or unworthy society and to start history over again with better men in control and finer principles to guide them.[4] Jack London, a congenital literary radical, used to end his personal letters with the words, "Yours for the revolution."[5] Had he lived before 1750 his correspondents would have thought him crazy. The twentieth century understands him readily.

What brought about this dramatic change of mind? In our own time of intense hostility between the Communist and non-Communist worlds many have quite simply charged it up to Karl Marx and his disciples. Others have ascribed it to the doctrines of the eighteenth century philosophes; or to the birth of the conviction that men need not, and therefore ought not, any longer endure poverty with patience and resignation. Still others have attributed it to the supposedly revolutionary quality of Christian principles in a modern context; or (more plausibly) to the increasing secularization of the modern world.[6] A remarkably able interpreter of modern European history ascribes it to the spectacles of the American and French revolutions and to the ideas that were generated and publicized in the course of these conflicts.[7] One scholar would even fix precisely the beginning of this remarkable reversal of human habits of thought. He dates it from that day in 1776 when a young Virginia slaveholder, Thomas Jefferson, wrote,

[4] A perfect example of a book suffused with this spirit is Charles H. George, ed., *Revolution* (N.Y.: Dell, 1962).

[5] D. W. Brogan, *The Price of Revolution* (N.Y.: Grosset and Dunlap, 1966), p. 2.

[6] These and other hypotheses are discussed by Hannah Arendt, *op. cit.*, pp. 15, 18, 217–19.

[7] L. C. B. Seaman, *From Vienna to Versailles* (N.Y.: Harper & Row, Colophon Books, 1963), pp. 32–33. This small book is the best short synthesis of nineteenth century European history. It strips away conventional mythology from half a dozen major episodes in modern history.

"All governments derive their just powers from the consent of the governed."[8]

The last contention is certainly exaggerated. The makers of the American Revolution were far more interested in the redress of specific grievances against a specific king and Parliament than they were in the universal establishment of noble principles of eternal validity,[9] though of course their example did help to establish a revolutionary tradition. So influential has that tradition subsequently become, that scores of millions of people no longer object to revolution as such; only to particular revolutions whose outcome they happen to deplore. Democrats cheer revolutions that overturn absolutism and condemn those that destroy democratic (or at least participatory) government. Communists support any revolution which gives promise of being turned to the service of some Communist cause and denounce any which forestalls some Communist takeover or gain. The political Right takes an exactly opposite tack.

The Causes of Revolutions

Revolutions are of many types and they arise from a variety of causes. Some, like the American Revolution, derive from protests against particular abuses; some, like the Chinese Revolution, are the culmination of many years of effort by ideologues; some, like the French Commune of 1871, develop chiefly out of military defeat compounded by social discontent; some, like the French Revolution of 1848, are undertaken to replace a monarchy with a republic; some are counterrevolutionary, like that in Hungary in 1919. In the nineteenth and twentieth centuries the commonest type has been the revolution undertaken to secure national independence.

[8] Brogan, *op. cit.*, p. 3. Brogan selects this incident because he thinks the Declaration of Independence was more coherent and historically influential than such similar proclamations as the British Bill of Rights or the French Declaration of the Rights of Man.

[9] Cf. *Infra.*, pp. 176–77.

Successful revolutions are a blend of several disparate ingredients. They require popular resentment of the status quo; an easily identified person or class (the king, the aristocracy, Jews, capitalists, foreigners) to blame for what is disliked; a conviction that it is possible to change the regime; strong faith in the future; and careful advance planning. Spontaneous outbursts of mass rage never succeed by themselves because the leaderless people soon vent their passion and, lacking practical plans or leaders, are quickly suppressed by the authorities they have momentarily frightened.

One of the hardiest myths about revolutions is that they are caused by intolerable grievances and popular misery. Who could have had more, or more justifiable, grievances for the past 6000 years than the peasants of Egypt? Yet the only revolution in Egyptian history, that of 1952, was undertaken not by peasants but by a clique of army officers who were humiliated by their country's defeat in the Israeli-Egyptian war of 1948. As for misery, most Frenchmen were worse off in the 1750s and again in 1795–1796 than they were in 1788–1789 when the storm clouds of the great French Revolution broke. The lot of the Russian peasants improved visibly after their liberation from serfdom in 1861. By 1914 they had acquired considerable land and their government was building railways, promoting industrialization, and providing education for a steadily increasing percentage of Russian children. Yet the Russian Revolution came in 1917, not 1861. It often seems that old grievances are most poignant when they are being redressed, when improvement has begun but is not moving fast enough to satisfy the discontented. Unpopular regimes are most vulnerable to revolution when they have begun to reform, whether in eighteenth century France or twentieth century Turkey and Russia. Those elements in a country most apt to rebel are usually not the most downtrodden but the envious and the frightened: those who resent the privileges of another class or caste or who fear the loss of their own special status. Among those who grumbled loudest about the eighteenth century French monarchy were bourgeois whose vanity had been wounded by slights suffered at the hands of aristocrats, businessmen disgusted with endless governmental regulations and taxes, and newly ennobled judges who wanted not freedom for everyone but the end of any effort to restrict the privileges of persons like themselves.[10]

In a famous study of four major revolutions (the English Puritan Revolution of the 1640s, the American Revolution of 1774–1783, the French Revolution of 1789–1799, and the Russian Revolution of 1917 and after), Crane Brinton[11] pointed out that none of the regimes overthrown was a black tyranny. In England, Charles I had been trying in his habitually ineffectual fashion to introduce into his government some of the efficiency and modernization being developed by Richelieu in France. A century later George III and his ministers offended the American colonists by trying to bring more order and system into imperial administration. Such ministers as Turgot and Necker had tried for years to rationalize eighteenth century French finances and develop a greater measure of justice in taxation. The reform efforts of Czarist Russia have already been noted. The revolutionaries against these regimes wrote and talked much about the "tyrannies" they were opposing with such valor, but much of this was the hyperbole common to all political strife. No reputable historian now accepts at face value all the charges made by revolutionaries against Charles I, Nicholas II, or Louis XVI. Nobody now considers George III to have been the capital scoundrel that American patriots (and smugglers) alleged. A comparison of these ineffectual men with some of the *real* tyrants of modern history is instructive. There were no successful revolutions against the likes of Henry VIII, Richelieu, Frederick William I, Hitler, or Stalin. The moral is clear: People "rise not against

[10] F. L. Ford, *Robe and Sword: The Regrouping of the French Aristocracy After Louis XV* (N.Y.: Harper & Row, Torchbook, 1965), is a good study of one of these privileged orders, the Nobles of the Robe. Cf. especially pp. 250–52.

[11] Crane Brinton, *Anatomy of Revolution*, rev. ed. (N.Y.: Prentice-Hall, 1952).

the wickedness of the regime but its weakness."[12]

Financial grievances and difficulties are often contributory causes of revolutions, but the establishment of clear cause-and-effect relationships is difficult. A study of six revolts in seventeenth century Europe (England, France, Spain, the Netherlands, Portugal, and Naples) has shown that all began as protests against taxation. The American and French revolutions were both preceded by short depressions, 1763–1774 and 1787–1789 respectively, and the Russian Revolution was precipitated by the exceptional economic and psychological strains that grow out of a losing war. Still, in the four major revolutions Brinton studied, the financial difficulties of the *governments* concerned were a far more important factor in bringing on revolution than any economic hardships suffered by most of the people of these lands. French peasants in the eighteenth century were better off than their fellows in any other Continental country save, perhaps, the Netherlands; and any kind of economic yardstick shows that the French nation grew more prosperous in that century. Only the French *government* wallowed in a steadily deepening morass of insolvency. Early seventeenth century England was prosperous for that age, and Englishmen paid lower taxes than other Europeans—though, again, the *governments* of James I and Charles I were in perpetual financial straits. By contemporary standards the eighteenth century British colonies in America were not sunk in depression and misery, though London was short of money for imperial defense. Russia has always been a rich land, though the government of Nicholas II was heavily in debt and notorious for its wretched incompetence in finance. Thus the greatest of Western revolutions came in societies that were relatively prosperous but which had incompetent governments unable to cope with financial pressures that were not *in themselves* overwhelming if attacked with intelligence and vigor.

[12] The words are those of Eric Hoffer, *The True Believer* (N.Y.: Harper & Bros., 1951), p. 42.

One feature common to all these societies was that their ruling classes were divided and inept. The class immediately below the rulers showed exceptional animosity towards their superiors. The intellectuals were more than ordinarily discontented, and more adept than usual at demonstrating that the shortcomings of the government were the result either of unjust usurpation or the deliberate wickedness of the rulers. In seventeenth century England many of the great lords and merchants, members of the natural ruling class, were either champions of parliamentary privilege against the king, or Puritans opposed to the High Church policies of Charles I. The philosophes were devastatingly effective propagandists against the Bourbon monarchy. Thomas Paine, Samuel Adams, Patrick Henry and the Committees of Correspondence spoke and wrote more ably for the American colonials than anyone did for the government of George III. Most of the pre-1917 Russian intelligentsia were hostile to the Czarist regime.[13]

Even more damaging was the attitude of many of the privileged orders. When new ideas become popular, or social changes occur, and the government fails to make desired adjustments to them, many members of the dominant class acquire a bad conscience. In eighteenth century France many of the nobility became convinced that their critics were right, that aristocratic class privileges *were* unjust. So did many of the "conscience stricken gentry" of Czarist Russia. In the case of the disaffected American colonies many prominent Englishmen obviously considered the rebels to have the better case. Edmund Burke, later the arch-foe of the French Revolution, defended the rebellious Americans. Lord Jeffrey Amherst, the commander in chief of the army, declined to take the field against the colonials. The Earl of Effingham refused to take his regiment to America. General Conway said the conflict was a civil war and that in such a case his duty as a citizen superseded that as a soldier; therefore he could not serve. The great war leader Chatham withdrew his son from General

---

[13] Brinton has much material on this, *op. cit.*, pp. 38–73.

Carleton's regiment in Canada and defended the colonists in the House of Commons because he held that they were fighting for the basic Whig principle of no taxation without representation.[14] When the ruling class so obviously loses its belief in the rightness of its own position, when the upperdog begins to sympathize with the underdog, it is "an indication that there is about to be a reversal in the position of the dogs."[15]

To repeat, the whole foregoing discussion indicates that revolutionary situations develop not because problems are insoluble but because governments are stupid and slack. Many people in Stuart England, in London and America in the 1770s, in France in the 1780s, and in Russia at the turn of the twentieth century, knew what their governments needed to do to disperse gathering storm clouds, and said so. But governments must listen, and in many societies they and the class from which their personnel is drawn seem to grow so blind, lazy, and unimaginative that they lose the instinct for self-preservation. Charles I, George III, Louis XVI, and Nicholas II were all upright men personally, but remarkably dull, unintelligent rulers. They managed to drive into opposition most of the able and imaginative people in their respective countries. George III's incapacity was so spectacular that he provoked into opposition the greatest English statesman of the eighteenth century, and made rebels out of both George Washington, the richest man in the American colonies, and that bastion of conservatism, John Adams.[16]

Above all, these rulers used force unintelligently: sporadically, half in shame, and always too late. Charles I dithered,

[14] These examples are cited by Katherine Chorley, *Arms and the Art of Revolution* (London: Faber & Faber, 1943), pp. 17–18.

[15] Brinton, *op. cit.*, p. 58.

[16] It is a characteristic of inept rulers that they customarily surround themselves with ministers and advisers as incompetent as themselves. One of George III's favorites was Lord North. An M.P., speaking in the House of Commons about North's policy towards the American colonies, declared that "The noble lord has exceeded even the exploits of Alexander the Great, for where Alexander conquered only nations Lord North has managed to lose an entire continent."

attempted an unconstitutional arrest of his leading parliamentary opponents—and then failed to get them. George III's government followed no consistent policy in the American colonies, mingling hesitant coercion and clumsy threats with periodic retreats and tardy concessions. Louis XVI lacked clear ideas of any kind. His commander of troops in Paris in 1789, General Besneval, had 30,000 men. This was more than enough to cope with disturbances of any kind, but Besneval did not know what he should do and his king never enlightened him. Willy-nilly, the men were allowed to fraternize with the people until they became politically untrustworthy: virtually a trained force of mutineers. In the February Revolution in Russia Nicholas II made no effort to remove 150,000 recently recruited young troops from close association with revolutionary civilians in St. Petersburg and Moscow. Soon they went over to the people. Two other cases demonstrate the same point. Charles X was overturned in the French Revolution of 1830 by an insignificant Parisian riot that could easily have been suppressed. Louis Philippe lost his throne in the same city in February, 1848 when contradictory orders were given to the troops, they were forbidden to fire on the people, and finally they were allowed to mingle with the people.

When governmental ineptitude is this flagrant it is more accurate to say that a regime committed suicide than to say that it was overthrown. Indeed, due to the overwhelming power of the weapons produced in the Industrial Age, and to the normal governmental monopoly of the best of them, no revolution in modern times has succeeded unless the regular army either disintegrated in a losing war, went over to the revolutionaries, was of such doubtful loyalty that authorities feared to use it against rebels, or was used stupidly.

A comparison with the action taken by other rulers in other crises is most instructive for making judgments about the successful revolutions enumerated above. In 1794 the Whiskey Rebellion in western Pennsylvania was put down with dispatch and the authority of the new American republic established. In June, 1848 the rulers of the newly founded Second

French republic dealt with a rebellious section of Paris by allowing General Cavaignac to surround it with Algerian troops and use heavy artillery to blast the rebels into submission. In the same year, the Austrian Marshal Radetzky was beseiged by Italian revolutionaries in Milan. He moved his troops outside the city to keep them from contact with civilians, regrouped, reinforced his army, marched back, and took Milan by storm. In 1871 the French President Thiers took similar action in successfully combatting the Communards. Because force was used promptly, the Russian revolt of 1905 was put down in short order, even though the Russian people had far more substantial grievances than the French had ever had against Charles X in 1830.[17]

The history of the Italian Fascist and German Nazi movements indicates the permanent validity of the foregoing analysis. Neither gained power by winning revolutions in the usual sense, but both movements were revolutionary in intent and method and both carried out revolutionary changes after coming to power. Both enjoyed considerable cooperation from the Italian and German national armies before they gained power. In both cases the regimes they supplanted declined to use force against them even though these movements obviously yearned to destroy the free societies that fecklessly allowed them to exist.

Hence it is clear that the occurrence of a revolution has much less to do with injustices than with such factors as the astuteness and morale of the ruling class, the temper of the intellectuals, whether or not men of ambition and ability are allowed to rise in a society, and, above all, how the national army is handled in crises.

---

[17] Chorley has an extensive discussion of the crucial role of armed force as a determinant in the outcome of revolutions. For most of the examples cited here cf. especially pp. 27, 39, 113, 154. The same point is also considered by Gustave le Bon, *The Psychology of Revolution* (N.Y.: G. P. Putnam's Sons, 1913), pp. 50–54.

What Sort of People Are Revolutionaries?

What kind of people foment revolutions and are attracted to them? An answer to this question should indicate a good deal about the worth of revolutions themselves. Conservative, satisfied people usually see revolutions as the work of a pack of vile conspirators who are supported by a scrubby assortment of irresponsible intellectuals, cranks, malcontents, criminals, and mere opportunists who hope to do better in a new regime than they have been able to do in the old. This view has considerable validity.[18] Yet, as we shall see, it is only half the truth. Moreover, it does not distinguish between those who actually instigate revolutionary movements and those who are subsequently attracted to them.

Conspirators, vile or not, do not really cause revolutions. Indeed, many of them do not expect a revolution to begin in their own lifetimes. More often than not they see themselves as analysts and planners developing the ideas and perfecting the techniques that others will some day use to smash some hated system. What usually happens is that an uprising takes place somewhere and gives them a chance. As soon as they recover from their initial surprise they abandon their books and clandestine newspapers, scurry out of their coffee houses, and rush to take part. Here they have great advantages. Most of them are educated and imaginative. They know what shape they want a new society to assume, and they have long ago laid plans to achieve it. They know how to dramatize popular grievances and to inflame mobs with resentment against their rulers. They have a far better idea than mere street rioters of

---

[18] Even the American Revolution, different in so many ways from its European counterparts, had its full quota of unruly and lawless types: smugglers, tar-and-feathers enthusiasts, mobs who smashed houses and intimidated officials, and of course the "Indians" who threw tea in Boston harbor. For a description of some of them cf. Claude van Tyne, *The Loyalists In the American Revolution* (Gloucester, Mass.: Peter Smith, 1959), especially pp. 1–47.

what revolutionary techniques are apt to be effective. Finally, the names of at least some of them are well known to the public. Thus they have a good chance to emerge on top in any revolutionary situation.[19] In the Russian Revolution of 1917 the abrupt collapse of the Czarist regime caught everyone by surprise. An exceptionally fluid political situation existed for several months, at the end of which the Bolsheviks, the most seasoned and ruthless conspirators, were able to seize power. The Puritan churchmen of seventeenth century England, the Merchants' committees and Committees of Correspondence in the American colonies, and the Freemasons in eighteenth century France, combined the roles of conspirator and revolutionary phrasemaker in their endeavor to overturn existing governments. None, however, were able to seize power cleanly as the Bolsheviks did.

Those who do the most to prepare the soil for revolution are alienated intellectuals. Some are keenly intelligent, genuinely creative persons who think their talents and contributions are not properly appreciated or used. Some are mere dilettantes anxious to do something "significant," or inveterate dreamers who want to redeem their drab lives by identifying themselves with some attractive "cause." Whatever the case, they sublimate their personal grievances and discontents by becoming impassioned idealists full of zeal to smash some rotten "system" which has failed both themselves and (by now) "the people" as well. They attack existing institutions, weaken loyalties, and break down support for a regime. One such man was the pamphleteer and phrasemaker of the American and French revolutions, Thomas Paine, a malcontent and professional radical who drifted from job to job all his life. Another was Samuel Adams, a failure by common reckoning in both business and a variety of minor political jobs, but an expert propagandist and rabble rouser and an ardent advocate of a restoration of primeval Puritan virtue, a talent and a cause for which there was little demand in stable eighteenth

---

[19] Arendt, *op. cit.*, p. 263.

century societies. Similar types were the Russian Jewish intellectuals who had been abused, persecuted, and shut off from positions and opportunities which ordinarily would have accrued to persons of their talents. More recent examples were Adolf Hitler, a vagabond misfit and fourth-rate artist nourishing his hatreds and twisted dreams; Josef Goebbels, a well-educated novelist and playwright whose works nobody would publish and who finally found his proper niche in life only when he became master of the propaganda apparatus of Nazi Germany; Mohandas Gandhi, the Indian victim of British and South African social and racial discrimination; and Benito Mussolini, the restless ex-socialist, ex-pacifist, ex-newspaper-man, ex-war veteran, looking about for a movement to join and dominate.[20]

Many people join or support revolutionary movements mostly because they are bored. In eighteenth century France there were aristocrats who added zest to their lives by patronizing the philosophes, discussing the "social contract," and applauding plays which satirized their own class. The wives of rich merchants thought it fashionable (not to say deliciously daring as well), to maintain salons where the intellectual avant-garde exercised their wit denouncing contemporary society. In the twentieth century many wives of rich German industrialists, mere idle society ladies, financed Hitler years before their husbands ever heard of him.

---

[20] In an interesting study of three revolutionists, Lenin, Trotsky, and Gandhi, E. Victor Wolfenstein has discovered suggestive correlations between the tribulations they endured at the hands of their families and various public authorities when young and the attitudes they assumed in public life as adult leaders. He argues that psychological analysis, in a deep and systematic sense, is the ingredient most often lacking in a serious study of politics. Of course this raises the practical problem of the accuracy of psychoanalytical procedures applied to persons long dead. Cf. *The Revolutionary Personality* (Princeton, N.J.: Princeton University Press, 1967), especially p. 318.

The checkered career and the persistent disappointments of Samuel Adams are related in detail by John C. Miller, *Sam Adams: Pioneer in Propaganda* (Boston: Little, Brown & Co., 1936), particularly Chaps. 1–4.

Twentieth century revolutionary movements have attracted many restless freebooter-adventurer types. Often they are war veterans unable to adjust to peacetime norms: men like the Italians who came home from World War I to fill the ranks of the squadristi and then the Blackshirts; or the German veterans who joined the Free Corps and then graduated to the S.A. and S.S., positions from which they could maltreat enemies with impunity and provide the physical force so useful in revolutionary movements. The characteristic most prominent among all these human types is frustration of some kind. Their remedy for frustration is not to change themselves but to chastise the world.[21] They fight not for freedom but for pride, for revenge, for the power to oppress others. In this connection it is noteworthy that most revolutions have begun in cities—the abode of multitudes who feel uprooted, cut off from familiar soil, community, and occupation.

Once a revolution has *begun* it quickly attracts more sinister types. These are unbalanced, unsavory characters, men who have disfigured every human society since the world began. Some are nihilists, chronically discontented people who love rebellion for its own sake, men who would rebel against their own principles if the latter were ever realized. Some are half-mad fanatics willing to shed oceans of blood in pursuit of some ideal, usually an unrealizable one. Many are thieves, beggars, outcasts, misfits, degenerates of every stripe, scoundrels to whom the present means nothing and who are therefore always ready for any kind of change, no matter how drastic or bloody. In normal times creatures of this sort are

---

[21] Thoreau once wrote, "If anything ail a man so that he does not perform his functions, if he should have a pain in his bowels even . . . he forthwith sets about reforming—the world." Henry David Thoreau, *Walden* (N.Y.: J. M. Dent, Everyman's Library ed., 1962), p. 67. An excellent analysis of the human types who are attracted to revolutionary movements, indeed to mass movements of any kind, and their motivations, is provided by Eric Hoffer, *op. cit.* There are also some interesting observations on the same subject by Gustave le Bon, *op. cit.,* pp. 70–71, 97–101, 151, 233–38, and Brinton, *op. cit.,* pp. 32–35, 42–44, 106–15, 118–22.

held in check by force, but once a revolutionary situation develops they become free to murder, rob, riot, burn, smash, rape, and otherwise vent their passions and manias. These are the people who personally shed most of the blood during revolutions. They are gangster-terrorists like the French deputy on mission (Jean Baptiste Carrier) who loved to kill out of sheer primitive barbarism and who drowned prisoners in wholesale lots because it was faster than the guillotine. Some are monsters like the Russian secret police chiefs Yezhov and Yagoda; soulless "technicians" like Adolf Eichmann, the Nazi murderer of several million Jews; men from the gutter like Julius Streicher, the professional pornographer who became an important Nazi propagandist; heartless machiavellian brutes like Josef Stalin, ex-seminarian and ex-bank robber, who inflicted more suffering on more human beings than any other man in history. The Russian Revolution abounded in these types at all levels. The wild, vengeful savagery with which many of the Bolshevik leaders celebrated their triumph disgusted Lenin, himself a man so relentlessly rational that he refused to read poetry or listen to the music he loved because he feared it would soften him and make him merciful to those whom the laws of history had destined for destruction.[22] For sadists and terrorists of this stripe revolution is less a matter of idealism than an opportunity for revenge, a rare chance to sate blood lust.

For others the cruelty *is* a matter of idealism. It is not comforting to reflect that the worst slaughters in modern history were not the haphazard work of sadists but were the result of careful planning by perverted intellectuals and extravagant "idealists," spartan monomaniacs for whom this world is never pure enough. St. Just was an ideologue of this type in the French Revolution, though he was vastly overshadowed by Robespierre, who employed terror remorselessly to eliminate enemies of his Republic of Virtue. Communist massacres have all been designed to hasten the day when everyone will

[22] Brogan, *op. cit.*, pp. 12, 122.

be comfortable and happy in the Marxist utopia. Even the Nazis were perverted idealists in that they slaughtered Jews, Slavs, and gypsies in order to speed passage to their ideal world run by Nordic supermen. If a nation is so unlucky as to fall under the control of such zealots it suffers horribly while they muddle towards heaven on earth through the blood of all whose vision is less clear than their own.

Social engineers of this same species cropped up in disturbances long before the 1790s, but the damage they were able to do was smaller than in more recent times. In the sixteenth century a smattering of religious cranks declared war on existing unregenerate society, incited mobs to pillage churches, and drew down upon themselves and their largely harmless followers so much wrath that it discredited the very name "Anabaptist" for four centuries. Many others of a similar caliber surfaced in the English civil war: "Freeborn John" Lilburne, Gerard Winstanley, the Diggers, the Levellers, and the Fifth Monarchy Men.

Revolutions also provide a stage for other persons less odious and less dangerous than the foregoing, but hardly people to build anything of worth. These are born demagogues, technicians of words, mouthers of the inflammatory phrases that mobs love to hear, incurably disputatious persons whose dearest joy is to harangue an audience. The English Puritans produced many such men; Patrick Henry was such a one in the American colonies;[23] so were Marat and Vergniaud in revolutionary France; Tseretelli in the Russian Revolution; and Goebbels in the Nazi movement. Both Hitler and Mussolini had this streak in their complex makeups too.

The final exhibit in our rogues' gallery of revolutionaries play no part in starting revolutions but are invariably spawned by them. They are the opportunists and profiteers, the men concerned only to find the winning side and to make as much

---

[23] Once more, it is indicative of the relatively restrained character of the American Revolution that Henry, one of its wilder spirits, was not devoid of the qualities of a statesman. After the Revolution, among other achievements he twice became governor of Virginia.

as possible for themselves out of upheaval. They are such persons as the amoral renegade noble Mirabeau; the cynical terrorist Fouche who outwitted Robespierre, headed the police successively under the Directory and Napoleonic Empire, and died the duke of Otranto; the dissolute Bishop of Autun, Talleyrand, who graduated to ambassadorships and the foreign ministry of several French governments, betrayed them all, and made himself rich in the process; the NEP men of Russia in the early 1920s; and the grafters and profiteers in every upheaval who pose as "patriots" when they seize the property of "enemies of the revolution" but usually manage to keep much of it themselves.

From the flavor of the preceding pages the reader has probably concluded by now that all revolutionary leaders and their sympathizers are irresponsible visionaries, bizarre cranks, and characters from the pages of the Marquis de Sade. To be sure, it is people of this caliber who attract attention at any time and who create revolutionary legends, but if revolution amounted to no more than the periodic liberation of mad dogs and buffoons it would hardly be revered so widely. The truth is that many intelligent, serious, respectable, and "practical" persons also become revolutionaries. They generally do so reluctantly, only when they have become so discouraged by the persistence of old wrongs, so desirous of getting seemingly necessary things done, that they turn to revolution as a regrettable last resort. The men who backed Parliament in the early stages of the English civil war were economically prosperous and socially respectable, often prominent. In the "Glorious Revolution" of 1688 many of the greatest magistrates, landowners, and soldiers of the realm deserted fumbling James II and welcomed William of Orange. In the American colonies thriving merchants joined radicals and visionaries in opposing the crown until they were frightened off by mob violence and such episodes as the Boston Tea Party. So did a majority of the non-Episcopalian clergy, hardly a giddy or bloodthirsty group. The signers of the Declaration of Independence are universally renowned as an exceptionally distinguished assemblage. Many were college graduates, in an age when such education was unusual. In France those who complained loudest about their government and refused to lend it money were prosperous bourgeoisie and discontented nobles.[24] Even the members of the Jacobin Club were a fair cross section of French society. Most were men in their thirties and forties who had displayed some ability before the Revolution and who were moderately "successful" in the ordinary sense—though less distinguished than their early compatriots and eventual enemies, the Girondins. Of the Russian revolutionaries, Lenin was the son of a school inspector, an important official in the Czarist regime; Trotsky and Kamenev were men of intellectual attainment; Sverdlov was a chemist; Felix Dzerzhinsky a noble. In the cases of the German Nazis and Italian Fascists, though the leaders were a scurvy lot the movements gained either the cooperation or sympathetic neutrality of such substantial elements of the community as army officers, industrialists, and prominent landowners. Thus ideologues and chronic malcontents may do a good deal to bring about a revolution; and perverted intellectuals and riffraff may be responsible for most of the violence that takes place during it; but few revolutions would ever take place if regimes did not thwart men of talent in some obviously arbitrary way and if sound, reasonable men did not periodically despair of ever remedying the condition by means short of revolution.

The Course of Revolutions

Once a revolution begins forces are released which are difficult to control. British, American, and French revolutions all began as efforts to restore what were regarded as original desirable conditions or to eliminate wrongs that were held to have developed in the recent past. It took some time before the fomenters realized that their enterprises were developing into something new and unforeseen. Originally, the Puritan revo-

[24] Cf. *Supra.*, pp. 144–45.

lutionaries wanted to end what they regarded as the unconstitutional innovations of Charles I. The American colonists
wanted to end those of George III. The early French revolutionaries wanted to reform the administrative and tax structure
of France and to deprive the nobles and clergy of some of their
privileges. What distinguished the American Revolution from
the other two in this regard is that it alone did not fall into
the hands of ideological dogmatists and social architects. Its
leaders had limited objectives, they pursued these by means
remarkably moderate in revolutionary climates, and they
managed to remain in power throughout. Hence the American Revolution stopped about where its original promoters
intended.[25]

A. *Split Between Moderates and Extremists*—Once the
original revolutionary leaders have formed a government and
instituted most of their program they are ready to stop. Many
of the parliamentary rebels of the 1640s were satisfied when
they had effectively clipped the wings of the king and Established Church. Most of the members of the National Constituent Assembly of 1789–1790 were content when they had
ended feudal privileges, abolished monasticism, confiscated
church lands, revamped the tax system, reorganized the French
administration, and made Louis XVI a constitutional monarch. In 1917 the Kerensky regime in Russia struggled val-
iantly to keep Russia fighting on the side of the Allies in
World War I and to develop democratic government at home.
But it is the nature of revolutions to break bonds, ties, habits
and customs on every side. Thus very soon the revolutionary
movement is torn between those who think things have gone
far enough and more radical spirits who want to push on to
some fundamental social transformation. The radicals begin to
cry that the moderates are no different from the old rulers who
have been overthrown or that they are just as bad in some new
way. The moderates find themselves being blamed by more

[25] This process is discussed by Arendt, *op. cit.,* pp. 37–39, and Max Beloff,
The Age of Absolutism, 1660–1815 (N.Y.: Harper & Row, 1962), p. 164.
Also cf. *Infra.,* pp. 176–77.

and more people who have not gotten all they expected from the revolution. This condition is virtually impossible to avoid since about all an honest, candid man can promise in a revolutionary situation is the proverbial "blood, sweat, and tears." By now, however, the masses have had their imaginations fired and are inclined to believe that the simple, dramatic, attractive solutions to complex problems proposed by extremists can be easily realized. Thus decent men are at a severe disadvantage and soon find themselves on the horns of a hopeless dilemma. Since they are, after all, *revolutionaries* they do not for a long time regard their wilder comrades as enemies. Because they are also *moderates* who believe in freedom they will not immediately deprive their radical colleagues of freedom of speech and press.[26] The radicals, unencumbered by such nice scruples, take advantage of this and howl constantly that the moderates have betrayed the revolution. Meanwhile the regime has usually fallen into a war of some sort, or is at least threatened by one. To raise, train, supply, and employ an army effectively in these circumstances requires single-minded ruthlessness which moderates, by definition, do not possess. Soon Parliament is routed by Cromwell, mere constitutional monarchists and Girondins by the Jacobins and Robespierre, and the well-intentioned social democrat Kerensky by Lenin and Trotsky. Even in twentieth century Germany where the revolution came *after* the acquisition of power, the German generals and businessmen who thought they could control the revolution Hitler promised to make were brushed aside once Der Fuhrer had become chancellor.

In some ways the American Revolution and the coming to power of the Nazis might seem exceptions to this pattern but the differences are more apparent than real. In the American colonies it was the more radical elements who pushed for the Declaration of Independence from the first. In Germany the early extremists, the real *social* revolutionaries—men like

[26] The dilemmas of the honest, moderate man in a revolution are explored by Nicholas S. Timasheff, *War and Revolution* (N.Y.: Sheed & Ward, 1965), pp. 256–60, 309–10.

Strasser and Roehm—did not overcome Hitler but were purged by him in 1934 at a time when he still considered cooperation with the regular army vital. Of course with Hitler this act was only a matter of machiavellian calculation. Always a fanatic at heart, he subsequently became sufficiently "extreme" for the taste of anyone.

B. *Extremists Gain Control*—If the extremists gain control, things assume a different tone. Hard, egocentric, and puritanical,[27] these iron idealists are certain that they can solve every problem and legislate human happiness forever after. They are convinced that anyone who opposes them does so out of malice: because he is corrupt and does not love humanity. They deem it their paramount duty to strike down without mercy these enemies of a bright future and thereby to perform a higher mercy by hastening the day when all exploitation of man by man will be ended and everyone will live in happiness and plenty. (In the case of the English Puritan extremists everyone would live righteously in the eyes of God.)

Unhappily for the rulers at this stage in a revolution, they encounter an array of impassable obstacles on the road to the perfect society. One of the worst is that they must try to do several full time jobs simultaneously. They must rout the remnants of the old regime, lay the foundations for a new era, usually fight a foreign war, and all the while keep everyone working and eating. And whether they are ardent Puritans in England, Jacobins in France, or Bolsheviks in Russia, they are painfully aware that they are only a small minority in the whole society, that most of their countrymen care little for their vision or program. Worse, if anything, they soon discover that their efforts to transform human nature by exhortation and legislation are not working; that pet schemes like wage and price controls in the French Revolution (1793–1794), "war communism" in Russia (1918–1921), and the "Parliament of the Godly" in England (1653), are hopeless failures

---

[27] "Every revolution is puritanical, for men's thoughts should be on 'higher' matters than those of the flesh." G. L. Mosse, *Nazi Culture* (N.Y.: Grosset & Dunlap, 1966), p. 22.

and must be abandoned. The leaders are chronically overworked, and they are dependent on a bureaucracy whose only
enthusiastic members are a clique of party hacks and tub-
thumpers of dubious competence. On every side opposition,
graft, slackness, waste, and muddle seem rampant. Under this
inhuman pressure and constant harrassment the leaders begin
to degenerate personally. They grow testy, make snap judgments, and increasingly settle problems by executions, a
method that is at least fast and final. People who would shrink
from cruelty as an individual act of individual judgment
undertake it willingly if it is institutionalized and enjoined by
a Great Cause. Members of revolutionary assemblies who
would not freely condemn men to death (save for the gravest
crimes) are cowed by these terrorists and fanatical visionaries.
What they fear above all is to appear to lack revolutionary
zeal. Hence they acquiesce in the destruction of thousands in a
desperate effort to save their own lives. Whether under Robespierre or Stalin, they are like men who push each other into
the sea to get places in lifeboats.[28]

At this juncture the desperate ideologues redouble their
efforts to make men worthy of the New Jerusalem, for only
thus will the blood they have already shed seem justified in
their own eyes. This missionary effort is always painful and
often absurd. It frequently begins by renaming everything to
accord with the revolutionary mode. Thus St. Petersburg becomes Leningrad and Tsaritsyn becomes Stalingrad. France
gets a revolutionary calendar with day one: year one being
the day of the victory of the revolutionary army at Valmy. A
Jacobin names his child Free Constitution Letruc, and the
luckless son of an English Puritan zealot is christened Put-
Thy-Trust-In-Christ-and-Flee-Fornication Williams.[29] Whether in France in 1792–1794, in Russia for years after 1917, in

---

[28] An excellent study of the mentality of revolutionary extremists and
their problems in the French Revolution, is R. R. Palmer, *Twelve Who
Ruled* (Princeton, N.J.: Princeton University Press, 1941). Also cf. *Supra.*,
pp. 131–32.

[29] The names are cited by Brinton, *op. cit.*, p. 196.

Germany in 1933 and after, in China for twenty years after 1948, or in Fidel Castro's Cuba, everyone must participate in an endless array of parades, festivals, and celebrations. Torrents of speeches and admonitions assail the eardrums of all and sundry. Fearing nothing so much as independent thought, the authorities labor to inoculate the masses with their own visionary passion. They seek to suppress even the minor vices of men and will leave nobody alone in their relentless search for secret enemies and hypocrites. Because the vices of men (major or minor) can never be suppressed for long, the search for hypocrites never ends and the terror employed against them becomes boundless. Cromwell's troops purge Parliament of all save their own supporters, then rout Parliament altogether. They seize the lands of the Royalists, disestablish the Anglican church, drive their remaining enemies into exile, close the theatres, and ordain a stern code of morality for everyone. The Committee of Public Safety, dominated by Robespierre, imposes maximum wages and prices, conscripts people into its armies to fight wars (something the Old Regime never dared to attempt), robs the same people by inflation to finance the wars, undertakes a savage repression of Christianity, and answers objections or disobedience with the guillotine. Communists, whether Russian or Chinese, go these earlier revolutionaries one better: they turn terror into an ordinary technique of government. Millions of "aristocrats," Kulaks, landlords, and "class enemies" perish in a hundred terrible ways. Millions more are packed off to concentration camps to be worked to death for the glory of the new society. All is justified by an appeal to the new secular god, Historical Necessity. Doubtless it was this state of things Aldous Huxley had in mind when he remarked satirically of intellectuals who admire revolutions, "Intellectuals of the world unite! You have nothing to lose but your brains."[30]

[30] Aldous Huxley, *The Devils of Loudun* (N.Y.: Harper & Row, Torchbook ed., 1959), p. 321. In the *Communist Manifesto*, Karl Marx advised the workers of the world to unite since they had "nothing to lose but their chains."

When a revolution reaches this stage, life becomes intolerable for the ordinary nonpolitical man. The regime badgers him incessantly; it will allow no one to escape the total politicization of life. In its frantic determination to close the gap between lofty revolutionary aspirations and prosaic human nature it sheds far more blood than the discredited Old Regime. Ordinary people cannot stand this for long. Fortunately revolutionaries, even the most violent, also have their limits. Soon they are quarrelling among themselves, partly because many of them are at heart nihilists who are happy only when attacking and tearing down. Soon they are purging and executing each other amid deafening accusations of crime and treason. In the twentieth century this is augmented by carefully arranged confessions of guilt and show trials.

C. *Thermidor*—This crisis in the Revolution (commonly called Thermidor after the month in which Robespierre fell) was followed in all the major European revolutions by the rule of a military dictator. Such a man gets his chance because revolutions usually break up the military system of the Old Regime and at the same time fall into civil or foreign wars, or both. Thus a man who may or may not have had previous military experience, but who has great latent talent for generalship, gets an exceptional opportunity to make a name for himself in war. This, in turn, sometimes provides him the means of seizing control of the government. The hitherto inconspicuous country gentleman Oliver Cromwell followed this path when he organized the Ironsides, routed the Cavaliers, made himself ruler of England, and executed Charles I. Kemal Ataturk, the ablest Turkish soldier in World War I, became the ruler of Turkey after that war. In the French Revolution Hoche was a sergeant in 1792, a twenty-four-year-old general in 1794; Jourdan a haberdasher in 1789, a thirty-four-year-old general in 1793; Pichegru a noncommissioned officer in 1789, a general at thirty-three in 1793; Napoleon Bonaparte a lieutenant in 1789, a twenty-five-year-old general in 1794, first consul in 1799, and "Emperor of the French Republic" at thirty-five in 1804. Men of this sort are sometimes ideologists (Cromwell), sometimes not (Napoleon, Kemal); but those who turn military into political power are invariably realistic and capable.

The circumstances under which soldiers gain power, and their relationship to the terror, however, often differ considerably. In England the terror period was brief and limited and it did not result in a transfer of power.[31] Cromwell was already the most powerful man in England before the execution of Charles I in 1649; afterward he merely consolidated his position and took the title of lord protector. In France the terror lasted nearly two years, took about 40,000 lives, and culminated in the overthrow of Robespierre in 1794. What to do next, most Frenchmen found puzzling indeed. All were in favor of "justice and moderation." But what did this mean? Punishing all revolutionaries and returning to 1789? A continuing battle against all "enemies of the revolution"? Anyway, did "moderation" mean merely the absence of violence while campaigns continued against religion, monarchy, and the nobility, or while they continued against "patriots" and ordinary people? Above all, "how does one come out of a regime of violence after having once been in it? How to get back on the road of justice and moderation once one has left"?[32] Five years passed before the problem was finally solved by the emergence of Napoleon Bonaparte as a military dictator.

The rise of Cromwell and Napoleon from the ashes of revolutions impressed the Bolsheviks. They studied earlier revolutions with great care in an effort to avoid having their own fall into the arms of a victorious general. Before 1922 Trotsky seemed the most likely Russian Bonaparte. Perhaps it

---

[31] Of course Cromwell's troops slaughtered half a million Irishmen, but this atrocity took place in a different country in the course of a religious and national war. It is, therefore, not strictly analogous to the massacres of the French Revolution and Leninist and Stalinist Russia.

[32] The words are those of the Count de Montlosier, uttered in 1796. Cited by R. R. Palmer, *The Age of the Democratic Revolutions*, II (Princeton, N. J.: Princeton University Press, 1964), 210.

was one of his chief sources of strength that the (then) self-effacing Stalin seemed least likely.[33] In Russia the terror lasted far longer than in France, and Stalin proved to be in many ways both the Robespierre and the Napoleon of the Russian Revolution. He drove Trotsky into exile in the 1920s, and then murdered Chief of Staff Tukhachevsky and thousands of other high ranking officers in the 1930s, probably because he feared Tukhachevsky as a potential Napoleon.[34] Thus, having liquidated all other potential Napoleons, Stalin became his own Napoleon. Like Bonaparte, he chained the revolution, consolidated its achievements, muddled its doctrines, and spread its influence far and wide.

D. *Reaction*—The ultimate aftermath was similar in all three cases. Once the revolution had run its course the dead dictator of the terror period became a convenient scapegoat. In the 1660s Cromwell's body was dug up and hanged, and historians for the next two centuries proclaimed him a tyrant and a villain. Only a small clique of French historians have ever tried to portray Robespierre as other than a monomaniac. In Russia Trotsky was an ideal villain as long as Stalin was alive. After Stalin's own death, Khrushchev and his cohorts officially blamed Stalin for everything Russia had suffered in the preceding generation, removed his body from its grand mausoleum, and renamed Stalingrad.[35] In all cases the relieved

---

[33] This is the opinion of the author of a scholarly four-volume study of the Russian Revolution and its aftermath. Cf. E. H. Carr, *Studies in Revolution* (N. Y.: Grosset and Dunlap, 1964), p. 89.

[34] Nobody knows for certain all the reasons that impelled Stalin to decimate his armed forces. Perhaps it was mostly the same paranoid suspiciousness that caused him to execute or maltreat millions of ordinary Russians. During the civil wars of 1918-1921 the Bolsheviks had dragooned Czarist officers into aiding them and training a generation of Communist successors. A decade later, when they were no longer needed, Stalin murdered most of them. Meanwhile, many of their Communist successors were trained in Germany in the mid-1920s. Like the Czarist officers, when they were no longer needed, and when they had come to seem a possible danger, they too were purged.

[35] Interestingly, Lenin's reputation has remained unscathed. His body is still (1968) on public display in Moscow.

people lapsed into a period of moral looseness in reaction against the enforced puritanism of the terror epoch. Restoration England (1660s and 1670s) and France under the Directory (1795–1799) have long been bywords for ostentatious frivolity and fashionable vice. Though the reaction was less obvious in post-Stalinist Russia, nonetheless the Communist party press has complained repeatedly about the prevalence of drunkenness, hooliganism, and idle writing without social content; conduct to be expected in "decadent capitalist" societies but most unseemly in the heavenly city of Marx and Lenin.

Is Society Improved By Revolution?

The fact that revolutions have occurred with great frequency in the modern world does not in itself prove that they are either inevitable, or ethically just, or that they have made the world a better place. Change always takes place, and there are innumerable ways of bringing it about. Hence we now have to consider the crucial questions: is revolution the best, or even a desirable, way of effecting change? Does anyone benefit from revolutions? If so, who? How much? Does the whole society benefit? Does the world benefit? Do the benefits, all told, outweigh the harm done?

Those who believe that revolutions are desirable and just, often point to the political imbecility of such rulers as Louis XVI of France (1772–1792) and Nicholas II of Russia (1894–1917). They contend that the regimes headed by such men were so rotten that revolution was a lesser evil. Even though revolution is accompanied by violence and bloodshed, they say, is it not sometimes the only practical way to cut some political or social Gordian Knot, to break through intolerable barriers, to eliminate antiquated practices, to create the flexibility of attitude and fluidity of circumstance in which a society's problems can at least be attacked intelligently? Even if utopia is not attained (and it never is), is not the way at least opened for men to examine anew their values and difficulties in a spirit of rededication and creativity? Indeed, was not the

168

Timeless Problems in History

very ease with which such old regimes were overthrown in 1789 and 1917 proof that they had long ago outlived their usefulness? Furthermore, does not revolution in one country often have salutary effects in others? Did not the spectacle of the French Revolution, and fear of a similar upheaval at home, have much to do with the willingness of nineteenth century British governments to gradually broaden the suffrage, reform the army, improve conditions of labor, and redress some of the grievances of the poor? Likewise, was not much of the social legislation of the 1930s in England, France, and the United States undertaken out of fear of revolution; or at least in an effort to inhibit the growth of domestic Communist or Fascist movements?

A. *Specific Improvements*—The foregoing line of argument contains much truth. The English revolution of the 1640s swept away feudal anachronisms like ship money, knight's fees, tunnage and poundage, and the Court of High Commission. The Glorious Revolution of 1688 clearly established that Parliament was the senior partner in the government. The American Revolution ended stamp taxes, the remnants of the Navigation Laws, ineffectual and unpopular control of colonial affairs from faraway London, and the belief that one must always obey his sovereign. It established the principle that man has inalienable rights, regardless of his sovereign. By the 1790s the ex-colonies were governed with greater efficiency and regularity than before the Revolution. Far more important for world history, independent America became in the nineteenth century the land of equality and opportunity, the mecca of Europe's politically discontented and her poor. A flood of immigrants of twenty nationalities soon built the world's wealthiest and most powerful nation. Had the land remained a collection of British colonies governed from London primarily for the benefit of British mercantile interests, this development surely would have proceeded at a much diminished pace.

In the case of the French Revolution, if one omits the despoiled privileged orders (perhaps 4 percent of the population) on the one hand, and a clique of intellectual visionaries on the other, a majority of Frenchmen got a fair portion of the equality they wanted in 1789, and some of the liberty—though not the fraternity, since differences and hatreds between Frenchmen were exacerbated rather than lessened by the Revolution. Many obsolete privileges were destroyed, a humiliating sense of personal and social inferiority was removed, some popular participation in government was achieved, the machinery of government was improved, promotion by merit was established in the army, economic opportunities were broadened, the Bank of France was established (something the Old Regime, pathologically inept in the field of finance, could never do), and many peasants—the backbone of an agricultural nation—secured clear title to much land.

In the twentieth century many benefits have obviously accrued from revolutions. The question is whether they have outweighed the cost. The Bolsheviks modernized and industrialized Russia and made her overwhelmingly powerful. Hitler brought Germany out of the depression and restored the national esprit de corps. Mussolini drained the Pontine Marshes, improved Italy's transportation system, started many new industries, and undertook an extensive development of the country's power resources. But in all three cases the price was staggering. Mexico also paid a high price for the revolution that began with the overthrow of the dictator Porfirio Diaz in 1911. The breakup of big estates caused a disastrous decline in agricultural production. The expropriation of oil concessions and the expulsion of foreigners deprived the country of needed technical help and ready income from which to accumulate needed capital. For a decade the country fell into civil wars that benefited no one but bandits like Villa and Zapata. Still, these sombre developments were a condition of throwing off foreign tutelage and making Mexico a nation. And progress has been real and steady—if not spectacular—since.

Perhaps the most clearly beneficial revolution of recent times was the one guided to completion by Kemal Ataturk in Turkey. Whether one considers the appalling problems he faced, the fervor and skill with which he attacked them, or even the barbarity of his personal life, Kemal was a Peter the Great and Stalin rolled into one. He preserved Turkey's independence at the end of World War I, thwarted a Greek effort to conquer and annex part of Anatolia, gave the country new political institutions, altered the alphabet, dress, names, customs, and family law of the Turkish people, provided the means for someone else to succeed him in an orderly manner, and managed to do it all without Turkey becoming militarist or a menace to her neighbors. It was an accomplishment of an extremely high order and one accompanied by less brutality than one would expect.

B. *Things Unchanged*—If revolutions usually produce improvements like these in some areas of human affairs (at whatever price) there are many more things they change only slightly, if at all. Of course to those who have lost their property, and perhaps their families, and who have been driven into exile, it appears that a revolution has changed a lot. To a detached observer, however, it is clear that many institutions, laws, and especially habits, are either left untouched or soon slip back into customary grooves. Generally, ideas are changed the most and social arrangements the least. The Industrial Revolution did far more to alter the everyday pattern of living of most people than all the political and social revolutions of history combined.[36]

Revolutions usually produce a considerable shift in economic resources but they never bring about an equalization of economic power. Much of the property of English Royalists was secured permanently by the supporters of Parliament in the 1640s and 1650s.[37] American "patriots" secured much of the property of the more vocal and active "Tories" during the American Revolution. French peasants, bourgeoisie, and land speculators eventually got most of the land taken from the church and emigre nobles in the 1790s. The state seized and

---

[36] Brinton discusses these points. Cf. *op. cit.*, pp. 264–65, 269–75.

[37] See Paul Hardacre, *The Royalists During the Puritan Revolution* (The Hague: Martinus Nijhof, 1956), and the numerous writings of Joan Thirsk.

disposed of the properties taken from Czarist supporters in twentieth century Russia. In all cases it might be claimed that these resources passed into hands that were more progressive economically, but nobody can claim that the transfers produced equality or justice for the whole population. The same old horse just had a new rider. It was precisely this quality of revolutions that aroused the ire of the early nineteenth century utopian socialist Saint Simon. He insisted that political revolutions were useless because they merely exchanged one ruling group for another. What was needed was a complete transformation of the whole economic order! (Saint Simon himself had made a fortune in land speculation during the French Revolution.)

Politically, revolutions never live up to their advance billing either. Everyone gets tired, and the old slogans gradually lose their appeal. Like the Old Regime, the new one is composed of imperfect, fallible men. They soon have to face many of the same old problems. Increasingly, they tend to deal with them in the same old way, to adopt many of the characteristics of those they have overthrown. They soon justify Lord Acton's disgruntled observation that every class is unfit to govern.

Since a nation's foreign policy flows primarily from its national interests, revolutions affect this but little. British foreign policy proceeded along the same lines in 1620, 1650, and 1690. The foreign policy of the French revolutionary government was much like that of Louis XIV: secure France's "natural boundaries" and whittle away at the power of the Hapsburgs. Russian foreign policy, whether under Czars or Bolsheviks, has always been to extend Russian influence westward in Europe and eastward and southward in Asia.

Even the "opium of the people" employed by revolutionary regimes has but a slightly different flavor from that allegedly purveyed by the old monarchies. The latter entities, said Karl Marx, allied with established churches and tried to induce people to accept hardships in this world by dangling before them the vision of an eventual heavenly reward. But what do revolutionary regimes do, and Communist ones above all?

They excuse their tyrannies by invoking visions of the Republic of Virtue, the Classless Society, or some other chimera.

The fundamental attitudes of people usually prove remarkably resistant to revolutionary change. After the Stuarts were
restored in 1660 all the old financial and religious quarrels
between throne and Parliament broke out again. James II
(1685–1688) tried to rule more arbitrarily than his father
or grandfather had done, and it finally required another revolution in 1688 to confirm the parliamentary victory of forty
years before. The American Revolution changed the machinery of government in the colonies but not its spirit. A limited
monarchy was thrown off; a limited republic replaced it. Both
England and America continued to draw philosophical suste-
nance from John Locke, and America retained English law,
language, and culture. Slavery and inequality in voting, which
had existed before the Revolution, continued to exist afterward. In France the revolution of 1789 overthrew an absolute
monarchy and replaced it with a succession of regimes heavily
influenced by the Rousseauan conception of the rightful omnip-
otence of the General Will. Nonetheless, a century ago Alexis
de Tocqueville, a prescient observer of both America and his
own country, pointed out how many of the institutions and
practices of the Bourbon monarchy had not been changed at
all. Either they had simply been renamed by the French revolutionaries, or else they were resurrected soon after being
initially discarded. He considered that far from the Revolution
representing a sharp break in French history, it had rather
been the bloody culmination of the process of governmental
centralization begun by Richelieu and Mazarin and continued
by Louis XIV in the seventeenth and eighteenth centuries.[38]
Recent studies have shown in minute detail how the French
administration in the twentieth century operates in much the
same fashion as it did in the eighteenth, and how the attitude

[38] Alexis de Tocqueville, *The Old Regime and the French Revolution*
(Garden City, N.Y.: Doubleday, Anchor Book ed., 1955). Arendt also has
a good short analysis of the persistence of a distinctive national spirit from
one regime to another. Cf. *op. cit.,* pp. 154–55.

of the French public towards all governments has remained relatively constant for centuries.

The case of Russia is the most interesting of all. The Communists have made many and important changes, and their propaganda is like nothing this world has ever before endured. Still, innumerable features of the new regime are the same as the old, or mere accentuations of earlier tendencies. The secret police of the Czars gave way to the vastly more efficient secret police of the Communists. The new Red Czars secure a greater measure of obedience from their subjects all the time than the old Romanoffs were able to command part of the time. The aristocracy was a privileged class in the old regime: Communist party members are in the new. Czarist Russia, like the rest of the world, had wage differentials. The Communists abolished them; then had to restore them to stimulate production. Stalin, the representative of a philosophy of history which holds that individual and national differences are trivial beside economic facts and class rivalries, eventually glorified Ivan the Terrible, Peter I, and Catherine II as great Russians, represented the war against Germany (1941–1945) as a patriotic struggle to save Holy Mother Russia, discovered that Russians had invented everything, and insisted that his subjects venerate him as the world's foremost authority on all subjects from Marxist science to wheat growing. As the French proverb has it, "The more things change the more they remain the same."

C. *The Price of Revolution*—Like everything else, revolutions have their price. They produce by-products for which the world must pay long after the revolutions themselves are over. Sometimes, as in the American, Mexican, and Turkish revolutions discussed above, the price appears worth paying. In the cases of Fascist Italy and Nazi Germany it clearly was not. In all cases, however, it is a sobering thought that after a revolution has passed "it is easy enough to tell who was defeated, but much harder to determine who was victorious."[39]

[39] Albert Guerard, *France: A Modern History* (Ann Arbor, Michigan: University of Michigan Press, 1959), p. 255.

One of the most obviously harmful features of revolution we have considered already is the opportunity which the breakdown of government gives to an assortment of neurotics, fanatics, psychopaths, and desperados to satiate their variegated manias and lusts at the expense of the rest of the population. Long after revolutions are over how easy it is to forget the crimes that accompanied them! What of the 500,000 to 1,000,000 Vendeeans who perished during the French Revolution, the half million Irishmen slaughtered by Cromwellian armies, a comparable number of helpless Armenians murdered by the Turkish revolutionary government in World War I, and the numberless victims of the successful Communist revolutions of our own age? All these were people like ourselves. They had flesh and blood, hopes and dreams. Their nervous systems reacted to pain just as ours do. They were mourned by parents and children and friends just as we would be. They had as much right to life as we—or as the revolutionaries who despoiled, tortured, and murdered them.

Apart from the justice or injustice of revolutionary massacres and confiscations, these events themselves bedevil the domestic life of a country because they leave behind a sizeable class of impoverished and embittered people. Here the United States was remarkably fortunate. While many worthy colonial royalists lost their property or were driven into exile they did not constitute a major public problem when the revolution was over. England had more trouble. The despoiled Anglican squires who filled the Cavalier Parliament of 1660–1677 seethed with hatred for their Puritan enemies. They failed to get back the lands they had lost in the 1640s and 1650s but they were strong enough to inflict harsh religious persecution on the defeated Puritans in the 1660s and 1670s. Within a generation, however, the persecution moderated, the old wounds gradually healed, and it cannot be said that English public life was permanently poisoned by the experience. The Bolshevik victors in Russia avoided the problem altogether by an expedient that would have pleased Caligula or Tamerlane: they simply exiled or murdered all their opponents.

France suffered much more. Ever since 1789 she has been cursed by factionalism of a dozen varieties, the product of the first and several succeeding French revolutions. The basic trouble arose from force-feeding. Most people can digest major changes only slowly and gradually. The changes effected in France between 1789 and 1792 were important and unsettling —and they came in torrents. Before the French people had had a reasonable opportunity to adjust to them the government fell under the heel of Robespierre. The hatreds engendered by this "Torquemada of democracy,"[40] have produced so many alternating bouts of reaction and revolution that France has had seventeen constitutions since 1789. In most of her subsequent revolutions, especially those of 1848 and 1871, more massacres have ensued. So much French blood has been shed by so many other Frenchmen, of so many different social and political persuasions, that the events themselves and the endless public controversies about them have poisoned all French public life. In the 1880s the great French historian Fustel de Coulanges wrote that all his colleagues were party men who feuded endlessly among themselves and wrote history primarily to support a cause or to attack an adversary. By now several generations of them have accused all major figures in the Great Revolution, and most of those in the 1848 and 1871 revolutions as well, of treachery, duplicity, and hypocrisy. This tradition has conditioned the French people to expect mostly dishonesty from public figures. Hence they have reacted to every national crisis by searching for the latest batch of "traitors" who have let the country down. In this way modern France has become a land of myriad rifts that are deep and passionate. There is the France of St. Louis IX and Joan of Arc versus the France of Voltaire; clericals versus anticlericals; monarchists versus republicans; legitimists versus Orleanists; both versus Bonapartists; Communists versus Fascists; and workers versus bourgeoisie. These people have not only hated each other for generations; they have a pro-

---

[40] The designation is that of Guerard, *Ibid.*, p. 255.

found intellectual horror of one another. They regard each other as either stupid, deliberately dishonest, or both. To foreigners it seems incredible that a play depicting Robespierre in an unfavorable light could have provoked furious demonstrations and counter-demonstrations in Paris more than a hundred years after Robespierre's death, or that a proposal to commemorate the two-hundredth anniversary of Robespierre's birth could at once give rise to savage verbal battles in the Chamber of Deputies.[41] Perhaps worst of all, for a century French workers have been fed a version of history which exalts revolution as a means of securing desired social and economic changes. At the same time they have seen every revolution in their own country end with the successful revolutionary leaders inheriting the spoils of the conflict for themselves. Little wonder that most twentieth century French proletarians have become politically irrational: profoundly individualistic yet pro-Communist.

Several times earlier in this chapter, passing reference has been made to the difference between the American and other revolutions. It is now time to consider the point in some detail. Hannah Arendt has an interesting analysis of the differing aftermaths of the American and French revolutions which spotlights one of the worst characteristics of most revolutions: their tendency to divorce expectations from permanent realities. It is ironic, she says, that the French Revolution, which ended in disaster, has shaped much of world history, while the American Revolution, an outstanding success, has remained much less influential. The differences lay partly in mere luck; more in the different objectives of the revolutionaries. The French Revolution involved much more theorizing than the revolt of the colonies, and theory has application everywhere while the experience of a single isolated state often does not seem to. The American Revolution took place in a society that did not know widespread grinding poverty. It

---

[41] For a vivid description of many of these passionate feuds cf. Pieter Geyl, *Encounters in History* (N.Y.: World Publishing Co., Meridian Books, 1961), pp. 87–142. Some of the specific examples cited here appear on pp. 117, 130, 132, 379.

broke away from a king nobody regarded as absolute. It took place within a political system in which everyone was subject to the same laws. Unlike Frenchmen, the American colonials already had long experience of self-government. But the crucial difference was the objectives of the revolutionaries. The Americans did not cherish the utopian vision of liberating all mankind. They merely strove to ensure, broaden, and strengthen the freedom to which they considered themselves entitled as Englishmen. Moreover, they interpreted "freedom" narrowly: the right to take part in their own government. Thus they pursued limited, attainable objectives and with the winning of the war against Great Britain these were secured.

A prominent American historian pursues this thesis further. He contends that many of his colleagues have exaggerated the features the American Revolution had in common with the French Revolution by overrating the international character of the Enlightenment. The American uprising, he argues, was not a revolution at all in the usual sense but a *colonial rebellion.* The rebels issued a Declaration of *Independence,* not a Declaration of the Rights of Man. Moreover, that Declaration, the Federalist Papers, and other writings of the founding fathers are technical, legalistic, and conservative in phraseology; not full of brief, ringing, emotionally charged phrases like so many of their European counterparts. It is only a few preambles and phrases taken out of context and quoted endlessly that have given an opposite impression. Where the great European revolutions have been clashes of fundamentally different ideas about how society should be organized and operated, and for what purposes, and where many of them were merely parts of a series in which ideological baggage was carted from each uprising to its successor, the American rebels saw their actions as an endeavor to affirm the same British constitution that king and Parliament also professed to be upholding. Hence the American Revolution did not rip apart the fabric of American life; did not in fact even interrupt the continuity of our thinking about politics.[42]

[42] Daniel Boorstin, *The Genius of American Politics* (Chicago: University Press, 1964), pp. 67–129.

These considerations point up dramatically the fundamental error of the wilder spirits among the French revolutionaries, and of innumerable other revolutionaries at other times and places: e.g. they try to do impossible things. They refuse to acknowledge that many of man's problems cannot be solved by revolution or anything else because they flow not from some *arrangement* of particular *things* but from the flaws in human nature. They will not admit that deficiencies exist in all governments; that some are inherent in the very structure of government. There never was a government that *some* of its subjects did not regard as unfair, unjust, or inattentive to their interests. There never was a regime that did not contain functionaries who were inefficient, dishonest, or partial in their administration. Moreover, for such problems as the clash of economic interests, racial animosities, or religious and ideological differences, there is no perfect solution. Often there is not even a *good* solution but only a choice of evils or unwelcome compromises. There is much wisdom in Dr. Johnson's couplet:

> 'How small, of all that human hearts endure,
> That part which laws or kings can cause or cure.'[43]

Revolutionary zealots, however, are remarkably naive. They ignore human weaknesses and passions, never pondering whether the existence of these might not render their own doctrines incorrect. Instead, they assume that if only their own program is enacted it will transform human instincts. If they are Communist they believe that man's psychological makeup and ethical outlook are products of society's economic substructure anyway and thus will change when it changes. If they are Syndicalists or Fascists they think that the very struggle involved in making the successful revolution will purify the human spirit. In any case, they are convinced that everything that is amiss can be put right by some *process,* by changing *things.* Hence they try to do such hopelessly utopian

---

[43] Lines added to Goldsmith's *Traveller.*

things as to combine power and law and yet leave everyone free. They try to make men free not only to govern themselves but to make them completely free in the nonpolitical sector of life as well. They proclaim that they will abolish poverty and secure universal human happiness. They try to build a new society, based on new principles, out of the same human material responsible for the deficiencies in the old society. They never ask themselves how such a subjective thing as "happiness," for example, can be guaranteed by any law, any system, any regime, any *process.* Instead, they oversimplify reality, reduce everything to sharp contrasts, and insist that they alone are competent to deal with all problems.

If adventures like this merely failed it would matter little. But to inflame the minds and hearts of millions with slogans, myths, and battlecries; to raise utopian hopes and expectations and then disappoint them, does not just leave the situation where it was before. It makes everything worse. It inhibits cool, rational thought. It renders more difficult the task of dealing with *real* problems and *real* possibilities. In practice it means that the revolutionary governments are soon doing worse things than the regimes they displaced. Those who made the Puritan Revolution protested against a small tax, "ship money." Soon they were themselves imposing taxes ten times as large. Out of power, they protested minor Stuart land confiscations; in power they plundered the English church and much private property, dispossessed multitudes of Irish, and conquered Scotland. With the capital secured by these depredations, Cromwell got the army and navy Charles I could never raise. With it he routed the Parliament men who had overturned the king and undertook European wars Charles I could never afford. The Russian Revolution buried the inept tyranny of the Czars and gave the world fanatical Communist evangelism and the ghastly tyranny of Stalin. The French Revolution relieved peasants of feudal burdens but then forced them to bear arms and hurled them against all Europe for twenty-two years. It abolished lettres de cachet and replaced them with the guillotine. It emptied the old Bastille of its handful of common criminals and built "more and better bastilles with fewer empty cells."[44] It sneered at the fanaticism of the Church and unleashed a torrent of revolutionary and nationalist fanaticism which has not abated yet. It killed Louis XVI and raised up, successively, Robespierre and Napoleon. Even in mild America, "patriots" dealt more harshly with "Tories" than the British government had dealt with *them* before 1774.

The crucial point here is that regardless of what successful revolutionaries may intend to do, the usual result of their activities is to accelerate the accumulation of power by the state. Because most revolutions create anarchy for a time, it becomes necessary to resort to tyranny to restore order: the worse the anarchy the stronger the tyranny. Hence the emergence of the Cromwells, Napoleons, and Stalins of history. English judges badgered the hapless Charles I with impunity but they said nothing when Cromwell seized their hands physically and made them sign Charles' death warrant. French kings strove for centuries to reduce the privileges of provincial estates, the clergy, and the nobles. The Constituent Assembly (1789–1791) suppressed them all in a year and despoiled them in the bargain. The Convention (1792–1795) then executed the king himself. A few years later Napoleon made all the important elective offices in the land appointive. The ways in which Lenin and Stalin outdid the Czars have already been recounted.[45]

---

[44] Brogan, *op. cit.*, p. 10.

[45] The contrasting patterns of the American and French revolutions is a major theme in Arendt's book. Cf. especially pp. 49, 55, 85–87, 123, 154–57, 210. The utopianism of most revolutionaries is examined thoughtfully by Hoffer, *op. cit.*, especially pp. 138–39; by James J. Maguire, *The Philosophy of Modern Revolution* (Washington: Catholic University Press, 1943), pp. 13–20, 100–01, 114–16, 126; and by Thomas Molnar, *Utopia: The Perennial Heresy* (N.Y.: Sheed and Ward, 1967). The role of revolution in adding to the power of the state is analyzed by Bertrand de Jouvenel, *On Power* (N.Y.: Viking Press, 1949), pp. 215–20, 231–35.

The Legacy of Revolutions Abroad

If a revolution affected only the generation that made it and the country in which it took place, it would not be difficult to total up in parallel columns the benefits it bestowed and the harm it did, and to conclude either that it was a good experience for that society or a bad one. But things are not that simple. Any major revolution produces repercussions that reverberate over the whole earth for generations afterward. The American Revolution stimulated later revolts in Latin America and helped bring about the French Revolution. The latter developed out of a crisis worsened by financing the American colonies against Britain and by the importation into France of the slogans and battlecries of the Americans. The French Revolution, in turn, has had an incalculable influence on all subsequent history. In both it and the Russian Revolution it was repeatedly insisted, at the time, that nothing so grand or significant had ever before taken place. In both countries the revolutionaries claimed that their activities had relevance for all men.

In all three cases it seemed for a time that everybody loved a revolutionary. European intellectuals of the Enlightenment lionized the virtuous, unspoiled, liberty-loving American colonists struggling for freedom against that mercenary old enemy of every Continental state, Perfidious Albion, the Carthage of the North. Everywhere people of the same sort rejoiced at news of the French Revolution, at the spectacle of "idealists" rising against injustice and obsolescence. Hazlitt, Fichte, Coleridge, and Kant were among the eighteenth century intellectual luminaries who joined poets, merchants, professional people and country gentry of a dozen nationalities in expressing their elation. Charles James Fox said of the fall of the Bastille, "How much the greatest event in the history of the world and how much the best."[46] Wordsworth welcomed the Revolution with a poetic outburst:

[46] Brogan, *op. cit.,* p. 8.

> France standing on the top of golden hours,
> And human nature seeming born again.[47]

Most of the Flemish and Walloon subjects of the Holy Roman emperor, and the German subjects of scores of petty princelings, rejoiced at the early victories of the French armies and waited complacently to be conquered by these Hosts of Liberation.[48]

It was the same with the Russian Revolution. Most literate Western people have a vague, but permanent, sympathy for "victims of oppression." Before 1914 the best known "victims of oppression" in the Western world were the subjects of the Russian Czar. Hence *any* Russian revolution would have been regarded with general favor in the West. More narrowly, many Western socialists were secretly ashamed that they had failed to carry out revolutions in their own countries. Now some of them could at least boast that they had helped "save" the Russian Revolution by calling strikes to prevent shipment of munitions to the White armies fighting the Bolsheviks.[49] For years afterward they and their intellectual allies praised every Bolshevik achievement. They attributed all the successes of the new regime to the grandeur of its principles, and explained all its failures and crimes by citing the enormous difficulties it had to face.[50]

Euphoria of this sort seldom lasts long. The revolution itself alienates all who profited from the Old Order or sym-

---

[47] William Wordsworth, *The Prelude or Growth of a Poet's Mind* (Oxford: Clarendon Press, 1959), p. 195.

[48] This attitude is discussed at length in Palmer, *The Age of Democratic Revolutions,* II.

[49] Even such a staunch defender of British interests as the Labourite Foreign Secretary Ernest Bevin (1945-1951) used to make this claim.

[50] The Western reception of the Russian Revolution is analyzed by Brogan, *op. cit.,* pp. 48–69. A perceptive Frenchman once summed up the psychology of westerners of this type by noting that they were still in mourning for the socialist ideal, and that "They flee to the Red Metropolis because they hate the societies in which they live." Raymond Aron, *The Century of Total Wars* (Garden City, N.Y.: Doubleday, 1954), p. 356.

pathized with it. Many of these people emigrate to other countries, preach hatred of the new regime, and hatch plots to destroy it. Meantime the excesses of the revolutionaries frighten an array of domestic and foreign peoples and seem to verify what the embittered emigres are saying. Soon the evidence is more tangible. The French revolutionary armies did not spend all their time scattering Liberty, Equality, and Fraternity in the lands they overran. They also established military governments, imposed crushing taxes on the vanquished, systematically stripped conquered areas of their defenses so they could not be used as bases for future attacks on France, plundered the churches, and carried art treasures back to France. Thus did the revolution which modernized so much else also modernize the technique of exploitation. For good measure, all was done with a maximum of arrogance towards those "liberated," the Committee of Public Safety (1792–1794) even complaining that French generals treated captured enemy officers with consideration.

Another of the harmful legacies of revolutionary regimes is that they drive other peoples and other governments to adopt some of their own hardness and intolerance in sheer self defense. Nonrevolutionary societies have to surrender many of the values they cherish in order to better defend the remainder against the revolutionary society. Gentleness and moderation decline on both sides. When Napoleon forced upon whole peoples savage struggles like the Peninsular Campaign in Spain (1808–1812) and the Russian Campaign (1812) the rest of Europe replied in kind. The English declared grain and raw materials contraband of war, thereby for the first time deliberately directing a war against the whole civilian population of the enemy country. The Spaniards and Russians answered atrocity with atrocity, massacre with massacre. By the time the revolutionary and Napoleonic wars were over possibly as many as 8,000,000 Europeans had perished and everywhere national hatreds had been intensified. Worse, nation worship had been born. Everywhere men were now told that their highest duty was to accept military conscription and die in battle for the race-nation to which they belonged.

The dissemination of revolutionary ideas has a similar effect. It tends to polarize politics, to make everyone either "progressive" or "reactionary," pro or antirevolutionary. Serious political thought decreases, hatreds deepen, men grow afraid, and everyone begins to react automatically in the presence of certain words and symbols. As early as 1791–1792 Parisian bombast about the destruction of monarchy aroused alike the ire and cupidity of France's neighbors. The governments of Austria, Prussia, and Russia discussed the danger that jacobinism might spread, and laid plans to invade France and destroy it.[51]

The polarization is as evident in the realm of ideas as in politics or diplomacy. Edmund Burke, who had defended the rebellious Americans only a few years before, was revolted by events in France and astounded at the official justification offered for them. As early as 1790 he replied with one of the most eloquent denunciations of revolution ever written. A decade later Joseph de Maistre turned out a similar work. This pair have been patron saints of conservative, antirevolutionary doctrine ever since.

Among many who are neither statesmen nor political theorists, reaction against the Revolution is still more intense. After 1800 the upper classes all over Europe were less enlightened, less liberal, less generous in spirit than they had been before 1789. No longer did French nobles coquette with the ideas of the philosophes. Those who survived the Revolution at home or trickled back into France during the Napoleonic era and after were not chastened and made wiser by their experiences. Rather, they were now "ultras": men "more Roy-

---

[51] It has long been thought that their primary interest was the partition of Poland and that their talk about suppressing jacobinism was mostly insincere. R. R. Palmer, however, contends that their concern was genuine and that the fact that they laid so many of their plans in secret proves it. The traditional view he ascribes to the penchant of nineteenth century historians to regard foreign affairs as more important than ideology. Cf. Palmer, *The Age of Democratic Revolutions,* II, 154–55.

alist than the king, more Catholic than the pope," as the phrase went. Many had become as savage and unbalanced as the worst of the revolutionary terrorists, capable of such acts of embittered madness as the public butchery of a live eagle to dramatize their hatred and contempt for Napoleon and the principles they imagined he embodied.

The harm done to the world by the ideas and example of the French Revolution may be best estimated by considering some specific events. The doctrine that every people has a right to a separate existence in an independent nation has opened scores of pandora's boxes that have never been closed and will not be in the foreseeable future. Immediately, it led to the mid-nineteenth century wars that ended in the unification of Germany and Italy. It also led to the insoluble problem facing Europe in 1914: Hapsburg insistence on the "right" to rule many peoples because they had always done so while their subject nationalities insisted on their "right" to unite all the members of their "race." This hopeless dilemma, aggravated by German nationalist vainglory, caused the First World War. And *that* conflict caused the Second World War. Who can say now that the Italian and German people are better off for having become united, when unification led to slaughter and defeat in World War I; inflation, chronic unrest, and fascism between the wars; and fire, bombs, greater slaughter, and worse defeats in World War II?[52] Who can say now that Europe gained from the wave of revolts which swept across the continent in the wake of World War I, overturning monarchies, breaking up empires, and leaving behind a dozen constitutional governments? These regimes were unstable because most of their people did not understand democratic government and lacked both the historical experience and the personal attitudes necessary to make it work. Soon many of

[52] Of course Italy was nominally on the winning side in World War I, but her armies were seldom victorious and the promises made to her during the war were not fulfilled afterward. Hence she emerged from the conflict with the psychology of a defeated nation. For a fuller discussion of the nationality problem in the Austro-Hungarian Empire, cf. *Supra.*, pp. 87–88.

them became convinced that the whole system was but a blind for connivance and corruption, was hopelessly rigged against them, and deserved to be destroyed. In a few years most of the regimes degenerated into open or thinly disguised dictatorships: Hungary in 1920, Lithuania in 1923, Greece and Poland in 1926, Austria in 1932, Germany in 1933, Latvia and Estonia in 1934, Spain in 1936. Between 1939 and 1941, all except Spain were conquered by either Nazi Germany or Stalinist Russia. Spain "escaped" with a mere three year civil war that blasted her cities, smashed her industry, disrupted her transport, and reduced her population some 3–5 percent. And what of the rest of Europe? Is it now better off for having, at a staggering cost, defeated Germany in two world wars? Has the rest of the world been improved because Europe bled herself white in these conflicts at a time when her guidance was most needed to aid in the transformations taking place outside Europe? Have we all benefited because modern totalitarians have studied the French Revolution and taken from it Robespierre's technique of "temporary dictatorship" to safeguard the gains of the revolution while the transition to ordinary constitutional usage is being prepared? Somehow the latter is unconscionably slow in arriving, and the "temporary" dictatorship remains.

The legacy of 1917 has been comparable. The Russian Revolution, the Bolshevik takeover, and the subsequent crimes of the victors have spread a fear of communism that has fouled the political atmosphere of our whole planet. In particular, fear of Communist revolutions has already led to several revolutions of the Right. Because Communists lie, subvert, and employ force without scruple they provide lessons in technique to all those lawless elements of the Right that exist in every country, and give them an excuse to strike first. Time after time, in Hungary and Bavaria in 1920, in Italy in 1922, in Germany in 1933, in Spain in 1936—to list only the best known cases—the Right has shown that it is just as adept at the employment of force as are Communist revolutionaries and just as ruthless once victory has been gained. These constant threats of revolution and counter-revolution tear societies to pieces.

Of all the legacies of revolution, the most harmful and the most enduring is the establishment of the *tradition* of revolt, of studied contempt for orderly legal processes, of the myth that revolution is the magic panacea for every public ill. The case has been pleaded with unusual eloquence by one of modern Europe's most famous liberal scholars and publicists:

Revolution is a word with a double meaning: sometimes it means a new orientation of the human mind, and sometimes the subversion of law and order. More and more, during the great peace of the nineteenth century, the Western mind came to confuse the two meanings of the word, and ended up by convincing itself that every subversion of law and order, every destruction of an existing legitimacy is, and must of necessity be, the beginning of a new and better orientation for humanity. The fallacy of this confusion is now apparent; if, by a lucky chance, the subversion of a long-established legitimacy be accompanied by a new and better orientation, nonetheless it is always, by its very nature, followed by universal panic. But the nineteenth century, made smug by its security, had forgotten even the notion of a general fear. As long as the order created by the Congress in 1815 lasted, that delusion cropped up in literature, in history, in philosophy, in the theoretical parts of political platforms, and was confined to a few attempts at fanciful revolts. When that order collapsed in the World War, the delusion swept through Europe. Young and old, rich and poor, wise and ignorant, conservatives and radicals, were all eager for revolution, were all seeking happiness in the total destruction of rules and laws in every phase of human activity. The most essential laws—the ones on which the legitimacy of government depended and therefore universal security—were almost everywhere violated and overthrown with astonishing ease, and illegitimate governments were hailed, even by the elite, as splendid innovations. The religious and secular authorities—the papacy, the universities, the courts and academies, the banks and tribunals— offered weaker and weaker resistance to the universal folly and allowed the total destruction of the world to be accomplished; sometimes they even helped to destroy it.[53]

The malign legacies of revolution spread and multiply, too, because revolutionaries carefully copy from each other. In our century the syndicalist Sorel got most of his ideas from the nineteenth century Marxists and anarchists. Mussolini drew heavily on Sorel and Lenin. Hitler learned from Mussolini, and openly admitted copying Communist propaganda techniques. Stalin adapted many of the features of Fascist Italy and Nazi Germany, particularly the "cult of personality," to his own regime.

Would the Benefits of Revolution Have Accrued Anyway?

When attempting to estimate the worth of revolutions it is necessary to consider whether their benefits would have come about anyway. Without the parliamentary victory in the civil war of the 1640s it is likely that the Stuart kings would have continued to try to add to royal power. It is not likely that they would have succeeded, for they were an inept dynasty and they were making their effort in a country where the parliamentary tradition was strong, where most of the wealthy and influential people opposed them, and where no standing army existed for use against opponents. Moreover, subsequent history has shown that royal absolutism is impossible to maintain once large numbers of people become educated, articulate, and determined to share in their own government.

Without the American Revolution, the history of the central part of North America would have been vastly different in many particulars. Industry probably would not have developed as rapidly in British colonies as it did in the new independent nation. Westward expansion almost certainly would have been slower, since the Proclamation of 1763 indicated

<hr />

[53] Guglielmo Ferrero, *The Reconstruction of Europe* (N.Y.: Norton, Norton Library ed., 1963), p. 347.

that the British wanted to keep a large area of the American continent as a fur trading preserve. Consequently some portions of the modern western United States might now be parts of Canada and Mexico. Immigration from Europe almost certainly would have been on a reduced scale. Probably democracy would have developed more slowly. Considering, however, the enormous natural wealth of America and the relatively generous treatment Britain subsequently accorded Canada and Australia, it seems likely that had there been no American Revolution we twentieth century Americans would have been little less prosperous or "free" than we are.[54] For the last 250 years, after all, British public life has been more moderate in spirit than that of most Continental countries. Nineteenth and twentieth century Englishmen have shown a general willingness to modernize their political practices and economic system rapidly enough to avoid the violence that has bedevilled the public life of such countries as France and Spain.

Of course it can be contended that they were frightened into this liberality by the American and French revolutions. Possibly; but it is significant that other Europeans were *not* frightened into a similar liberality. Moreover, many prominent Englishmen sided with the rebellious colonials well before the French Revolution. Thus it seems probable, though unprovable, that Britain gradually would have shown a more accommodating spirit in her dealing with the Americans and would eventually have treated them much as she did the Canadians.

A more telling indictment of revolutions is the easily observable fact that all sorts of important improvements in the human condition have occurred without revolution. They

---

[54] Of course, if an independent United States had not existed in 1803 Napoleon could not have sold the Louisiana Territory to President Jefferson. Still, in default of that transaction it is likely that Britain would have gotten the Territory at the Congress of Vienna in 1815 to add to her existing American colonies. Hence all the foregoing arguments from probability are not seriously affected by the question of the Louisiana Purchase. Cf. *Supra.*, pp. 76–77.

have come merely with the passage of time and gradual changes in men's minds. Slavery ended in the Western world without violence (save in the United States) partly because it grew economically unprofitable, partly because the consciences of men were increasingly revolted by it. With the· growth of labor unions and the advance of education, laissez faire capitalism has moderated without revolution all over the Western world. Woman suffrage has become close to universal in Western countries without women rising in revolution. There are many ways of effecting change; revolution is only one.

Viewed in this light, the French Revolution in particular seems tragically futile. All over Europe in the late eighteenth century "enlightened despots" were codifying the laws, abolishing torture, curtailing the privileges of churches and nobles, endeavoring to promote the prosperity of their nations, and displaying a social consciousness new in the annals of monarchy. These tendencies were at work in France too. In time they would have produced equality before the law, suppression of the privileges of birth, and the rest of the gains that came to so many other peoples without the bloodshed and ruinous fragmentation of French politics produced by the Revolution. In fact, the Revolution probably slowed down progress along these lines by scaring the European ruling classes into the reactionary attitudes that typified them for a generation after 1815.

In the case of Russia, it is obvious that the Bolsheviks have made her a mighty world power. But since the Czarist government was beginning to attack the country's fundamental problems before 1913 is it not likely that most of the Bolshevik achievements would have come eventually, albeit more slowly? When we justly admire the remarkable economic and scientific achievements of Russia since the revolution of 1917 it is easy to forget that similar advances have also taken place in many other countries in the same years—without regimentation and oppression. And these have not been only literate, "advanced" Western countries like Belgium, Britain, and the United States. Brazilian industrial output, or Indian, or Turkish, has also grown vastly in half a century. Perhaps most striking of all, Japan, a medieval Asiatic land in 1860, within a generation became a literate, industrialized, westernized nation without recourse to concentration camps, the terror system, or indoctrination in Marxist mythology.

That revolution is not the only road to material accomplishment is easily demonstrated by references to Latin America as well. Though we are still too close in time (1968) to the events to be dogmatic, Puerto Rico's prosperity increased more rapidly during the era of peaceful reforms undertaken by Governor Munoz Marin than Cuba's did for a decade after the Castro Revolution. The Bolivian revolution of 1952 threw that benighted land into a worse state than ever, a morass of confusion and inefficiency which for years defied all efforts at remedy.

Finally, even if revolutions always produced economic improvement (which they do not) this would still beg the most important question: is economic efficiency, or even economic equality, the most worthy goal men can pursue? Or, for that matter, is political liberty? Does not pursuit of these objectives, when carried to the length of undertaking sanguinary revolutions, destroy more important and nobler qualities of the mind and spirit? These are essentially *qualitative* questions, questions of relative human values. They have no precise answers, but no one who is either a Christian or a secular humanist can ignore them or opt *automatically* for the gains of revolution regardless of cost.

Is Revolution Obsolete?

Whether we like them or not we cannot undo the revolutions of the past. But ought we to have more of them? Yes, say the temperamental romantics who think of revolutions as liberating forces and who have not given up the dream that the imperfections of men can be cured by changing the ways they are educated, organized, and governed. Yes, say the Communists and all their allies, for their thoughts are on a communized world and they envision revolution as a promising tool for its achievement. No, say an increasing number of thoughtful people everywhere. Desirable or not, revolution has become too dangerous. In the nuclear age it is increasingly likely that some revolution will ignite a war fought with weapons that will undo 6000 years of history in a few days— or hours. Besides, they add, science is providing solutions to more and more of our problems. What is needed is not incessant revolutionary tumult and fanaticism which undermines civilized attitudes and conduct but a long period of quiet, careful adjustment. Even if this means postponing some things that are desirable in themselves, it is better for people to make gains peacefully and at a rate slow enough for them to be assimilated than to rip the fabric of society apart in the headlong, bloody pursuit of utopia. Besides, revolutions—particularly social revolutions—fail to deliver on their promises anyway.[55]

In summary, then, one does not need to be an Ultimate Conservative[56] to conclude that revolutions usually do more harm than good. They destroy old evils and overturn ineffectual governments. Sometimes they liberate economic resources and energy and give able people opportunities they previously lacked. Sometimes they promote a greater degree of justice. They may even frighten other governments into making salutary reforms in order to avoid further revolutions. But most of the time the price seems too high. Too much blood is shed and too many of the old ills simply reappear in a new guise or are replaced by things even worse. Too many opportunities are provided for fanatics and butchers. Too many enduring hatreds are burned into the souls of everybody concerned. Revolutions set an example of organized lawlessness. They

---

[55] "Nothing, we might say today, could be more obsolete than the attempt to liberate mankind from poverty by political means: nothing could be more futile and more dangerous." Arendt, *op. cit.*, p. 110.

[56] An Ultimate Conservative has been defined as a man who, had he been present when God brought order out of chaos, would have favored retaining chaos.

thereby beget other revolutions. These, in turn, incite enemies of revolution into counter-violence, in a vicious circle. All this has been destructive enough in the past. The world ought no longer to risk it in the nuclear age.

But having said this we must conclude regretfully that few are apt to pay much attention. Norman Angell "proved" that war did not "pay" in 1910, but World War I began in 1914 anyway.[57] It is not difficult to demonstrate that the world would be much better off now if all governments disarmed down to the weapons required for domestic police work and did not attempt to interfere in the domestic affairs of other nations, but they will not do so. The vices of unrestrained nationalism are evident to any intelligent person, but men do not abandon nationalism on that account. Thus, harmful or not, revolutions are apt to be with us a long time simply because many people still believe and hope in them and because the world's supply of restless, bored, and thwarted people is as great as ever.

[57] Norman Angell. *The Great Illusion* (N.Y.: G. P. Putnam's Sons, 1933).

V

WHAT CAUSES "NATIONAL CHARACTER"?

The Issue

Thousands of history books have been rendered more color-
ful, but hardly more accurate, by writers who refer knowingly
to "Celtic melancholy" or the preternatural "clarity" of French
thought. If describing some crisis, such scribes are apt to exult
that the day was saved because a key party had a "cool Nordic
temperament." If making a reference to Princess X, they do
not fail to inform us that she "inherited her mother's fiery
Spanish soul." If the narrative happens to involve a Scot the
adjectives "dour" or "canny" are invariably appended. This
sort of thing is bound to raise doubts. If all Scots were "dour"
one would expect that such an unsociable people would by
now have become extinct from sheer failure to reproduce. If
all of them were "canny" they ought to have long since become
the rulers and financiers of the world since most other people
are not paragons of shrewdness. To take another case, how
many times has one heard or read that "southern" peoples
are more lazy, excitable, and sensuous than "northerners," and
that people from northern countries usually work harder and
prize liberty more? To be sure, millions of Americans from
north of the Mason-Dixon line hold this opinion of themselves and southern Americans, the Scots hold it of themselves
and the English, the Dutch of themselves and the Belgians,
northern Frenchmen and Italians of southern Frenchmen and
Italians, northern Europeans of themselves and southern
Europeans. Yet, save for the North and South Poles, every
spot on the face of the earth is north of some other and south

of still another. Moreover, how many lazy southern sensualists who happen to move 400 miles north immediately become hard working defenders of liberty?[1]

If writing of the type described does serious violence to historical truth, what are we to do? Are we to say that because all normal human beings need food, clothing and shelter, have the procreative instinct, are attached to their families, and will defend their possessions and interests, that they are therefore so much alike that we ought to forswear all qualitative distinctions among branches of the human family? Surely peoples and nations possess *some* distinctive and meaningful group characteristics? After all, anyone who is not blind or cretinous is aware that Greeks, Germans, and Englishmen differ significantly in appearance, manners, habits, and attitudes. The differences between white and black peoples, or Europeans and orientals, are even more obvious. If we are forbidden to generalize, how are we to perceive any meaning in history? If every human being and every historical event is quite unlike any other, how can we even reflect on human affairs? The real problem lies between these two extremes. What this chapter seeks to explore is whether certain "races" and nationalities are by nature noble, cruel, brave, treacherous, or gloomy. More particularly, we need to consider whether the inhabitants of particular national states have a true national character: e.g. are the differences between, say, Englishmen and Frenchmen, permanent and of such importance that they constantly shape the basic character of English and French national policy? And if they are such, from what sources do such differences spring? Racial heritage? Physical environment? Historical experience? Some other?

Carelessness

It is mildly reassuring that nonsense of the "fiery Spanish soul" variety is less common in historical writing now than it

---

[1] The example is taken from Jacques Barzun, *Race: A Study in Superstition* (N.Y.: Harper & Row, 1965), p. 94.

used to be, though it is still by no means extinct. Sometimes it is due to mere carelessness. For instance, the author of a generally valuable book on sixteenth century Spain remarks that in Philip II the Hapsburg jaw was less noticeable "than in the majority of his race."[2] Obviously, what he means is not "race" at all but the Hapsburg dynasty. Elsewhere the same writer declares that "The age long infusion of Semitic blood from Carthaginian, Moor, and Jew may have contributed its share to making Spain a land of mystics, and to making northern Spain the proverbial 'land of rocks and saints'."[3] Other portions of the book, however, explain clearly and at some length that most distinctive Spanish national characteristics were the fruit of centuries of battling the Moslem Moors, and of the ruinous economic policies of many Spanish governments.[4] In another book, which provides a generally distinguished treatment of its subject, the author falls into a rhapsody about the Welsh politician David Lloyd George. It begins thus: "His words, filled with the instinctive music of his race. . . ."[5] Doubtless the writer himself would be as hard pressed as the reader to explain or justify this ornate phraseology.

Sometimes the attribution of a distinctive national or racial characteristic has a solid basis in fact but is overdrawn. For instance, a scholar prominent in Renaissance and Jewish studies declares that the great massacre of Jews in Spain in 1391 was "an early illustration of that innate violence of character . . . which distinguished Spanish life throughout history, and rendered Spanish civil wars noteworthy for their ferocity in the annals of the human race."[6] Now the Spanish national character does have some distinctive features, which we will

[2] R. Trevor-Davies, *The Golden Century of Spain* (London: Macmillan, 1964), p. 118.

[3] *Ibid.,* p. 9.

[4] Cf. *Infra.,* pp. 229–31.

[5] George Dangerfield, *The Strange Death of Liberal England, 1910–1914* (N.Y.: Capricorn Books, 1961), p. 275.

[6] Cecil Roth, *The Spanish Inquisition* (N.Y.: W. W. Norton & Co., 1964), p. 22.

discuss in due course and for which there are compelling reasons in Spain's historic experience, but to claim that the Spaniards are naturally more prone to savagery than other peoples is nonsense. To some extent the writer corrects his own distortion by noting that there were massacres of Jews in England in 1189, and in Germany both during the First Crusade and in the twentieth century. However, he appears to forget entirely such similar atrocities as the anti-Jewish pogroms in late Czarist Russia, the Turkish massacres of Bulgarians in 1876 and Armenians in 1915, the slaughter of Moslems in Jerusalem by the Crusaders in 1099, Communist massacres of "class enemies" in twentieth century Russia and China, and the propensity of Assyrians, Huns, Vikings, and Mongols to massacre enemies of any kind. As for civil wars, that of Spain (1936–1939) was undeniably brutal and bloody, but so were the French civil wars (1560–1598), the French Revolution (1789–1795), the Thirty Years' War in Germany (1618–1648), the American Civil War (1861–1865), the Russian Revolution and civil wars (1917–1921), the conflicts that followed the T'ai P'ing Rebellion in China in the 1850s, and the Roman civil wars of the first century B.C. and the third century A.D.[7]

Race

Discussions notoriously get nowhere until the main terms are defined. "Race" is not really the same thing as "nationality," though numberless people *think* it is. They are also convinced that "racial" differences between themselves and other members of the human species are profoundly important and that their own assumed superiority over other people is due to a nobler racial heritage. Hence if we are to reach any valid generalizations about national traits and psychology we

[7] Nor are things looking up. The Indonesians slaughtered somewhere between 200,000 and 400,000 domestic Communists in 1965, some 100,000 Nigerians reputedly perished by mass murder in 1966, and after 1966 the government of Nigeria tried hard to starve to death the whole population of rebellious Biafra.

must consider whether the observable physical and psychological differences between the "races" of men reflect important and permanent genetic differences.

One of the permanent characteristics of the human mind is that it seeks to bring comprehension, order, and regularity out of the chaos of existence. About 200 years ago the scientific classification of all living things was first undertaken in earnest. Given the obvious diversity of mankind it was in no way surprising, unreasonable, or disreputable to expect that if the human species could be accurately divided into races, and the races compared carefully, that permanent, meaningful differences between them might be revealed. Given the millenia of human existence and the cultural and geographical isolation of many peoples it seemed quite possible that races of widely differing *natural* capacities and psychologies might have grown up.

The first efforts to classify mankind were made on the basis of the most obvious criterion: skin color. It was soon recognized, however, that differences in other physical features were equally pronounced. Further efforts were then made to categorize humans according to the new criteria or to combinations of them. None of these efforts has ever been very successful or convincing.

Racist Absurdities

In informed circles in the Western world, racist doctrines are currently held in low repute. For this the imtemperate prophets of race have chiefly themselves to blame. The literature on every aspect of racism is enormous, but the race pundits have never been able to agree on even the fundamentals of their "science."[8] For two centuries they have classified people by color of hair, skin, and eyes, type of hair, shape of skull, form of eyes, stature, type of blood, even height of arch. Some

[8] Barzun, *op. cit.,* is an excellent, brief, entertaining summary of the whole subject. Louis L. Snyder, *The Idea of Racialism* (N.Y.: D. Van Nostrand Co., 1962), is also good. Both books are written from the liberal point of view: i.e. by unbelievers in "race science."

have gone even further; subdividing their fellows into races according to diet, climate, the kind of soil where they live, even the way they pronounce words—though it is not explained how anyone knows the way words were pronounced centuries ago.[9] As a result of such industry some race scientists have discovered that mankind consists of three races; others that it is divided into five—or eight, or fifteen, or thirty-three. None appear to have been troubled by the fact that the more closely human populations are studied the less clear-cut "races" become. Likewise, the easily observable fact that individual Negroes, Indians or Caucasians differ dramatically from other Negroes, Indians and Caucasians in height, color, and personality is treated as of no account, while the much smaller differences between the *average* of one race and the *average* of another are held to be highly significant.[10] The most obvious points of general agreement have been that each "scientist" is convinced that the particular "race" to which he happens to belong is superior to the others and that all race scientists but himself misunderstand the sources, twist the meanings of terms, and avoid obvious conclusions. Perhaps it is more than coincidental that several of the most extravagant and outspoken racists of the nineteenth century, notably the Frenchman Gobineau, the German Nietzsche, and the Germanized Englishman Houston Stewart Chamberlain, died insane.[11] The words and deeds of many others cause one to marvel at the ingenuity displayed by men anxious to inflate personal, tribal, or national egos. Vuk Karadzic, an early nineteenth century Serb nationalist, insisted that his people were the greatest on the planet, that they had a culture 5000 years old, and that Christ and the twelve apostles had been

[9] Some insight into pronunciation in times past may be gained by examining old poems in which the words at the end of each line rhyme, but the limitations of this technique are evident.

[10] A good general survey of the biological aspects of racism is Theodosius Dobzhansky, *Heredity and the Nature of Man* (N.Y.: Harcourt, Brace and World, 1964). Some of the matters above are considered on pp. 80–84.

[11] In fairness, it must be acknowledged that in their disregard for common sense and ordinary observation some of the dogmatic environmentalists of our own age appear equally ill-balanced.

Serbs. Between the two world wars, a Hungarian patriotic organization discovered that modern Hungarians were a "Turanian" people, descended from the ancient Persians, Sumerians, Hittites, and Egyptians. Since Christ had been a Scythian, he was therefore a "Turanian" too, as were all the early Christians. In the same years the Greater Finland Society concluded that precisely because Finns were a *mixture* of Scandinavian and East Baltic "races" they were more dynamic than "purer" races and were therefore destined eventually to gain control of northern Europe.[12] Not to be outdone in absurdity, some of the political and "intellectual" leaders of contemporary Africa have been revealing to a hitherto unsuspecting world such priceless lore as the Egyptian Negro ancestry of Moses and Buddha, that Christianity was derived from a Sudanese tribe, and that Nietzsche, Bergson, Marx, and Sartre were all descended from hitherto unknown Bantu philosophers.[13]

The fact that most racists have had (and still have) some political axe to grind has further reduced their repute. Such French aristocratic racists as Boulainvilliers in the eighteenth century, deBonald at the turn of the nineteenth, and Gobineau in the middle of the nineteenth, argued at inordinate length that the French aristocracy was a separate "race" from other Frenchmen because they wanted thereby to justify domination of French government and society by their own social class. With the coming of the Industrial Revolution in the nineteenth century, a development which wrenched millions of people from their native soil, some astute politicians con-

---

[12] These fantasies are described by Hans Rogger and Eugen Weber, eds., *The European Right: A Historical Profile* (Berkeley: University of California Press, 1966), pp. 378, 394, 417–19. One wishes he could say that it indicates the relative sanity of the Greater Finland Society that its members should argue that Finns were a particularly able and dynamic people because they were a *mixed* rather than a "pure" race. Among people, as among plants and animals, hybrids often seem particularly long lived, sturdy and physically resistant. More likely, the Society was just making a virtue of necessity.

[13] We owe these particular accomplishments to one Dick Akwa. Cf. *The New York Review of Books*, May 12, 1966, 24.

sidered that race could be employed as a new principle to unify the nation politically and emotionally. Such late nineteenth century figures as the British imperialist Cecil Rhodes and the German clerical reactionary Adolf Stocker viewed race in this light. In the twentieth century such perceptive dictators as Mussolini, and especially Hitler, used emotional racism to distract people from pressing social and economic problems, to weld modern society's divergent interest groups together, to inflate everyone's ego, to justify man's persistent desire to hate and persecute other men, and to develop a national esprit de corps.

The most appalling example of the cynical manipulation of race notions for political ends occurred in Nazi Germany. Hitler's belief in the superiority of the "Nordic" race was notorious. Nazi race scientists, however, found that pure "Nordic" types existed in Germany only in a few small communities around Berlin—an awkward discovery for a movement which hoped to lead all Germans. Before long the race researchers refined their studies sufficiently to conclude that *all* Germans were true Nordics. Then in the late 1930s Nazi Germany became allied with Italy and Japan. It would hardly do to refer in public to one's allies as contemptible inferiors so the race scientists hurriedly discovered that both Italians and Japanese were basically Nordic types. Eventually Hitler decided that anyone who had ever exhibited such qualities as courage, resourcefulness, artistic imagination, and intellectual acumen must have been a Nordic since these were distinctive Nordic traits. This elastic conception enabled Nazi racists to adopt as their own such remarkable Nordics as Julius Caesar, Michelangelo, Leonardo da Vinci, and Genghis Khan. Even Jesus Christ was discovered to have been an "Amorite Nordic".[14] If one follows Nazi logic perhaps the purest of all races

[14] Other students of the "Nordics" have been equally imaginative. At times Nordic has meant only Germans and Scandinavians, but at other times it has also included one, several, or all of the following: Dutch, Flemings, most Englishmen, some of the Irish, Anglo-Americans, white south Africans, Thrako-Hellenes, "true" Kurds, most West Persians, and Afghans. Snyder, *op. cit.*, pp. 50, 84.

is the one composed of "race scientists" themselves. Numerous studies have shown that people who have marked antipathies towards certain categories of men or certain occupational groups usually have them against many other categories and groups too.[15]

The fully developed Nazi conception of race highlights the patent absurdities which distort the whole subject. Even if there are biological features or processes which truly mark off some categories of men from others (itself a highly controversial matter), how are these necessarily connected with all sorts of other phenomena? For instance, how can artistic or psychic qualities be transmitted hereditarily within a race? If a man inherits the ability to paint expertly, why weren't his parents equally accomplished painters? Not surprisingly, some white liberals have grown so outraged by such nonsense, by the racial arrogance of their fellow Caucasians, and by the practical injustices that have been spawned thereby, that they have become inverted racists. They blame all the wickedness in recorded history on white people and attribute all virtue to the maligned colored peoples of the world, forgetting that the history of the latter is quite as replete with greed, stupidity, oppression, and general nastiness as the saga of the self-satisfied "Nordics."

Does Racism Have Any Validity?

Despite the grotesqueries of the ardent racists one cannot say that *all* racist concepts are nonsense, or even that they are unimportant. The importance of heredity in animal breeding and in the improvement of plants is well known. That the character of a human being is formed by heredity as well as environment is equally obvious. The hereditary character of various diseases is established beyond question. It is a matter of common observation that members of the "Mongolian race"

---

[15] Clyde Kluckhohn, *Mirror for Man: The Relationship of Anthropology to Modern Life* (N.Y.: McGraw Hill, 1949), pp. 138–39.

have a particular fold of skin about the eye which gives them a slant-eyed look, and that Negroes possess woolly hair and thick lips. Careful tests and surveys have shown such things as differences between the "races" in average cranial capacity and brain size; marked variation between "races" and cultures in performances on I.Q. tests; wide variations among "races" in susceptibility to certain diseases and resistance to others; and marked differences in the frequency with which certain blood types (A, B, O, AB, RH factor) are found among different "races."

The difficulties arise not from recognizing such facts but from interpreting them correctly. Selective breeding readily produces dogs or cattle of markedly differing physical features, capacities, and temperaments; but the key factor is that the whole process is controlled throughout by men who select the qualities they want in the animals, crossbreed those individuals who possess the desired traits, and rigorously exclude the rest. No attempt even remotely like this has ever been made to direct human reproduction, and we cannot even experiment with human beings in ways that are routine with animals and insects. Moreover, human beings have a long life-span compared with many animals and most insects. There have been only about 200 human generations in recorded history. For these reasons less is known about human heredity than about animal heredity. Finally, the qualities that are most desirable among humans are often the opposite of those prized (by humans) among animals. It is desirable for men to be even tempered, to be socially adaptable, and to learn many different things readily, while animals are usually bred to accentuate a few particular qualities and to suppress others.

Arguments about the relative importance of heredity and environment are interminable. An individual inherits his genes from his parents, but he inherits only some of them and these in haphazard combinations. Thus, theoretically, parents might have thousands of children but no two would be identical. Even "identical twins" have different fingerprints, and often widely different personalities as well. About all that can be said for certain in the present state of genetic knowledge is that environment can operate only on the raw material bequeathed to it by heredity, but that nothing inherited expresses itself in a vacuum; it is always shaped by environment. The degree is still uncertain.

Arguments about skull capacity and brain size are inconclusive because big people of whatever race tend to have larger heads than small people of the same race. Moreover, nobody has ever shown that intelligence is linked to head or brain size anyway. Intelligence tests are unquestionably significant within a particular culture but nobody has ever solved the problem of using them to make meaningful distinctions between peoples of different cultures since the very structure of the tests reflects certain values, skills, and kinds of knowledge that are more pertinent to some societies than to others.[16]

To summarize: biology and genetics cannot demonstrate that the marked differences among human types necessarily indicate "superiority" or "inferiority." Indeed, the latter are not biological phenomena at all. They are subjective evaluations: ethical, social, and political judgments. Only since the middle of the nineteenth century have men tried to support them by linking them to biology.

Biologically sound or not, hostility between cultures, between peoples who think of each other as belonging to different "races," is one of the most deeply rooted of all human instincts. Just *how* deeply is shown by the fact that American medical doctors, among the most highly educated people in Western societies (and presumably those most aware that differences between races and nationalities are neither of genetic origin nor of fundamental importance), nonetheless discriminate against their Negro colleagues. Negro doctors have long had their own medical association, have frequently been denied hospital privileges, and have been doomed to generally inferior training, in most of the northern United States as well

[16] Dobzhansky considers these matters in some detail. Cf. *op. cit.*, pp. 102–10.

as in the south. Clearly, race feeling is nonrational, something close to instinctive.

Every racially mixed society has had to wrestle with this problem. The ancient Greeks regarded the Persians with contempt, as barbarians, brutes, "stammerers" who uttered elemental, incomprehensible sounds like dogs or birds. Hindu writings also reveal race hatred and discrimination thousands of years ago. Our own century has been suffused with the antipathies of English and Irish, Poles and Russians, Flemings and Walloons, Greeks and Turks, Castilians and Catalans, Malays and Chinese, Moslems and Hindus, Jews and Arabs, Singhalese and Tamils in Ceylon, East Indians and Negroes in Guyana, Ibos, Yorubas, and Hausas in Nigeria, and everywhere blacks and whites. The reasons are usually ignoble: fear, vanity, frustration, economic rivalry, greed for land, cultural rivalry, the desire of political rulers to distract attention from other matters, mere dislike of those who are different, and sheer human irrationality. But the hatreds are not lessened on that account.[17]

The whole subject of race has been muddied further by changes in intellectual fashion. Two or three generations ago the vast majority of educated men, whether biologists, sociologists, historians, anthropologists or some other, were unabashed racists. Such journalists as Maurice Barres, W. T. Stead, Katkov, and Danilevski; literary figures like Rudyard Kipling; the historians Treitschke, Seeley and Fiske; the military writers von der Goltz, Bernhardi, and A. T. Mahan; Kaiser William II; President Theodore Roosevelt; Senators John C. Calhoun and Albert Beveridge; British Colonial Secretary Joseph Chamberlain; and Confederate President Jefferson Davis are but a sampling of hundreds of public men from many countries who spoke and wrote openly of the natural superiority of certain races (invariably their own) to

---

[17] Some of these points are discussed briefly in a fine, thoughtful book by William H. McNeill, *Past and Future* (Chicago: University Press, 1964), pp. 170–71. Cf. also Snyder, *op. cit.,* pp. 35–39, and Eric Kahler, *The Meaning of History* (N.Y.: Meridian Books, 1968).

others. Millions of people of every social class and political stripe agreed unquestioningly. In our own time, by contrast, any educated person who expresses racist ideas is at once denounced by his compatriots as stupid, heartless, bigoted, anti-intellectual (the ultimate offense) and often, for good measure, neo-Nazi. Yet our knowledge of genetics will surely increase, and the attitude of men towards their fellows is always in flux. Who can guess what will be both scientifically persuasive and intellectually fashionable fifty or a hundred years from now?

The term "intellectual fashion" is used here deliberately, since at any given time social and political desires have at least as much to do with shaping beliefs and attitudes about race as does scientific evidence. All those who yearn to improve man's condition in this world and who believe that dramatic improvement is possible—Communists east of the Iron Curtain, democratic socialists, liberals, and undifferentiated optimists west of it—*must* hold that environment counts far more heavily than heredity in shaping human beings. If it does not, then how can one hope to build significantly finer human societies? Both Communist and democratic theory insist upon racial equality. So does the United Nations and its myriad branches, the U.S. Supreme Court, numberless religious bodies, organizations for the advancement of minority groups, and crusaders and humanitarians of every stripe. In the face of this avalanche of "official" opinion and "interested" doctrine, the small minority of scientists, in no way frauds or fanatics, who have serious doubts about the whole matter have difficulty finding listeners—much less getting financial support for research which might produce conclusions with embarrassing political or social implications.[18] Other scientists hesitate to jeopardize their careers by even questioning the

[18] One such has been the Nobel Prize winning physicist William Shockley who has called for more research to determine whether there really are important genetic differences between Negroes and white people. Reported in *TIME*, February 3, 1967, 65.

"official" and socially acceptable view.[19] Geneticists who hold that class and national difference are the result of hereditary tendencies and that the only way to get rid of unwanted nationalities or social types is by controlling their rate of reproduction, usually get short shrift from book reviewers—if their books are noticed at all.

Still, one has to judge such questions according to the best knowledge available in his own time, not what was in vogue fifty years ago or what men may possibly think a century hence. It is possible that some of the conclusions about race reached by past speculators may eventually be proved sound, but at present there is little indication that this is likely. The great majority of biologists and geneticists, sociologists and anthropologists, testers and estimators, are currently convinced that there is no scientific basis for holding that one race is naturally superior or inferior to another. They insist that from what is known now the obvious differences between the various branches of the human family are mostly the product of physical and cultural environment rather than genetic difference. An unprejudiced layman may not refuse to accept this.

Summary

This whole excursion into the morass of "race" may strike the reader as an irritating irrelevance, particularly since the boundaries between races are notoriously fuzzy and fluctuating,[20] and every existing political state contains more than one

[19] Harry E. Garnett, a former head of the Department of Psychology at Columbia University and past president of the American Psychological Association, argued in 1961 that all sorts of tests clearly indicate natural Negro inferiority. The American Anthropological Association denounced his conclusions by a vote of 192–0, declaring them to be not merely scientifically unsound but *politically undesirable* as well. Cf. Snyder, *op. cit.*, pp. 68–75, for a discussion of the case.

[20] Consider the following sequence: Norwegians, Germans, Austrians, north Italians, south Italians, Greeks, Egyptians, Sudanese, Ethiopians, Kenyans, and Congolese. Where is the dividing line that clearly marks off Nordics from non-Nordics or, for that matter, blacks from whites?

"race." Nonetheless, the proverbial "man in the street" thinks of race and nation as the same. He assumes that all citizens of the Spanish state are members of the Spanish "race"; that all English citizens of whatever ultimate ethnic derivation are now "Englishmen." This may not be good science but it is attuned to the real world. What influences the course of international events is not what "Celts" or "Aryans" think or do, but what is done by those political entities that appear on a map as Germany, Russia, Great Britain, China, and the United States. Thus in the following discussion when we speak of the national character of England or Spain we shall mean what the ordinary person means: the collective national habits and attitudes of those people who live in England and Spain.

Nations Are Not Homogeneous

The previous section has indicated the unlikelihood that biological inheritance is responsible for the social and psychological differences between the "races" of men. It is doubly difficult to ascribe *national* traits to heredity because all "nationalities," save possibly the Eskimos, are the product of ethnic mixture. Unlike animals, who seldom willingly mate with other than their own type, even within a species, humans have always intermarried and interbred freely. Moreover, all parts of the earth have experienced mass migrations at various times. Most areas have been fought over repeatedly. Every invading army leaves behind it some of its own members as permanent settlers—not to speak of a host of illegitimate children. Every army takes away with it some of the women of the invaded area. Likewise, individual traders, land seekers, missionaries, refugees, and adventurers have wandered over the earth for centuries, often putting down roots far from their original homes. Of the four most populous nations in the world, the Soviet Union, India, and the United States are notorious conglomerations of dozens of the most dissimilar peoples. Yet they are all "Russians," "Indians," and "Americans." Those in the United States have already intermarried extensively, and all of them speak an Americanized form of English.[21] China is somewhat more homogeneous than the other three states, but it still contains quite different Mongol, Manchurian, Tibetan, and South Chinese types.

Centuries ago when the Germanic barbarians overran the western Roman Empire some of them settled in northern Italy, abandoned their native tongue, and became "Italians." Others settled in Gaul and became the ancestors of modern Frenchmen. Still others settled in Spain and became "Spaniards." A few centuries later the Vikings repeated the process, settling in such disparate places as England, France, and Sicily, adopting the native languages, and becoming "Sicilians," "Frenchmen," and "Englishmen."

Sometimes, imaginative students of race and nationality questions have become so impressed with the heterogeneity of a nation that they have insisted that its inhabitants cannot possibly be one "people." The examples of Boulainvilliers, de Bonald, and Gobineau, and their political motivations, have been noted earlier. A more interesting case, because the "expert" had no such axe to grind, is that of Henry Mayhew, an English journalist who in the 1850s published a two volume study of the London poor in which he argued that the flotsam and jetsam of big city British society (peddlers, prostitutes, beggars, actors, laborers, and the like) belonged to a different race than the rest of Englishmen. He based his case partly on the arguments that these outcasts were nomadic in their habits and parasitic on the productive elements in society, but more on claims that they spoke a secret language of their own and that they were physically different from other Englishmen—

---

[21] Of course cross-breeding between American whites and Negroes is less than it used to be but the great majority of U. S. Negroes have some white ancestors. In the U.S.S.R. such peoples as the Georgians and Ukranians cherish a separate identity to a greater degree than do, say, the descendants of Czech or Irish immigrants to the U.S.A., but both the Russian government and the outside world consider them "Russians" for all practical purposes.

particularly in the greater development of their jaws and cheekbones. Mayhew marvelled only that these "facts" had so long remained unnoticed.

In Europe the frequency with which one encounters incongruous names indicates clearly the extent to which the whole continent has become ethnically mixed. There are Frenchmen who bear the English name "Waddington," the Italian name "Viviani," or the German names "Koenig" and "Schmitz." There are Italians with such Slavic names as "Suvich," Poles with German names like "Wagner," and Germans with such Slavic names as "Brauchitsch," "Treitschke," and "Nietzsche." One encounters even such curious Franco-Teutonic hybrids as "von Francois." The World War I German Field Marshal von Mackensen bore a name that one might think Danish save for the "von," yet Mackensen was descended from a Scottish family named Mackenzie that had settled in Prussia two or three centuries earlier. Many people around the Baltic have names that end in "ius," yet by "nationality" some of them are Lithuanians, some Finns, some Swedes, some Danes, some Dutch, and some Germans.

All such examples are pallid, however, beside that extraordinary phenomenon, the "Sicilian." Omitting all such mavericks as tourists, merchants, and slaves (themselves of twenty different origins), since ancient times Sicily has been settled and ruled successively by Phoenecians, Greeks, Carthaginians, Romans, Byzantines, Moslem Arabs, Norman French, Germans, Angevin French, Aragonese, Castilian Spanish, Austrians, and modern Italians. What sort of "national character" does a modern Sicilian possess?

Moreover, "nations" are like "races" in that variations are greater between individuals within the same nation than between the *averages* of different nations. This fact is easily forgotten because of our deep rooted habit of stereotyping certain peoples: e.g. we think of Swedes as being blond and ignore all those who are not; ignore in particular certain areas in Sweden where dark haired people are a majority. It is noteworthy that if one is asked to describe briefly the characteristics of his own countrymen he finds this difficult in direct proportion to the extent of his knowledge about them. It is always easier to generalize broadly and confidently about people of whom one knows little.

National Characteristics Change

The conception of "national characteristics" has still another serious drawback: the attitudes of nations and the public reputations of whole peoples have often changed. About 1800 it was a common gibe that "the French rule the land, the English rule the sea, the Germans rule the clouds." As Madame de Stael put it in 1810, the Germans are "loyal, good and simple, but dreamy, melancholy, full of sentiment, music, abstract thought. . . ."[22] In 1870 Thomas Carlyle wrote a letter to the editor of the *London Times* that went thus: "That noble, patient, deep, pious, and solid Germany should be at length welded into a Nation, and become Queen of the Continent, instead of vapouring, vainglorious, gesticulating, quarrelsome, restless, and over-sensitive France, seems to me the hopefullest public fact that has occurred in my time."[23] Who would have subscribed to these sentiments in 1914 or 1940? In 1940 there would have been a more general disposition to see the Germans as essentially a tribe of barbarians perpetually scowling at civilization from across the Rhine.[24]

The Scandinavian Vikings were the scourge of Europe in the ninth and tenth centuries, murdering, pillaging, and burning their way along thousands of miles of seacoast from Russia to Gibraltar and eastward to Italy. Their remote Swedish

[22] Barzun, *op. cit.,* p. 82.

[23] Cited in Milton S. Mayer, *They Thought They Were Free: the Germans 1933–1945* (Chicago: University Press, First Phoenix ed., 1966), p. 241.

[24] This was the view of many French writers after 1870 and of at least one major English historian. Cf. A. J. P. Taylor, *The Course of German History* (New York: Coward-McCann, 1946), p. 14. Of course this indictment of the Germans ignores all the French invasions of German states in the thousand years separating Charlemagne and Napoleon.

descendants repeated these fearsome performances in central and eastern Europe on several occasions between 1600 and 1709. Yet twentieth century Sweden, Norway, and Denmark are three of the earth's model nations: peaceful, prosperous, democratic, internationalist—a veritable lexicon of the liberal virtues. Twentieth century Switzerland is, like Sweden, a paragon of national wholesomeness and international rectitude. Few recall that fifteenth and sixteenth century Swiss mercenary troops were not the ornamental Papal Guard of our time but the most skilled soldiers and heartless plunderers of their day.

Seventeenth century Englishmen regarded the Scottish Lowlanders as a coarse, cruel, animalistic people. Not long afterwards the designation was transferred to the Irish. George Washington disdained New Englanders as "an exceedingly dirty and nasty people"—a reputation they have scarcely maintained. In the 1930s most Western peoples thought of the Japanese as intelligent and industrious, but rather weak, imitative, and sly. During World War II their slyness was accentuated, but they became strong, tough, and treacherous as well. Since 1945 they have suddenly grown less sly and more gullible![25]

Of all such cases, however, the most interesting and instructive is that of Great Britain. Modern Englishmen like to think of themselves as an even-tempered, sensible people who understand government and respect it. In consequence of this moderation and wisdom they are blessed with the world's best government. Frenchmen, by contrast, are a constitutionally undisciplined, rebellious lot whose chief public preoccupation is overthrowing their governments. Consequently, and predictably, the French are badly governed. If one thinks of the

---

[25] For these and other examples cf. Dobzhansky, *op. cit.,* pp. 80–81; Kluckhohn, *op. cit.,* p. 126; and Mayer, *op. cit.,* p. 239. The quotation is from Mayer. Sometimes peoples *do* change; not merely in the opinions of others, but physically. German and Russian children after World War I differed in stature and head form from their parents. The reason derived from their physical environment: they were the survivors of the famines that racked both countries after the war. Cf. Kluckhohn, p. 118.

history of England and France only since 1789 this view has some plausibility. France has had several bloody revolutions in that period and more than a dozen different governments while England has had no revolutions at all and only gradual, peaceful changes in her governmental structure. A little reflection on the earlier history of the two nations, however, and the vision evaporates. In the eight centuries before 1789 England endured more civil wars, more changes of dynasty, and more general domestic violence than did France. Sixteenth century continental Europeans regarded Englishmen as an extravagant and ungovernable people, an opinion that seemed vindicated in the seventeenth century when the volatile islanders staged two revolutions and horrified Europe by executing their king. Even in their "well behaved" centuries, the nineteenth and twentieth, the English barely staved off a social revolution in 1848 and probably would have fallen into a civil war in 1914 save for the outbreak of World War I. Nor did they show much of their proverbial "common sense" in the 1930s when they appeased the Fascist dictators so long that they nearly ensured that Hitler would win World War II. Ironically, in that decade of Britain's national abasement, the Nazi Propaganda Minister Josef Goebbels, declared that the English "are a race of people with whom you can talk only after you have first knocked out their teeth."[26] Less than a generation before, English and American diplomats had grumbled that it was useless to talk to German colleagues unless one first banged his fist on the table.

The private reputations of the British have changed even more dramatically through the centuries than their public character. About 1500 Erasmus, who loved Thomas More and a few other English scholars, thought the rest of Englishmen shiftless, untrustworthy, and remarkably dirty. Cellini compared them to wild beasts, and other Italians and Frenchmen considered Britons (especially Scots) to be barbarous, uncouth, and addicted to hard drink. If they had any saving

[26] Mayer, *op. cit.,* p. 239.

social grace it was the amorousness of their women![27] Three centuries later the same Continentals were sneering at the same Englishmen as a nation of sexually frustrated shopkeepers and clock watchers—a designation subsequently inherited by Americans.

Most absurd of all, peoples sometimes have several different, even contradictory, reputations at the same time. The most tragic example is that of the Jews. At various times in the last century the Jews have been depicted (simultaneously) as a race of (1) grasping capitalists and financiers who milk society dry for their own profit, (2) Communist sympathizers and leaders of social revolution who persistently seek to undermine society, (3) irreligious liberals and Freemasons, and (4) sinister plotters of the destruction of the whole Gentile world. Now of course some Jews have been and still are grasping businessmen. Other Jews were undeniably prominent in nineteenth century revolutionary movements, especially that in Russia which culminated in the 1917 revolutions. Still others have been and are now liberals, secularists, and Freemasons. But this is not the point. Anti-Semites try to indict the whole Jewish people in each case. The comic irreconcilability of the same people trying to simultaneously exploit, transform, and overthrow the same societies is the best commentary on the general validity of any of these stereotypes. Alas! The whole matter is not just a bad joke. Adolf Hitler, a despicable man but an immensely intelligent propagandist withal, perceived that successful propaganda must be simple,

[27] Erasmus recorded that the floors of English homes "are commonly of clay, strewed with rushes, under which lie unmolested an ancient collection of lees, grease, fragments, bones, spittle, excrements of dogs and cats, and everything that is nasty." Ralph N. Major, *Disease and Destiny* (N.Y.: D. Appleton Century Co., 1936), p. 31. For other estimates cf. John U. Nef, *Cultural Foundations of Industrial Civilization* (Cambridge: University Press, 1958), p. 134; and John Gage, "England In the Italian Renaissance," *History Today,* October 1960, pp. 713–21. Francesca M. Wilson, *Strange Island: Britain Through Foreign Eyes: 1395–1940* (N.Y.: Longmans, Green & Co., 1955), is an interesting study of England as it appeared to foreigners through the centuries.

direct, packed with emotion, and attuned to the most vulgar and elemental prejudices of thoughtless millions. He repeated endlessly all the contradictory cliches about the Jews, stressing the particular one with the most appeal to a particular audience. Thus he aroused a widespread, furious hatred of the Jews, and eventually murdered some 6,000,000 of them.

Variations In Fortune

If the reputations and alleged "national characteristics" of peoples and states have often changed so have their political and military fortunes. Indeed these changes have been so numerous among all the major European peoples that they argue strongly that all "nationalities," or at any rate all political states, have far more similarities than differences. Sixteenth century Europe was dominated by Spain, but France overshadowed the Continent from 1659 to 1815, Germany from 1870 to 1945, and Russia since 1945. In the nineteenth century, northwestern Europeans had the biggest and most thriving colonial empires, from which it was often argued that they were therefore better colonizers than central, eastern, or southern Europeans and quite likely superior peoples as well. This assumption was not only unwarranted scientifically but was historically untrue in the bargain. In the fifteenth century, Portugal—a tiny state with negligible resources and a naval tradition confined mostly to fishing—led the world in exploration and empire building. The accomplishment could hardly have been due to any distinctive national characteristic, since Portugal has never led the world in anything else of significance before or since. The real reasons for her exceptional achievement then were that she had settled her domestic problems earlier than other European states and, above all, to the historical accident that Prince Henry the Navigator devoted state resources and his own entire life to the promotion of exploration. In the sixteenth and early seventeenth centuries not the British but the Spaniards and Portuguese had the world's two largest colonial empires. The third largest, that of the Dutch, had been mostly taken away from Portugal. France acquired a huge overseas empire in North America and India in the eighteenth century but lost it all to England because inept political and military leadership caused her defeat in the Seven Years' War (1756–1763). Still, she set to work and acquired another immense and completely new empire in the nineteenth century. The only factor common to all these western European states was that they were all maritime powers fronting on the Atlantic Ocean. Central and eastern European states, by contrast, were either landlocked or else were discouraged from trying to become naval and colonizing powers because other and often hostile nations controlled the entrances to the Baltic and Black Seas. Moreover one of the most imposing of them, Austria-Hungary, always had too many domestic problems to indulge in the luxury of overseas empire building. Still another, Russia, was at least as avid and successful in colonization as Western states, but she had no incentive to expand overseas when she could more easily build a contiguous land empire from the vast and nearly empty reaches of Siberia. Moreover, of all the erstwhile imperial powers only Russia and Portugal had not (1968) either lost or given away most of their colonies. Who would argue that this proves the natural superiority of Portuguese and Russians to other Europeans?

The reputations of national armies have often fluctuated in a similar fashion. It has been common in recent times to make jokes about the poor fighting quality of Italian armies, the implication being that Italians lack courage. A typical jibe was that of a Russian diplomat about 1880 who, when told that Italy was clamoring for the South Tyrol, sneered, "Why on earth should Italy demand an increase of territory? Has she lost another battle?"[28] Those who jeer seldom remember that modern Italian armies have come from a land that is much the weakest of the Great Powers, a poor country lacking

---

[28] William L. Langer, *European Alliances and Alignments* (N.Y.: Knopf, 1956), p. 220.

in iron, coal, oil, money, and food; that the armies have usually been poorly equipped and supplied; that they have been led by politicians and generals whose abilities have run the gamut from mediocre to lacklustre. Their ancestors, the legions of Julius Caesar, were the finest troops in the world 2000 years ago. Moreover, soldiers of modern Italian descent in the American army have performed quite as well as those of other national derivations.

In the seventh and eighth centuries, Arab armies were the terror of the Western world. In that age there were no Jewish armies at all. There was not even a Jewish state. Individual Jews scattered about Europe, western Asia and northern Africa were everywhere regarded as a particularly unwarlike people. Who would then have guessed that three times (so far) in the twentieth century, 1948, 1956, and 1967, brilliantly led and tightly disciplined Israeli armies would overwhelm Arab armies that could only be described as wretched on every count? The Chinese army in the nineteenth century was a subject for comic opera, but the Korean war of the 1950s showed that modern Chinese troops, given good organization, leadership, and a cause to fight for, perform bravely and capably. Russian troops in World War I demonstrated great physical bravery and endurance but were eventually crushed by the Germans due to lack of equipment and the prevalence of incompetence and corruption in Russia's political and military leadership. In World War II the sons of those Russian soldiers fought with equal bravery and much better success against the sons of their German conquerors because this time they were supported by more and better equipment, abler field commanders, and a more efficient political state. French armies were markedly superior to German armies in the reigns of Louis XIV (1643–1715) and Napoleon I (1799–1815), but markedly inferior in the Seven Years' War (1756–1763), the Franco-Prussian War (1870–1871), and the world wars of our century. Again, this had nothing to do with the innate quality of either Frenchmen or Germans. It had much to do with numbers, comparative morale and state efficiency at various times, and with the personal abilities of Turenne, Frederick the Great, Napoleon, and Moltke the Elder. The famed Turkish janissaries were the best infantry in eastern Europe about 1500, a time when Turkish military technology was abreast of that of the rest of Europe. Though the janissaries continued to be recruited from the same peoples and to receive the same training, their effectiveness declined rapidly in succeeding generations as the Ottoman government relaxed its discipline over them and as European military technology pulled well ahead of that of Turkey. Clearly, the important differences between armies at different times have been those of organization, training, equipment, leadership, supply, and morale—not race or nationality. Whether in political leadership, empire building, or military expertise, there is little evidence of consistent superiority on the part of any nation or people.

The situation is the same in the realms of intellect and culture. During the Renaissance, Italy was the most advanced and civilized part of Europe; the home of the world's most splendid art and literature, the originator of modern diplomacy and court etiquette, and the society that introduced silverware and table manners. In a century this preeminence passed to France.

Sometimes nobody "leads." Consider the "scientific revolution" of the sixteenth and seventeenth centuries. Among the greatest scientists of the age, Copernicus was Polish, Tycho Brahe Danish, Kepler German, Galileo Italian, Leeuwenhoek and Stevin Dutch, Napier Scottish, Descartes and Pascal French, Bacon, Boyle, and Newton English. A mere listing of the names indicates that the "revolution" was a phenomenon common to most of Europe.

The Real Causes of National Differences

Despite the foregoing observations any alert, knowledgeable person is aware that marked physical and psychological differences between nationalities *do* exist. Moreover, they are pronounced and long-lived. It is not that all members of a given nation are alike; only that enough of them are sufficiently alike in enough ways that it does not do violence to the truth to speak of their "national character." Yet, as our consideration of "race" has shown, these differences do not appear to have a genetic basis. Where, then, do they come from? How do nations acquire them?

We must begin by making a distinction between mere provincialism, a virtually universal human sentiment, and modern nation worship. The twentieth century is so suffused with nationalist vainglory that it is startling to be reminded that nationalism, the *real* religion of our age, is less than two centuries old. Provincialism is a different story. For centuries the English have been a parochial people, as evidenced by the condescension with which they have commonly regarded foreigners and the willingness of many of them to support the endeavor of their sixteenth century King Henry VIII to establish an English *national* church free from Roman domination. In the same age Protestantism became established in Sweden and in much of Germany because Martin Luther and King Gustavus Vasa were able to play on the dislike of the German and Swedish people for Italian ecclesiastical overlords and tax collectors. Still, the religious wars of that age showed clearly that religious allegiances often overbore attachment to one's own locality or to people of the same language and customs. Whether the wars were in Germany (1531–1555, and 1618–1648), France (1558–1598), or the Netherlands (1568–1648), individual Catholics of many nationalities flocked in to fight on the Catholic side against as varied an array of Protestants in the enemy armies.

Many Europeans had no national feeling at all. In the Middle Ages most of them thought of themselves primarily as Gascons, Tyrolese, or Lubeckers, inhabitants of towns or provinces, rather than as Frenchmen or Austrians or Germans. In the sixteenth century Erasmus wondered idly whether he was French or German. It did not occur to him that he might be Dutch. In the long Dutch wars against Spain (1568–1648)

and France (1660–1713) most people in the Low Countries
either kept out of the wars entirely, did as they were forced to
do by whatever power dominated locally at a given time, or
took sides in terms of their personal interest. Dutch pirates
preyed on everyone's shipping; Dutch farmers and merchants
traded with all parties impartially. This was regarded as in
no way exceptional. Well down into the eighteenth century
all European armies were composed of anyone who could
be induced or coerced to serve. Civilians traveled about unmolested in enemy lands during wartime because everyone
assumed that war was the business of kings and courts; that
it did not concern what the twentieth century would call the
"nation." That Napoleon I (1799–1814) interned enemy
civilians in wartime was everywhere regarded as conclusive
proof that he was only a half-civilized Corsican adventurer;
definitely not a "gentleman." In Russia both the government
and the army were top-heavy with foreigners well into the
nineteenth century.

All this was changed by the French Revolution and the Age
of Romanticism. The Revolution invested "the people" with
a sacredness and grandeur heretofore reserved for kings and
showed the world how national patriotism could be employed
to create mighty armies, vast in number and zealous to spread
a secular gospel. The intellectuals of the Age of Romanticism
(roughly 1790–1825) loved to trace contemporary institutions and practices back to their real or supposed medieval
origins. They insisted that each nation or people had a distinctive spirit or "genius." They urged each people to develop
an awareness of its own glorious past, to cultivate its ancestral
language, literature, and culture, and to strive to establish its
own free and independent national state. Soon small children
all over the Western world were committing to memory oaths
of allegiance; learning to recognize national birds, animals,
and emblems; saluting national flags; studying "patriotic" history books; and (doubtless) breathing sighs of relief when
they got an occasional day off school because of some national
holiday. Thus much of the national character of the people
of any modern state is merely the product of careful education

and deliberate indoctrination in a national folklore. It may be true that "Frenchmen are not born with an innate skill at making love, Englishmen are not born law-abiding and full of political common sense, Germans are not born . . . with an innate feeling for authority,"[29] but they have been educated and indoctrinated as if they were, so the result is much the same.

Other national qualities are of natural growth, obviously the product of historical experiences. A people whose rule over another is long, unchecked, and officially unquestioned easily become arrogant. Colonial masters of "natives" have been notoriously so. So were the Hungarian masters of subject Slavic peoples in the old Austro-Hungarian Empire, and the Ottoman Turkish rulers of Christian Balkan peoples. The official mode of address of the latter to their subjects was "Obstinate and Stiff-Necked Dogs." Those long oppressed and systematically robbed by foreign rulers (or who believe themselves to be such, which amounts to the same thing) readily become volatile, rebellious, guileful, prone to conspiracy, and unwilling to work regularly. The Irish languishing under English domination, or the Poles under the Russian and German yokes, are cases in point. The formation of a state by the conquest or coercion of many small principalities easily creates a cultural tradition of admiration for military prowess, as in modern Germany. It was surely no accident that the totalitarian ideologies of the twentieth century developed to the fullest in Russia, Germany, and Japan—lands where there were long traditions of iron discipline and submissiveness to force. In states that have been established as a result of successful revolutions, or where governments have been so hated that revolutions against them have broken out repeatedly, there easily develops a cult of revolution, a glorification of the very concept of revolution—and thereby a potent cause of future revolutions.[30]

[29] Crane Brinton, *Ideas and Men* (N.Y.: Prentice-Hall, 1950), p. 417. The same point is discussed by Herbert Butterfield, *Man On His Past* (Cambridge: University Press, 1955), pp. 125–26.

[30] Cf. *Supra.*, pp. 181, 187–88. For a fuller discussion of this point cf. Nicholas S. Timasheff, *War and Revolution* (N.Y.: Sheed & Ward, 1965), pp. 43–47.

Differences Between Cultures

Many of the most easily discernible and important differences between peoples are those which separate not nations but whole cultures or civilizations. Of all the obstacles which the underdeveloped parts of Asia and Africa have to surmount if they are to achieve the material standard of life of western Europe and America, none bulk larger than the intangibles. Many underdeveloped peoples envy and want Western industry, scientific expertise, and material power; but they reject the rest of Western culture—they reject the philosophical attitudes and practical habits that are responsible for the material achievements. Unlike the West they do not welcome change as desirable. If they are Arabs they think Islam is already Allah's perfect society. If they subscribe to any of several oriental religions they strive to come to terms with the existing world rather than to change it for the better. Many peoples have no real concept of the necessity for precision, accuracy, logic, promptness, and predictability in speech and deed, without which advanced industrial societies cannot exist. They see nothing incongruous or harmful in habitual exaggeration, in saying "1000" when they may mean only 100 or 50, since they seek only to convey a general impression of size or magnitude. Habits like this may have a certain antique charm, but who can run a factory or laboratory thus? People in many parts of the earth still regard physical labor or the manipulation of mechanical things as demeaning. Hence most of the educated people in their societies become lawyers, politicians, or government officials rather than sorely needed doctors, engineers, or agronomists. Often this prejudice is so deeply ingrained that not only do such people almost never build anything new or useful: they do not even learn to use or take proper care of the machinery given them by more advanced nations. A vivid recent example was the complete failure of Arab armies to make effective use of first-rate Russian military equipment in the Arab-Israeli war of 1967. In most parts of the world there is still no real tradition of civic morality (public honesty). Elected officials routinely make themselves and their families rich, and little public business proceeds without systematic bribery.

Of all major parts of the earth, southern Asia seems least apt to "progress" in the Western sense. The area is already overpopulated and has a high birth rate which steadily aggravates all its existing problems. A worse difficulty is the attitude of most of the people. Unpredictable, irresponsible, fatalistic, corrupt in a financial sense, unpunctual, unaccustomed to either planning or systematic work, superstitious, indifferent to "efficiency," they personify most of the qualities that stand in the way of the acquisition of wealth, power, or even physical comforts.[31]

A much briefer but equally severe arraignment of Latin Americans has been delivered by one of the most stimulating of contemporary historians. Latin America's problems, he insists, are not really due to lack of wealth, lack of education, an unprogressive Church, exploitation by the United States, or any of the other conventional whipping boys. They are due to deficiencies in the Latin American character, personality, and psychology. The vast riches of Central and South America's land are nowhere exploited rationally. The great wealth of the dominant few in each country, in itself not necessarily a barrier to progress, is not invested productively as was, for instance, the wealth of nineteenth century England. Instead, it is dissipated in social display or hoarded abroad.

The reasons for this state of affairs are rooted in the cultural inheritance of Latin America, which goes back centuries, even millenia. The Latin American outlook is derived from Spain, that of Spain from her medieval Arabic enemies, that of the Arabs from the ancient Middle East. All ancient Asiatic societies were despotisms consisting of two classes: a ruling bureau-

---

[31] This bleak assessment represents the considered judgment of the famous Swedish economist, Gunnar Myrdal, a man by no means unfriendly to the aspirations of disadvantaged peoples anywhere. Cf. his *Asian Drama: An Inquiry into the Poverty of Nations* (N.Y.: Pantheon, 1968), 3 vols., an immensely detailed work which distills the research of ten years.

cracy of scribes, priests, soldiers, landlords, and money lenders; and the other 90–95 percent of the population who were systematically exploited by the former. This has remained the prevalent social form in Arab lands down to the present and it is still typical of most of Latin America as well.

Among the Arabs the political structure was tribal and the predominant social form was patriarchal despotism. Within a given tribe, blood ties were extremely important, while people outside the tribe were scarcely regarded as human beings. Arab society was largely an agglomeration of tribes, larger social units coming into existence as various families, and then whole tribes, became linked by intermarriage. Since these units could be easily dissolved, any advanced conception of the state was inhibited. Everywhere rule was personal. If one secured a high position he took care of his relatives and retainers—essentially the Mediterranean (and Latin American) view of politics to the present day.

Within the family the position of women was dramatically inferior to that of men. Sons brought up in such an atmosphere were hopelessly spoiled by their mothers and female relatives. Egocentric, self-indulgent, immature, petty, lacking self control, sharing to the full the disdain of ancient Europe and Asia for manual labor, lacking respect for vegetation, soil, or animals, inhumane to other men, and submissively resigned to fate, the Arabs, and to a considerable degree the Latins as well, have become anachronisms in the modern world.

Such has been the heritage of Latin America. Such is the culture pattern that still prevails from the Himalayas to Peru, to such a degree that it is not inaccurate to speak of a Pakistani-Peruvian axis. These attitudes have survived all the efforts of three great religions, Judaism, Christianity, and Islam, to soften them. Christianity, with the highest ethical aims, has fallen farthest short. Very few of the people of the Pakistani-Peruvian axis pay any attention to the Christian injunctions of love, brotherhood, humility, cooperation, the sanctity of work, regard for women, community fellowship, respect for other men as creatures of God, and the rest. In practice they esteem the opposite of these principles. In particular, the Latin American ruling class treats Indians, Negroes, and the urban poor much as ancient Asiatic despots treated the masses of their subjects. Hence the French saying that "Africa begins at the Pyrenees" is culturally true, and quite as true of Latin America as of old Spain and Portugal.

The author of this crushing indictment of several civilizations and a whole culture freely admits that his statements are hateful to Spaniards and Latin Americans. He insists only that they are factually accurate.[32] Apart from the question of accuracy in this case, it is obvious that the qualities themselves are a litany of precisely what is *not* needed if material conditions of life are to be improved in our time.

Unhappily for "progress," such traits (which presently characterize hundreds of millions of people) show little sign of disappearing in the foreseeable future. However, there is no reason to think that they must last forever. After all, many of these attitudes once characterized Western peoples too. Ancient and medieval Europeans showed little concern for numerical accuracy in their writings, and the practice of keeping statistics is only about 200 years old. Civic morality in much of Europe two centuries ago was no more elevated than in much of the non-European world today. Because they had slaves to do manual work for them, the ancient Greeks of the Periclean Age and Romans of the Imperial Age disdained physical labor and were generally uninterested in mechanical things. Because they had serfs or servants, the same was true of the European aristocracy clear down to the twentieth century. Thus there is no reason to think the presently underdeveloped societies incapable of *ever* changing; it is merely that their present attitudes, sharply distinct from those of the West, prevent them from becoming Westernized and prosperous *now*. In this connection, some scholars consider Christian-

---

[32] Carroll Quigley, *The World Since 1939: A History* (N.Y.: Collier Books, 1968), pp. 453–67. For the present writer's briefer and more prosaic account of the development of the Spanish national character cf. *Infra.*, pp. 229–31.

ity to have been the crucial factor in the establishment of the material preeminence of the West. They argue that of all the world's great religions only Christianity sought to change the world rather than merely to come to terms with it, thus inculcating in Christian societies acceptance of change and a desire for it. Furthermore, Benedictine monasticism, by enjoining physical labor on monks as a religious duty, gave to regular physical toil a dignity which it never before had in the world and which it has never enjoyed in non-Christian societies. Thus it made Western peoples more systematically industrious than others.[33]

Different Areas Within the Same Civilization

Frequently, different historical experiences and traditions have caused pronounced variations between different nations within the same general culture. In modern times the French army has generally fought best in furious offensives in which spirit and elan are crucial. It has usually been much less effective during retreats, fighting withdrawals, or in hanging on grimly and absorbing punishment while the means for a greater effort are being slowly manufactured. The British army and people, by contrast, have long been renowned for their bulldog tenacity in the face of adversity. In 1940 their morale was positively strengthened by defeat, though of course there was still hope of eventual victory. Many reasons could be adduced to account for such differences, but two or three are indisputable. The French have long thought of themselves as a temperamental, spirited people. Moreover, their military theorists between 1815 and 1914 were virtually unanimous in ascribing the victories of the French revolutionary and Napoleonic armies to the elan produced by the ideas of the Revolution and to the doctrine of the everlasting offensive which Napoleon allegedly followed. Hence the French army

[33] The case for Benedictine monasticism is urged by Arnold Toynbee, *A Study of History,* 2 vols. (London: Oxford Press, 1947), I, 225–26. (Abridgement by D. C. Somervell).

was systematically taught that its past successes were due to the offensive spirit and that Frenchmen were by nature peculiarly suited to take the offensive. The British, however, from the time of Robert Bruce (a Scot) and the spider have prided themselves on their tenacity, determination, and ability to "muddle through" despite difficulties and adverse prospects. Since England is an island, morever, more time has generally been available to Britons to mount a serious war effort after initial reverses than has been the case with Continental states.

It is a matter of common observation, frequently discussed by political analysts, that "Latin" Europeans, as distinguished from Englishmen and Americans, tend to lack public spirit, to be almost instinctively hostile to any government, to have an underdeveloped sense of philanthropy, and to see little connection between their personal interests and those of the whole society. Notoriously, many French and Italian businessmen keep two sets of books: one for themselves and one for the tax collector. Many Frenchmen still try to turn their valuables into gold and tuck it away in cans, jars, and mattresses like their peasant ancestors of bygone centuries. Spain is the only modern nation where anarchism was ever a mass movement. Sicily is the only part of the Western world where bandits were still popular heroes in the middle of the twentieth century. Why? Most of the American descendants of Spanish, French, and Italian immigrants have either abandoned these traits or are in the process of doing so.

The reasons are rooted in their historical experience. All three peoples have been systematically misgoverned for centuries. During the last 1500 years Italy has been invaded and conquered by half the peoples of Europe. Whenever the foreigners happened to be preoccupied elsewhere she was vexed by political strife among her own small political entities. No part of the Western world has been so frequently overrun and thoroughly exploited in the interest of the conquerors as Sicily. Not surprisingly, centuries ago Sicily produced the Mafia, an informal, secret, "outlaw" government among natives to resist the "legal" government of foreigners. For centuries Spaniards were subjected to one of the most pervasive and extortionate tax systems Western ingenuity ever devised. To survive at all they had to become experts at evading it. The bad effects of this were worsened by the fact that Spain was abominably misgoverned: between 1598 and 1931 she had only a couple of rulers of even average ability. French peasants in the Old Regime were expected to pay as much as 80 percent of their income in taxes of one kind or other. Only by systematic tax evasion could they live. It has also been estimated that between 814 and 1726 French governments, by a bewildering variety of currency manipulations, coinage devaluations, and inflationary dishonesties (which governments deny to their subjects but freely practice themselves), managed to cheat the French people out of seventy-one times the value of all French currency in circulation in 1726.[34] When people have been treated like this for anywhere from ten to thirty generations it is not necessary to appeal to blood, soil, or germ plasm to comprehend their lack of public spirit.

Certain differences between American public attitudes and those of Europeans are also quite marked. Continental Europeans assume that international politics is mostly about money and power, that its procedures are largely "machiavellian," and that its decisive ingredient is force. American attitudes have been more ambivalent. Though we have generally been pragmatic in dealing with domestic public questions, and quite as "hardheaded" as the Europeans when some particular American national interest seemed at stake, there has always been a strong tendency in America to think about international affairs in terms of noble ideals and grand abstractions, to imagine that all people really want to settle international disputes by reason, logic, majority votes, and compromise, and to preach to foreign governments on the necessity of their adopting this vision. This proneness to sentimental emotionalism does not prove that Americans are better men than Europeans; only that our historical experience has

[34] J. B. Perkins, *France Under the Regency* (Boston: Houghton, Mifflin & Co., 1892), pp. 357–58.

been different. All European peoples save the English have been packed close to strong, hostile neighbors for centuries. All have conquered others and been conquered by others. All have known severe governmental oppression in their historic past. Those who left Europe and came to America wanted to leave this legacy behind. They wanted to found a new society based on finer principles. They were fortunate in that America was geographically isolated, had plentiful land for expansion and, after the mid-nineteenth century when immigrants began to come in floods, had no strong, hostile neighbors. Finally, those classes or groups (mostly Anglo-Saxon) who have dominated American society and government were never seriously oppressed in the New World. Not surprisingly, these happy circumstances produced in American attitudes towards foreign affairs a strain of naive idealism which has been shaken seriously only since World War II.[35]

It is time now to come to the heart of the matter, to examine the real or alleged "national character" of the people who live in some modern nation-states, and to account for the origin and formation of that character. We turn first to the Iberian Peninsula.

A. *Spain*—When a certain nineteenth century Latin American despot lay in his deathbed he was asked by a priest if he forgave his enemies. He replied, "I have no enemies. I have had them all shot."[36] The answer indicates one reason why

[35] That it has been shaken is beyond question. The tensions of the Cold War have made American domestic politics more ideological than before, and the hard necessities of that conflict have introduced into American foreign policy many machiavellian elements. One astute student of the nuclear age considers that particularly in the 1950s when John Foster Dulles was secretary of state, German rather than British concepts for the first time began to dominate American foreign policy. He regards the tendency as evidence that the American national character has not yet completely jelled. John Lukacs, *A New History of the Cold War* (Garden City, N.Y.: Doubleday, 1966), pp. 371–83.

[36] Salvador de Madariaga, *Spain: A Modern History* (N.Y.: Creative Age Press, 1943), p. 62.

northern Europeans and Americans have long regarded Spaniards with a certain wonder. To Anglo-Saxons they have always seemed remarkable for their fierce individualism, racial pride, religious exclusiveness, disinterest in economic efficiency, and aversion to physical labor. While many individual Spaniards have never fit this description there is no question that it has considerable applicability to the Spanish people as a whole. But the explanation of it does not demand excursions into biology or genetics. The Spanish national character derives directly from Spain's past history. Where other Europeans fought Moslem Arabs or Turks occasionally in the Crusades or after 1453, Spaniards fought them in every generation for seven centuries. This constant aura of warfare, frequently punctuated by actual bloody fighting, gradually burned into the Spanish national character—and into the Spanish church—an essentially tragic view of life and a spirit of lofty crusading enthusiasm mingled with cruelty and intolerance. Due to the same situation a sense of racial and religious pride—of separateness from the hated Moslem infidels —developed to an exceptional degree. The last was intensified by resentment of another religious minority, the Jews, who were prominent in medieval Christian and Moslem Spain. The resentment increased as superficially Christianized Jews began to work their way upward in Old Christian Spanish society.

The Spanish aversion to work, though exaggerated in Anglo-Saxon folklore, is real and has several easily traceable origins. For centuries in the Middle Ages marauding armies destroyed crops. For generations Spanish governments favored the Mesta (a guild of nomadic sheep raisers) over settled family-type farmers. Herds of sheep belonging to the Mesta ranged over wide areas in Spain, breaking down fences, destroying gardens, and ruining the labor of settled farmers. Eventually it came to seem to the ordinary Spanish peasant that work was useless. It also seemed socially degrading for the most menial jobs had always been performed either by serfs, by Moslem captives taken in the endless wars, or by the hated Moriscos (Moors nominally converted to Christianity). Steady physical toil lost further prestige in the sixteenth century when Spanish explorers and adventurers began to come back from the New World laden with fame and riches after an occasional lucky strike in Peru or Mexico. Finally, the extortionate taxes levied on sixteenth century Spanish peasants provided a strong incentive for anyone who could possibly scrape together the money to purchase his way into the hidalgo class (minor nobility). Hidalgos not only had more social prestige than peasants; they were exempt from most taxes as well. Thus many of the distinctive features of the Spanish national character have little to do with biological inheritance, but a great deal to do with the historic experiences of the Spanish people.[37]

B. *Germany*—A very different people, the twentieth century Germans, have been viewed by the rest of the world with mingled admiration and disgust, but above all with a mixture of fear and puzzlement. Their diplomats have seemed peculiarly brusque and bullying, their national manner singularly aggressive, their conduct of war gratuitously brutal, their people methodically industrious but politically naive, their businessmen extraordinarily resourceful and fiercely competitive. Foreigners have been awestruck by a Germany whose agricultural production in the 1930s was greater than that of Russia—though Russia was thirty times as large, three times as populous, and endowed with richer soil. They have also had serious misgivings about the character of a people whose response to the Great Depression of the 1930s was to embrace nazism with all its abominations and to support its half-mad leader in a six year war to the death against most of the rest of the world. Other nations, after all, endured the depression too, but they did not turn Nazi and plunge into national insanity on that account. Can the English historian A. J. P.

[37] We have attempted here only to trace particular Spanish national traits; not to pass judgment on Quigley's thesis about the whole cultural heritage of Spain and Latin America—a much larger and more complex question. Cf. *Supra.*, pp. 223–25.

Taylor be correct in his claim that the Germans are only the most westernized of the barbarians; that they are a people permanently distinguished by their lack of restraint; that they have sought to master only the intellectual and technical side of Western civilization, rejecting its spirit and ethical norms; that the only constant in German history is violent oscillation between extremes?[38]

While the foregoing description—really an indictment—of a whole people is obviously a grotesque libel on millions of individual Germans who are no more offensive or inhumane than people of any other nationality, still, anyone who has lived through much of the twentieth century will hardly deny that a considerable portion of the description fits the German nation-state. Again, as with Spain, there are clear historical reasons for this. Just as Spain fought the Moslems for 700 years so the Germans struggled for 1000 years to gain "living room" in central and eastern Europe by forcibly pushing the Slavs eastward. As in Spain, a strong military tradition was created among many elements in Germany. The most important of these were the Prussians. In the seventeenth century Prussia was a small, poor, thinly populated land with few natural resources or elements of national strength. Over a century and a half (1640–1786), three rulers of exceptional ability and determination painstakingly pieced together the scattered territories of Prussia and made their kingdom a Great Power, the only artificially manufactured state in Europe. It was one of the most remarkable achievements in the annals of state building. It was possible only because the rulers saved and scrimped, cut costs, eliminated waste, eschewed the expensive courts of other monarchs, worked hard themselves, and worked and taxed their subjects to the limit of human endurance. One of the kings, Frederick William I, even beat idlers personally with a royal cudgel. Gradually they built a national administration of exceptional industry, honesty, and efficiency and, even more important, a sizeable army

[38] The thesis is argued most congently, and with all of Taylor's habitual verve, in *The Course of German History, op. cit.*

of high quality. By the skillful use of the latter in diplomacy and war they added East Prussia, Halberstadt, Minden, Magdeburg, West Pomerania, Silesia, portions of Poland, and various smaller places to the Prussian domain.

The modern German nation was formed between 1864 and 1871 by an astute combination of diplomacy and war, under the leadership of the brilliant Prussian Chancellor Bismarck. It would be only a slight exaggeration to say that Prussia, the most warlike of the German states, conquered and absorbed all the others save Austria, and gradually imposed her own habits and traditions on them. Thus modern Germany seemed to owe her whole national existence to order, planning, hard work, unquestioning obedience to able autocrats, and the intelligent (if unscrupulous) use of force. Furthermore, the stunning political and military triumphs of nineteenth century Germany came at the very time when German industrial, scientific, and technological development was accelerating at an unprecedented rate. This, in the opinion of some perceptive scholars, produced a basic coarsening in the German national character, an erosion of the nation's sense of right and wrong, an intensification of the tendency to revere sheer power and success.[39]

Moreover, more than most peoples, the Germans have had a dualistic, even schizophrenic, historic tradition. Like other Europeans they became Christians and were westernized, but more than most they have continued to cherish their pre-Christian traditions and heroes clear down to the present. Two such are Arminius, who defeated Roman legions in the Teutoberg Forest in 9 A.D.; and Widukind, the king of the Saxons who resisted the armies and Christian missionaries of Charlemagne in the eighth and ninth centuries. Both exemplify the old Teutonic tribal warrior ethos which antedated either Christianity or westernization and whose values were

[39] Ludwig Dehio, *The Precarious Balance* (N.Y.: Random House, 1965), p. 221. This is also the opinion of the foremost authority on the growth of the Prussian and German military machine. Cf. Herbert Rosinski, *The German Army* (N.Y.: Praeger, 1966), pp. 88–95.

antithetical to it. At the turn of the nineteenth century, the Romantic Movement, so full of admiration for ancient traditions, so suffused with emotion-packed abstractions about "Kultur" and "blood," became more influential in Germany than any other European country. In the latter part of the nineteenth century the great composer Wagner expressed all these diverse elements in the German national heritage in music of exceptional emotional appeal.[40]

Viewed against this historical background, German willingness to follow militarists and dictators and to wage aggressive wars in our age is merely a continuation of deeply rooted habits in domestic and international politics, habits that produced great dividends before 1914. It is also the product of a national mythology two thousand years old, one which glorifies force, heroism, and tribal solidarity.

In this connection it has often been said that Germany got the wrong kind of national hero. Nobody denies that the Great Elector (1640–1688), Frederick William I (1713–1740), Frederick the Great (1740–1786), and Bismarck (1862–1890) were men of outstanding ability and accomplishment. But they were all hard machiavellians, heroes only to other Germans. By contrast other peoples' national heroes (Washington, Lincoln, Gandhi, Joan of Arc, Garibaldi, Mazzini, John Sobieski, Churchill, to name a few at random) have been persons of obvious ethical stature as well as worldly accomplishment, figures widely admired in countries other than their own. One prominent student of German history has even advanced the thesis that the constant strain of generations of intense toil, interspersed with the taking of desperate chances in war, each crucial in building the German nation,

---

[40] The struggle of Western and anti-Western, Christian and anti-Christian, traditions for mastery of the German "soul" has been a prominent theme in scores of books about modern Germany. One of the better treatments of it is Peter Viereck, *Metapolitics: From the Romantics to Hitler* (N.Y.: Knopf, 1941).

has been responsible for the frequency of nervous instability among the rulers of modern Germany.[41]

C. *England and the United States*—If a nation's policy is shaped considerably by its national character that character is revealed by the nation's own image of itself, by the way it would like to be regarded by other nations and peoples. Nineteenth and twentieth century Englishmen have generally been more moderate in the conduct of their domestic politics than most continental Europeans; more generous and tolerant in their attitude towards human diversity in general and political opponents in particular. British diplomats have been as zealous as others to defend and advance their country's interests but they have been less harshly and narrowly nationalistic in manner than most. In foreign relations, British diplomacy normally does not seek showy triumphs over others but a profitable deal of some kind. Its practitioners are customarily ready to negotiate, mediate, compromise. These attitudes are easily recognizable reflections of the British national character. They are the human qualities held up for admiration for generations in British schools, newspapers, magazines, and public speeches. They are also a clear reflection of the code of conduct of the tight clique of aristocratic families who have dominated all phases of British public life since the sixteenth century: a code emphasizing honesty, discretion, fair play, good sportsmanship, and all these nebulous qualities that are supposed to characterize a "gentleman."

---

[41] Taylor, *op. cit.,* pp. 28, 65–66, 164. Frederick William IV's bouts of hysteria became so severe that he had to be removed from the throne in 1858. Bismarck, for all his superficial calm, was prone to extreme nervousness and fits of weeping during crises. William II (1888–1918) was notoriously mercurial and unpredictable. When World War I began, Moltke the Younger, the chief of the general staff, suffered a nervous collapse. The frequency of nervous breakdowns among other high ranking German officers was the subject of much comment inside and outside Germany and caused the Nazis in the 1930s to subject officer candidates to careful psychological screening. Hitler's frequent outbursts of rage and hysteria are well known.

From what source did all this moderation spring? Is it due to some splendid quality inherent in the germ plasm of Britons? Hardly. The readiness to negotiate and compromise, the search for "deals," is an obvious reflection of habits developed among a people who have lived for generations by foreign trade. The "sporting" attitude, more ruinously exemplified in the twentieth century by Britain's disinclination to "kick Germany while she was down" in the 1920s, is an outgrowth of the longtime addiction of Englishmen, particularly the aristocracy, to sports. A large portion of the whole British outlook is due to nothing more complex than the location of three bodies of salt water: the North Sea, the English Channel, and the Atlantic Ocean. Because England is an island and for 300 years maintained the biggest navy in Europe she was immune to successful attack from the Continent and thus free to enter or stay out of Continental wars as she chose. Hence, unlike the Continental powers, she did not need to maintain a standing army. Thus a militarist tradition never took root in England. This, in turn, meant that in her seventeenth century struggles for power between king and Parliament the king did not have a royal standing army at his disposal to crush his opponents before they could become effectively organized. Consequently, Parliament was able to win the wars. In this way, limited parliamentary government was gradually established in England much earlier than in the major Continental states. It was crucially important that this political system became firmly rooted before the Industrial Revolution. All the tangled social and economic problems created by that titanic upheaval horribly complicated all other public questions in the nineteenth and twentieth centuries and constantly bedevilled the efforts of Continental countries to introduce effective representative government. Finally, perhaps because the stability of the nation's political system allowed the habit of moderation to become rooted, British aristocrats gave way more gracefully than did Continental aristocrats before the political and social demands of the democratic, Industrial Age. Thus England avoided much domestic bloodshed and the growth of the bitter class and ideological hatreds that still disfigure the public life of so many Continental countries.

Due to this exceptional historical heredity, of which the island position and invincible navy have been the most important ingredients, Britain could always afford to be more casual —even downright inept—in the conduct of her foreign relations than Continental powers. Generations of Continental diplomats (and historians) have marvelled at the massive ignorance of dozens of prominent British public figures: their failure to learn foreign languages, the dilettante character of their education, the spirit of idle nonchalance with which they approached foreign relations. Gladstone, the "grand old man" of British liberalism and one of the great figures of British politics, in the 1880s and 1890s conducted the nation's foreign affairs with a mixture of impeccable moral rectitude and ghastly practical incompetence. Foreign Secretary Sir Edward Grey and others muddled the Entente Cordiale with France from 1904 to 1914, and Grey displayed pathetic slowness of mind in the world crisis of July, 1914. Prime Minister David Lloyd George, an able war leader, showed himself at the Versailles peace conference in 1919 to be ignorant of even the fundamentals of European geography. Another prime minister, Stanley Baldwin, refused to read newspapers in 1934 because he was "on vacation." Still another, Neville Chamberlain, has already become legendary for his incomprehension of either Hitler the man or the Nazi movement.[42] Such ineptitude in the conduct of foreign relations came close to destroying England in 1939–1940. It would have destroyed any Continental nation generations ago.

Many English attitudes have become rooted in the United

---

[42] For these examples and many others cf. Langer, *op. cit.,* p. 300; L. C. B. Seaman, *From Vienna to Versailles* (N.Y.: Harper & Row, Colophon Books, 1963), p. 183; John Terraine, *Ordeal of Victory* (N.Y.: Lippincott, 1963), pp. 61–62; Luigi Albertini *The Origins of the War of 1914,* III (London: Oxford Press, 1957). Hermann Kantorowicz, *The Spirit of British Policy* (London: Allan & Unwin, 1931) is an interesting analysis of the English character and British public attitudes.

States. This has not been due to biological transmission but to the fact that people of English speech and culture dominated the Republic in its formative years. Many other American traits are unique—the products of the particular American environment. Most immigrants to the United States were not aristocrats, not members of any social or educational elite. They were ordinary men. Once here, most of them had to do much hard physical labor to establish their homes and raise their families. Consequently, most of our national heroes have been ordinary men who possessed ordinary virtues to an extraordinary degree. Such figures as Washington, Lincoln, Jackson, and Theodore Roosevelt were red-blooded outdoor types, "regular fellows" who would have made the varsity team. They were not erratic geniuses like Michelangelo, Cromwell, or Napoleon.

Likewise, it has always been a part of American folklore that ours is a nation which God has singled out for a special destiny. We are the Land of the Free, a haven for the politically and religiously oppressed of the Old World, and a living image of the social and political cravings that all men have in their hearts. Consequently it has never seemed necessary to Americans to devise elaborate political theories of the European kind which are supposed to possess eternal validity. The grandeur of our national ideals has seemed to us self-evident. It has caused us to inject into our politicking, even when defending the most material of national interests, what seems to Europeans an insufferable excess of synthetic religiosity and moralizing.[43]

Like the English, we Americans have been lucky. Until

[43] The peculiarities of the American tradition are examined perceptively and in detail by Daniel Boorstin, *The Genius of American Politics* (Chicago: University Press, 1964), pp. 1–3, 25, 29, 34, 163. Lukacs argues that the proneness of American presidents from Wilson to Kennedy to practice imperialism while intoning floods of sanctimonious phrases is not hypocrisy. Rather, he argues, both practices have long roots, belief in both is widespread and genuine, and the contradiction between the two is hardly perceived by either presidents or most other Americans. *A New History of the Cold War, op. cit.,* pp. 371–72.

recently we have lived in sufficient relative isolation that moderate democratic traditions and habits have had time to take root; and we have been able to dispense with the expensive luxury of a permanent, massive military establishment. If one considers these factors he will then understand why it has always been the British and the Americans who have supported pacifist movements, lavished praise on the League of Nations and United Nations, insisted that other countries ought to disarm and trust their neighbors, advocated the abolition of war and the peaceful settlement of international disputes, pleaded for the interjection into international affairs of the spirit of law rather than mere power and force, urged the rest of the world to emulate the thirteen American colonies and form an international society, and insisted that all people everywhere really want to adopt democracy. To be sure, all these are noble ideals, and it is not this writer's purpose to deride them. However, as one of America's ablest students of international relations has pointed out, they all grow directly out of the British and American historical experience. Thus whatever their abstract grandeur, they are of little practical importance simply because other nations and peoples, with different historical experiences and different national objectives, do not share them and will not accept them.[44]

Sometimes it takes but a few years for the implacable facts of geography to fasten a certain reputation on a whole nation —or at least to strengthen an existing one. World War I provides an excellent example. In that conflict the British surface fleet (then the world's strongest) blockaded Germany. The Germans retaliated in the most effective way available to them: they clamped a submarine blockade around the British Isles. Each nation determined to weaken her foe by stopping neutral shipping to her. Now surface warships, without firing their guns, could stop neutral ships, board them, search them for war materials declared contraband, and then either bring them into port or let them proceed on their way. Thus their

[44] George Kennan, *American Diplomacy, 1900–1950* (Chicago: University Press, 1951), pp. 95–103. On the same point cf. also Crane Brinton, *Ideas and Men, op. cit.,* pp. 500–501.

interference with neutral shipping and their violations of neutral rights cost only annoyance and some ruffling of the national pride of neutral nations—but no bloodshed. Submarines, however, faced incomparably more difficult problems. They had thin hulls and they carried only light guns. They were forced to observe enemy or neutral shipping through tiny periscopes barely poked above the waves. Often they were unable to distinguish between enemy warships, enemy merchantmen, neutral merchantmen, armed merchantmen, unarmed merchantmen, or warships camouflaged as merchantmen. If they surfaced and demanded to board what appeared to be an unarmed merchant ship, only to discover that it was a warship or an armed merchantman, submarine and crew would be at once blasted to their doom by the superior guns of the surface ship. Thus submarines often had to shoot first and investigate afterwards. This necessarily shed blood. Inevitably, too, mistakes were made. Neutral ships were hit. Innocent neutral lives were lost. The world then howled in outrage at German "callousness," and the United States entered the war on the Allied side.

Yet who would claim now, fifty years after the naval duels of 1914–1918, that their use of submarines proved that the Germans are by nature cruel and heedless of human life, while employment of their surface fleet showed that the British are naturally compassionate and humane? Who can doubt now, that with national survival seemingly at stake, had the geographical situations of Germany and England been reversed that England would have used the submarines much as Germany did, and thereby reaped much of Germany's infamy? World War II displayed the matter in its true light: all major participants had submarines and all used them freely against their enemies. In all countries moralists said little.

Conclusions

Separate nations and peoples resemble each other in more ways than they differ. If one wants to understand a nation's policies the best course is to consider its national interests and objectives; not whether its people have "fiery Spanish souls," Nordic self-control or, perhaps, only American "tired blood." Nonetheless differences in national character are real. So far as science knows now they are not biological. They arise mostly from geographical environment, historical experience, and deliberate indoctrination. Consequently, they are not necessarily fixed forever. However, they are so deeply ingrained and they change so slowly that, at any given time, they might as well be treated as if they were inborn and permanent.

VI

THE CONDITIONS OF CULTURAL ACHIEVEMENT

One of the perennial puzzles of history is why certain ages produce brilliant cultural achievements while others do not; particularly why one society in a given age will excel culturally while another, superficially similar, will not. Since "culture" is a notoriously elastic concept it is essential to define immediately what is meant by culture in *this chapter*. "Culture" as used here, primarily means brilliant achievements in painting, sculpture, architecture, and the literary arts; secondarily, other triumphs of the human imagination and intelligence. The natural sciences are excluded from the discussion not because they are unimportant or because attainments in them do not qualify as victories of the human intellect and spirit, but because the *reasons* for progress here are much clearer and simpler than in the fine arts. Accomplishments in the natural sciences tend to be geometrically progressive and to depend heavily on material wealth. Biologists, physicists, and chemists build directly on the work of their predecessors far more than do poets or sculptors. Extensive financial support produces "results" more readily in engineering than in painting. Finally, most science is closely tied in with technology. Thus, at least in recent centuries, the natural scientists of each generation know more than those of the one preceding, and the wealthiest countries tend to be the most advanced scientifically.

It must also be stressed that judgments about artistic excellence are highly subjective. What one age applauds another deplores. What one person thinks entrancing, another regards as absurd. Lecky, the great nineteenth century English social historian, declared that eighteenth century English architects had "touched the very nadir of taste." These same architects are held in high esteem in our own time. Renaissance men sneered at medieval building and called it "Gothic" to indicate its barbarism. John Evelyn, a famous seventeenth century diarist, deplored its "heavy, dark, melancholy, monkish piles, without any just Proportion, Use or Beauty compared with the Ancient." Yet ever since the Romantic Age at the turn of the nineteenth century, Gothic architecture has been regarded as one of the truly magnificent triumphs of medieval Europe.[1] The same violent differences of opinion exist about the worth of non-representational sculpture and painting in our own time. Despite these subjective factors, however, there has always been sufficient general agreement on the whole matter to make meaningful analysis possible. No sane person, after all, contends that sixth century Europe was culturally superior to fifteenth century Italy, or to Athens in the age of Pericles.

Geography

Those who claim that climate and goegraphy are the primary determinants of a peoples' culture and civilization, invariably point out that the world's great civilizations—from ancient Egypt and Mesopotamia to modern Europe and America—have thrived in temperate climates. At the turn of the eighteenth century, one such geographical determinist, Fontenelle, contended that the arts and sciences could prosper only between the Atlas Mountains and the Baltic Sea; that great achievements could never be expected of the Laplanders who lived in the Arctic or the Negroes of tropical Africa. The idea was soon expanded and popularized by the French philosophe, Montesquieu. Obviously it contains considerable truth. Eskimos and other far northern tribes have never produced anything intellectually or culturally noteworthy because

[1] The examples here are taken from A. R. Humphreys, *The Augustan Age* (N.Y.: Harper & Row, 1963), pp. 217, 223–24.

all their energy and imagination is consumed in keeping alive in their harsh surroundings. Inhabitants of the tropics, on the other hand, find it so easy to collect enough food to eat, have such limited needs for clothing and shelter, and find heat and humidity such an effective deterrent to energetic activity of any kind that they seldom get in the habit of developing their faculties or working persistently at anything. Thus they achieve little. It may be objected that the Babylonian, Egyptian, Aztec, and Inca civilizations rose in the tropics, but this is hardly conclusive. Ancient Egypt and Mesopotamia probably had a more temperate climate than those areas have now, the Incas lived chiefly in the high mountains of Peru, and the Aztec capital was on the site of present day Mexico City at an altitude of 7500 feet.

Wealth

Cultural brilliance is certainly related to the wealth of a society. For millenia before the Industrial Revolution advances in every sphere of human activity were hindered by sheer lack of money. Kings wanted to make government more extensive and efficient, and to build bigger and more effective armies. Scientists needed both better equipment and greater economic security to pursue their researches. Businessmen wanted capital for investment. Charitable souls longed to distribute more largesse to the poor. Everywhere the same roadblock interposed: insufficient wealth.

This iron necessity has shaped the history of culture too. Artists and intellectuals need food, clothing, and shelter quite as much as other men. Hence a certain minimum of surplus wealth must exist if any society is to support an appreciable number of people who are not economically productive. In the Arctic or in poor, mountainous, desert, or frontier areas, everyone must exert himself to the fullest to secure the bare physical necessities of life. Little or nothing remains to devote to cultural pursuits. The latter become possible only when some men are able to command the labor of others. Contrary to the common assumption, most of the centuries' old English ballads that have come to be called "folk art" were not written by depressed commoners but by leisured aristocrats whose descendants have long since turned to other diversions.[2]

Above a certain level, however, the relationship between wealth and cultural splendor becomes far more complex than the simple equation "more wealth: greater achievement." For example, in the Middle Ages the main patrons of the arts were ecclesiastical bodies and individual churchmen. Such patronage was possible because the Church as an institution was both richer and better organized than secular governments or private enterprises. Yet every medievalist acknowledges that the intellectual and artistic triumphs of that time owed quite as much to deep religious feeling as to ecclesiastical money.

Likewise, the magnificent outburst of cultural activity that is called the Italian Renaissance took place in the richest, most economically advanced part of Europe, a place where many popes, merchant families, and political rulers had sufficient resources to patronize hundreds of artists and writers. Yet economic historians are generally agreed that the period 1300–1450 was an age of economic decline in most parts of Europe. Most of the great Italian banking houses went bankrupt in these years. Moreover, Venice and Genoa were two of the most prosperous cities in Italy; yet artistically and intellectually they lagged well behind Florence and Rome until about 1500. An economic revival got underway throughout Europe after 1450 but the products of the late Italian Renaissance are not markedly superior to those of a generation or two earlier. Furthermore, if some of the arts progressed dramatically in the fourteenth and fifteenth centuries, others did not. The stately simplicity of earlier Gothic architecture became lost in a swamp of intricate designs and striving for impossible effects. There was much evidence of literary and artistic decadence too: the cynical poetry of Francois Villon, the Dance of

---

[2] These matters are considered in some detail by Clement Greenberg, *Art and Culture* (Boston: Beacon Press, 1961), pp. 8–18.

Death motif in painting, and such writings as Sebastian Brant's *Ship of Fools*. These phenomena were most pronounced in northern France, the Low Countries, and western Germany, the second most prosperous area of Europe after Italy.

The Netherlands enjoyed remarkable economic growth in the sixteenth and seventeenth centuries. In the same age it produced a galaxy of talented painters and a considerable number of literary and philosophical luminaries. Cause and effect relationships, however, are not entirely clear. The greatest of modern Dutch historians holds quite simply that cultural achievement followed directly from economic prosperity; that in the late sixteenth century the cultural center of the Low Countries had been in the southern provinces of Flanders and Brabant but that in the seventeenth century it shifted to the northern provinces because they remained unconquered, unoccupied, and therefore unexploited by Spain.[3] An equally important consideration appears to have been that the Netherlands then contained many people who had money to spare but who lacked attractive investment opportunities. Consequently many Dutchmen bought pictures: for prestige, for enjoyment, and because they could be sold again. Unquestionably this condition provided employment for scores of artists. It did not mean, however, that the painters were necessarily held in high regard by their countrymen. On the contrary, prices for their works were very low, and most painters had to supplement their meager incomes in other ways. Steen and van der Velde made a living as innkeepers, van Goyen was a tulip merchant, Hobbema was a tax collector, van de Velde was in the linen business, Hals was poor most of his life, Rembrandt went bankrupt, and Vermeer had to pawn his paintings to a baker. The brilliance of Spanish arts in the reigns of Philip II, III, and IV (1556–1664) is universally recognized. Some of it was unquestionably due to lavish royal

---

[3] Pieter Geyl, *The Revolt of the Netherlands, 1555–1609* (London: Williams & Norgate, 1932), pp. 233, 239, 256–57; *The Netherlands Divided, 1609–1648* (London: Williams & Norgate, 1936), pp. 35, 156–65.

patronage. The country's sharp cultural decline in the last half of the seventeenth century has been ascribed by some to the decline of that royal patronage as the government approached bankruptcy, by others to the decline of private wealth in Spain. What nobody can explain in either the Dutch or Spanish cases is what produced the exceptional artistic talent in the first place. In the twentieth century the United States is much the richest nation in the world and can give private or public financial support to more persons and projects than any other nation, but it is difficult to draw a compelling conclusion from this. The general level of American literature, music, painting, and theatre is by no means contemptible but neither is it obviously superior to that of several other parts of the world. What American wealth *will* provide has drawn tens of thousands of extremely talented foreigners to our shores, but more of them have been scientists and engineers than artists or litterateurs. Many Americans of the latter genre have migrated to France. Few French literati have come to the more affluent U.S.A.

A consideration of the ancient Greeks is no more enlightening. The magnificent building program of Periclean Athens was financed out of the treasury of the Confederation of Delos, a loose alliance which the Athenians were able to dominate and exploit after the Persian wars. It is often contended that slavery accounted for the intellectual and cultural brilliance of Greek society since the slaves did much of the physical work, thereby liberating many of the free citizens of the community to devote themselves to things of the mind and spirit. The trouble with this argument is that most other ancient societies, not to speak of the antebellum American South, were also based on slavery. None of them produced an intellectual or cultural efflorescence remotely comparable to that of ancient Greece. Even a comparison of Periclean Greece with the later Hellenistic Age is inconclusive. More wealth existed in the later era, and its artistic expression was more individualistic, but achievements of an exceedingly high order were common in both ages.

War and Peace

Despite its destructive character war has never lost its charm for men. To many it has been so entrancing that they have envisioned it as a positive good, a great quickening agency, a phenomenon which stirs ordinarily sluggish men to do valiant deeds and strive mightily to solve old problems. In some fields the claim is valid. Modern wars usually increase medical knowledge. War also promotes certain types of industrial efficiency, and it stimulates any kind of scientific research even remotely connected with weapons-making. Never has the latter been so obvious as in the twentieth century when, for the first time in history, the level of scientific development in the military sphere often outstrips that in civilian production.

If one attempts to argue that war promotes cultural advancement, however, he is on much shakier ground. It is of course true that the cultural splendor of ancient Greece, and particularly Athens, was never brighter than in the fifth century B.C. during the Peloponnesian Wars. The brilliance continued into the fourth century B.C. even though the Greek states were immersed in constant wars and domestic strife and were unable to solve any of their major political problems. Some scholars have compared this condition with the generally peaceful state of the Roman Empire at its zenith in the second century A.D., concluding that war must quicken cultural development.[4]

Most history, however, seems to indicate the opposite: to show that warfare usually tends to produce cultural and intellectual sterility. The reason is that an aura of turmoil, passion, and violence leaves little room for the reflection and contemplation that produce great works of the mind and spirit. Notoriously, hard, militaristic, predatory societies like those of the ancient Assyrians, Spartans, and Huns, and the medieval Seljuk and Ottoman Turks, never produced anything culturally noteworthy. Rather, they usually destroyed what-

---

[4] For example cf. C. Warren Hollister, *Roots of the Western Tradition* (N.Y.: John Wiley & Sons, 1966), p. 172.

ever they found among the peoples they conquered. The brilliant Provençal culture of southern France was obliterated by the crusading armies that suppressed the Albigensian heretics in the thirteenth century. The great age of Irish manuscript illumination and fancy gold work came in the eighth and ninth centuries, a time of peace immediately preceding the destructive Viking invasions. The increasing cultural superiority of the northern over the southern Netherlands after about 1585 has already been noted. Conditions of life in the northern provinces were generally more stable, peaceful, and secure than in the south, even though both areas were at least nominally at war most of the time. During the French religious wars of the late sixteenth century only two writers of any consequence appeared. One was Montaigne, a skeptic who held aloof from religious and political movements of any kind. The other was Jean Bodin, who was so thoroughly discouraged by the destruction and chaos caused by the wars that he wrote one of the most famous of all defenses of absolute government. Germany was notoriously backward culturally and intellectually for half a century after being ravaged in the Thirty Years' War (1618–1648), though this condition also owed considerably to plagues and to a general economic decline which antedated the war.[5] Finally, the case of Renaissance Italy seems equivocal. The Italian states were egoistic and warlike throughout the Renaissance, yet the peak of the Italian Renaissance came in the forty years after the Peace of Lodi of 1454, an era of comparative quiet in which wars were short and seldom destructive. Whether Florence would have shone less brightly in these years had she been conquered by Milan or Venice, or whether the whole Italian Renaissance would have been stimulated or stifled by more serious warfare, is impossible to say for certain. One of the outstanding mod-

---

[5] For a consideration of this much debated issue cf. C. V. Wedgewood, *The Thirty Years War* (N.Y.: Doubleday, Anchor Books, 1961), pp. 485–506, and especially Robert Ergang, *The Myth of the All Destructive Fury of the Thirty Years War* (Pocono Pines, Pa., 1956).

ern students of this age thinks the relative peace of 1454–1494 was probably beneficial.[6]

Revolutions

The effect of revolutions seems less in doubt. Both Napoleon and Hitler regretted that literature and art so poorly reflected the "greatness" of their regimes. John Milton wasted twenty years as a pamphleteer for the parliamentary side in the English civil war of the 1640s and 50s. Only afterward, when things had quieted down and when he was personally in retirement and disgrace, did he write the works which have assured his immortality. The reasons are not hard to find. Revolutionaries are usually a zealous and often puritanical lot, anxious to remake a whole society according to splendid new principles. They subordinate every other consideration to the advancement of the movement. They regard artists and intellectuals as soldiers to be mustered into the service of the Great Cause. Soon literary works lauding the makers of the revolution and their holy principles flood from the printing presses, while painters and sculptors busy themselves immortalizing the marvels on canvas and stone. After the tide of revolution has ebbed little of this is usually regarded as an important addition to mankind's cultural treasury. This has been particularly true in the cases of the revolutionary regimes of the twentieth century. In the reign of Stalin (1924–1953) Russian artists and litterateurs dutifully turned out a vast amount of hack writing and many movies. Some of the latter had merit, but most were of the genre "boy loves tractor" and "girl loves production quotas." "Stalin modern" architecture was universally derided west of the Iron Curtain both during the dictator's lifetime and afterward.

The legacy of the French revolutionary era, however, is more equivocal. For a generation after the upheaval most of

[6] Garrett Mattingly, *Renaissance Diplomacy* (Baltimore: Penguin Books, 1964), pp. 82–83.

Europe was hostile to intellectual innovation. Writers and "intelligentsia" in general were far less heeded than they had been in the preceding century, mostly because they were widely blamed for the bloody deeds of the revolution and the ideas it had loosed. For France the era was a time of overall artistic decadence. Yet there were counter-currents too. Napoleon patronized the arts, even to taking painters with him on his campaigns to immortalize his triumphs. At least one artist of real stature, Jacques Louis David, was genuinely inspired. His best work had a strong political coloration and was done during the revolutionary and Napoleonic period. Nothing he produced afterward was of much value. Moreover, the Romantic Age was roughly coterminous with the revolutionary era (1789–1815) and was, to some degree, a reaction against it. Romantic artists and literati like Wordsworth, Keats, Shelley, Byron, Delacroix, Herder, Fichte, and Chateaubriand turned out many works of a high order.[7]

Religion

The relationship of religion to cultural development is considerably more complex, partly because it has been the subject of so many polemics. The English historian Christopher Dawson holds that religion is the heart of any true culture, and the historian-prophet Arnold Toynbee has stressed a similar theme in his epochal work, *A Study of History*. Others, most notably missionary secularists, have maintained that religion has always sought to stifle man's free spirit and thus has consistently had an inhibiting effect upon all intellectual and artistic expression. In their view excellence is achieved in spite of religion rather than because of it. There is considerable evidence to support each contention, and a lot more which indicates that both views should be moderated.

[7] For an evaluation of the French Revolution and its effect on the arts cf. Arnold Hauser, *The Social History of Art*, II, trans. Stanley Godman (N.Y.: Knopf, 1951), 641–63.

One of the strongest bastions of the secularist thesis is ancient Greece. The Greeks produced one of the most brilliant cultures the world has ever seen. This achievement has often been credited to their alleged secularity and rationalism, to their belief in "the primacy of the intellect—the supremacy of the spirit of free inquiry."[8] Unquestionably, the Greeks were more concerned with this world than the next one. They wrestled with ethical problems but not theological ones. They produced neither a major religious prophet nor a divinely ordained creed. Those of the Hellenistic Age (fourth to second century B.C.) generally denied that such moral restraints as society imposed had any divine basis. Their artistic motifs were highly physical. Yet Greek accomplishments of the intellect and spirit were quite as remarkable in the fifth century B.C. as they were to be later, and in the fifth century, Greek society was still fundamentally religious.

The same ambivalence is evident in the Italian Renaissance (approximately 1325–1550). Many of the great artists (especially the writers) of the age were openly or covertly pagan. The flavor of such books as Boccaccio's *Decameron,* Machiavelli's *The Prince,* Castiglione's *Perfect Courtier,* Cellini's *Memoirs,* and Guicciardini's *History of Italy* is distinctly modern and secular. Landscapes, personal portraits, and scenes from the pagan ancient world became common themes in painting, though these by no means displaced the episodes from the life of Christ and biblical lore that had been the stock in trade of painters for centuries.

The same ambiguity prevailed in sixteenth and seventeenth century England. The intellectuals of the Elizabethan age still lived in a medieval thought world, believing in Original Sin and the decline of the world from a primeval Golden Age. Their prevailing theory of knowledge was still authoritarian. Theology was the queen of the sciences, and all other learning was related to it. A hundred years later, however, in the age of Locke and Newton, intellectuals were beginning to model

[8] Edward McNall Burns, *Western Civilization,* I, 6th ed. (N.Y.: Norton, 1963), 183.

their thought processes on the natural sciences, particularly mathematical physics. Many argued that "modern" writers and thinkers were superior to the "ancients." Theology, while still respectable, had become merely one of several sciences, each of which tended increasingly to go its own way. Yet both were ages of noteworthy intellectual and cultural achievement. Things were no different across the Channel. "Irreligious" nineteenth century France produced great art—but so did "religious" thirteenth century France.

The crucial weakness in the thesis that culture springs from rationalism lies elsewhere. Its Achilles heel consists in the fact that a society which deifies reason thereby persistently questions the most fundamental assumptions on which it is itself based. It thereby generates skepticism and courts ultimate self-destruction. It has been claimed that this was the fatal flaw in the culture of the ancient Greek city states: the principle which brought about their internal disintegration. Interestingly, those patron saints of modern political conservatism, Edmund Burke and Joseph de Maistre, were the first among many historians and polemicists to claim that not merely the culture but the whole society of eighteenth century France destroyed itself because it embraced the rationalism of the Enlightenment.

The claim that religion is the core of any culture is similarly double-edged. It is not hard to demonstrate that religion can be and, indeed, often has been, a positive inspiration for intellectual and artistic accomplishment. Dante's *Divine Comedy,* one of the greatest half dozen literary works in all history, is profoundly religious in theme. The world's first true universities were outgrowths of the cathedral schools of medieval Europe. The painting and sculpture of the Middle Ages was almost entirely religious in theme, both in Western Christendom and in the Byzantine Empire. Gothic architecture, the most advanced art form of medieval Europe, was employed primarily in the building of churches. The most impressive single intellectual achievement of that era was the development of scholastic philosophy, primarily by Thomas Aquinas

(1225–1274), the result of an endeavor to reconcile Christian theology with newly acquired knowledge of the pagan ancient world. Many of the Renaissance popes, most ostentatiously Julius II and Leo X, deliberately sought to embellish the grandeur of the papacy by encouraging and subsidizing artists. In Islamic lands, where religion was an even more pervasive force in the lives of people than in Christian Europe, the arts and sciences throve well beyond European norms until the dreadfully destructive conquests of the Seljuk Turks in the eleventh century.

However, if religion is sometimes the mother of cultural achievement, religious animosity and strife can be the death of it. There is no doubt that the hatreds, persecutions, and wars of the Reformation era, and particularly the foreign conquest and domination that often came in their train, had an inhibitory effect on cultural and intellectual development.[9] The very atmosphere of the age turned men's minds away from culture. Henry VIII of England (1509–1547), for instance, became so absorbed in religious controversies that he gradually abandoned his early humanistic interests and patronage of literary men.

Within Christendom it has often been claimed that this or that denomination is particularly hostile to intellectual and cultural development. In some cases the assertion is unquestionably sound. Such groups as the Anabaptists of the sixteenth century and some of their Fundamentalist descendants have long specifically disavowed most of the intellectual and cultural products of the modern world. With the major Christian churches, however, almost any generalization is shaky. Many Renaissance popes were generous patrons of the arts, but other popes of the Counter-Reformation were not. Science

---

[9] Such students of the Renaissance as C. M. Ady and the great nineteenth century scholar Jacob Burckhardt think this was the case in sixteenth century Italy too. Cecilia M. Ady, *Lorenzo de'Medici and Renaissance Italy* (London: English Universities Press, 1960), pp. 163–65; Jacob Burckhardt, *The Civilization of the Renaissance In Italy* (London: Allan and Unwin, 1937), pp. 163–65, 175. For the Netherlands cf. *Supra.*, p. 249.

flourished in Catholic Italy in the early sixteenth century, but this preeminence was lost a century later when the papacy stumbled clumsily into a policy of repressing unfamiliar scientific ideas, notably in the famous persecution of Galileo.

With important Protestant groups, things are not much clearer. Reformation Calvinist mobs smashed churches and destroyed their contents in the Netherlands in 1566. Lutheran mobs had wrought similar havoc on a smaller scale in parts of Germany some years before. Wherever Calvinist churches were thoroughly established and organized they tried to impose a rigid intellectual and moral orthodoxy that was incompatible with the sensual exuberance and zest for intellectual inquiry that had typified the Renaissance. In the seventeenth century Netherlands few great litterateurs and scholars were strict Calvinists.[10] Ornate church decoration was condemned on theological grounds, and Calvinism had a depressing effect on most literature save religious poetry. But did the Netherlands become a cultural desert on this account? Hardly. For a time the southern provinces, still Catholic, surpassed the north in literary and artistic production, most of it inspired by southern Europe and the Counter-Reformation. Painting still remained popular in the Protestant north, however, and science flourished in these provinces where it was less circumscribed by veneration of Scripture and Aristotle.[11] In most Protestant lands art did not decline in any absolute sense: it merely ceased to be religious in theme. Such Dutch Protestant painters as Rembrandt, Hals, Brueghel, and Van Eyck, and such English Protestants as Gainsborough and Joshua Reynolds compare favorably with earlier and contemporary Catholic painters.

Partly in reaction against the Protestants who disliked elaborately ornamented churches, partly from a deliberate design to leave viewers awestruck by sheer magnificence and

[10] Pieter Geyl, *Revolt of the Netherlands (1555–1609)*, pp. 261–62.

[11] For many references to the situation in the Low Countries cf. Geyl, *The Netherlands Divided (1609–1648)*, pp. 40–41, 66–67, 211–12, 224, 227–28.

splendor, Catholic Europe embraced the ornate style known as the baroque. The opulent paintings of Rubens and the complex, convoluted sculpture of Bernini are among the finest baroque productions. Whether they are superior, inferior, or equivalent in quality to the works of Rembrandt and Hals is impossible to say. All evidenced genius.

One of the great ages in British literature is that of the late Elizabethan and early Jacobean period (1580–1620). It was the generation of Shakespeare, Marlowe, Jonson, Bacon, and many others. England at that time was a Protestant country engaged in the repression of Catholicism. Yet at about the same time there occurred a considerable literary and artistic renaissance in Poland, a country religiously mixed but in the process of becoming mostly Catholic again.[12] More markedly, it was also the Golden Age of Spanish culture, and great era of Suarez, Mariana, el Greco, Calderon, Cervantes, Velasquez, Murillo, Zurbaran, Cano, and Lope de Vega. Spain was neither Protestant nor religiously mixed. She was determinedly Catholic: the heartland of the Counter-Reformation.

Censorship

Measuring the effect of censorship upon intellectual and artistic production is as difficult as gauging the influence of religion. That writers should dislike censorship is not hard to understand, since it restricts their capacity to spread the ideas they cherish and it reduces their incomes from the sale of their books. The real case against censorship, however, does not lie here but in the claim that it inhibits human intellectual and cultural growth by preventing the dissemination of valuable knowledge and challenging ideas. So it does to *some* extent, but how much no one can say for certain. A lot of what has fallen to the censor through the ages would have added little to the stature of anything. More pertinent—and important—

[12] O. Halecki, "The Renaissance In Poland: Cultural Life and Literature," *Cambridge History of Poland,* edited by W. F. Reddaway, J. H. Penson, O. Halecki, and R. Dyboski. (Cambridge: University Press, 1950), pp. 279, 282.

it is extremely difficult to estimate the influence of censorship in times past because the practice was virtually universal and, at the same time, usually ineffective. Until near the close of the eighteenth century, civil governments took it for granted that it was a natural prerogative of rulers to control what was published in their jurisdictions. Churchmen assumed that they had a duty to employ the censor to safeguard the souls of the faithful.

Such censorship could be both harsh and capricious. A sixteenth century Englishman, John Stubbs, expressed his disapproval of a contemplated marriage between Queen Elizabeth I (1558–1603) and a Catholic prince by composing a pamphlet entitled *Discovery of a Gaping Gulf, Wherein England Is Like to Be Swallowed Up by Another French Marriage, If the Lord Forbid not the Banns by Letting Her See the Sin and Punishment Thereof.* Elizabeth was not amused; she had his hand cut off. The philosophes of eighteenth century France suffered less dramatically for their irreverent criticisms of contemporary society, but most of them spent some time in prison. Yet Elizabethan censorship did not stifle Shakespeare, and no philosophe's message was destroyed because its author languished for a time in the Bastille. Most noteworthy of all, the great age of Spanish literature occurred 150 years after the Inquisition was established in Spain.[13] Being on the Papal *Index of Forbidden Books,* then or later, did not prevent circulation of many outstanding European writings or markedly diminish their influence—even in Catholic countries.

Probably the principal reason was that censorship in the historic past was always grossly inefficient. Of the censors of eighteenth century France, "Never have so many officials pro-

---

[13] It is sometimes urged that Spain's cultural decline at the end of the seventeenth century was the inevitable result of the *cumulative effect* of the Inquisition. Cf. Cecil Roth, *The Spanish Inquisition* (N.Y.: W. W. Norton & Co., 1964), p. 274. Perhaps so, but any age of cultural brilliance is bound to decline *sometime.* A century and a half is a long time. In this case it is likely that Spanish poverty was more important than the influence of the Inquisition.

hibited so much with so little effect."[14] Some of them were even in collusion with those whom they were supposed to police. Diderot, the editor of the famous *Encyclopedia,* collaborated so closely with Malsherbes, the chief government censor, that he sometimes deposited offending materials in Malsherbes' house for safekeeping. Some of his colleagues observed wryly that Diderot was not only mistaken in denying the existence of Divine Providence but ungrateful as well. What other agency could have bequeathed him a censor like Malsherbes?[15]

Modern governments that wish to censor can, of course, do so more efficiently than their predecessors for the same reason that they can do everything else more efficiently: they have the products of the industrial revolution at their disposal. Moreover, untold millions of pious folk have always acknowledged the right of religious authorities to proscribe books and movies deemed harmful to morals or religious beliefs and have followed their injunctions.

Still, censorship frequently tends to be "counter-productive," as contemporary jargon has it. Often it merely calls attention to works whose suppression is desired by authority. "Banned in Boston" has long been an advertisement coveted by American publishers, whether the books in question be "advanced" works of worth or mere printed garbage. Even the stifling censorship of Stalinist Russia did not prevent the young people of that country from learning about the ways and works of the "decadent capitalist" West, and admiring and emulating many of them.

Personal Morality

Despite the vulgar stereotype of the intellectual as an otherworldly "egghead," and the artist as an unkempt sexual anarchist prone to drink, it is hard to draw any convincing conclusions about the relationship of personal morality to

[14] Peter Gay, *Voltaire's Politics* (N.Y.: Vintage Books, 1965), p. 73.
[15] Arthur M. Wilson, *Diderot: The Testing Years* (N.Y.: Oxford Press, 1957), pp. 121–22, 339.

artistic or intellectual eminence. The ancient Greeks were more permissive in sexual conduct than Western people have been at any time in the Christian era; but since they were so both at their cultural zenith and during their decline, this factor can hardly have been crucial for either their accomplishments or their decadence. Many Renaissance Italians deliberately imitated the sexual profligacy of the ancients, and the political morality of the age was no more elevated than its sexuality, but again there seems to have been no marked change from one stage of the Renaissance to another. It has been claimed that Ireland became intellectually and culturally preeminent in Europe in the centuries after the fall of Rome because she had never been part of the Roman Empire, and thus her inhabitants were unstained by the vices of antiquity. It seems more likely, however, that the vital factor was her geographical isolation which saved her from being inundated by the Germanic barbarians who overran England and the Continent.

On the level of individual morality, judgment is impossible. Michelangelo, Bracciolini, Byron, Diderot, deMaupassant, and Gauguin were libertines. St. Augustine, Boccaccio, Rousseau, and Tolstoy were so in youth, but reformed later in life. Blaise Pascal was an ascetic Jansenist, and Boyle and Newton were singularly upright men. John Calvin was, of course, the archtype Puritan. John Milton was a Puritan, and so were such early American literary figures as Jonathan Edwards, Cotton Mather, and Samuel Sewall. Ruskin and Carlyle were neither puritans nor libertines, but their personal lives would have been of surpassing interest to psychiatrists. One can conclude only with the irrelevant bromide that a great artist may be either a puritan or a wastrel, but if he is the latter he is not apt to live so long.

Political Power

Montesquieu once remarked that the human mind is never so free as in a time of decaying despotism.[16] This is merely a

[16] Cited in F. L. Ford, *Robe and Sword: The Regrouping of the French Aristocracy After Louis XV*, (N.Y.: Harper & Row, Torchbook, 1965), p. 233.

picturesque phrasing of a common belief that the culture of a people shines brightest when their society is in political decline. In many past societies the belief seems sound. Ancient Greek civilization reached its peak at a time when the little city states were battling to mutual exhaustion in the Peloponnesian and other wars, were passing under the harrow of domestic despots, and finally were being conquered by the half-barbarous Macedonians. Aristotle, we must not forget, was the tutor of Alexander the Great (d. 323 B.C.). The most productive period in the cultural life of the Byzantine Empire was the fourteenth and fifteenth centuries, a time when that decadent empire was under constant pressure from the Turks and tottering towards its destruction in 1453.[17]

The Golden Age of Spanish culture (1580–1650) is a less obvious demonstration of the principle, but still a largely valid one. As late as the Peace of the Pyrenees (1659), Spain was still feared by her neighbors as one of the most powerful states in Europe—though she had really been long in political decline. The kings who succeeded Philip II (d. 1598) were inept, Spanish trade stagnated, the government's financial problems grew more desperate with each passing year, many of the country's most productive citizens (the Moriscos) were expelled (1609–1614), and the quality of the army declined. To be sure, it is easy to exaggerate the degree of Spain's seventeenth century decline, since it followed hard on the heels of her preeminence in sixteenth century Europe. Nonetheless the facts are plain: Spain in 1600 was the mightiest power in the world; Spain in 1700 was a second-rate state; and the age of greatest Spanish cultural brilliance came in the first half of the seventeenth century. Comparisons with twentieth century Spain only muddy the waters. Modern Spaniards enjoy higher living standards than their sixteenth and seventeenth century ancestors but their cultural achievements are less impressive and Spain is no longer even a second-ranking power politically.

[17] Steven Runciman, *The Fall of Constantinople* (Cambridge: University Press, 1965), pp. 5, 14.

The case of Germany is similar. The era 1775–1830 is unique in German history for its amazing outburst of spiritual energy. It was the age of Kant, Hegel, Mozart, Beethoven, Goethe, Fichte, Schiller, Scharnhorst, and many others; also the period when German universities became the world's finest. Yet the German states were weak and divided politically. In the years 1870–1940, by contrast, Germany was politically and economically powerful but her cultural eminence gradually dimmed, especially in the Nazi era.

But, once more, many examples can be cited which do not support this thesis. Worse—they support the opposite thesis: that a nation's cultural zenith tends to coincide with its political strength. The great literary age of Rome, the era of Cicero, Livy, Horace, Seneca, Marcus Aurelius, and others came in the first century B.C. and the first two centuries A.D., the time of Rome's greatest territorial extent and political might. The period of Rome's political decline, the third, fourth, and fifth centuries of the Christian Era, was also an intellectual and cultural wasteland. Little was accomplished in the fine arts, and literature was mostly imitative. The ablest minds of the time, Saints Ambrose, Jerome, and Augustine, were figures whose importance was primarily religious. A millenium later, Petrarch was so convinced that culture and power are necessarily interdependent that he strove to follow in the footsteps of the Roman poets in the hope that his example would help to revive the Roman spirit in all spheres: in the arts, in politics, and in martial ardor. Late Elizabethan England was in the process of becoming a European great power and an expansionist one in the bargain: victor over the Armada and preparing to begin the colonization of America. The Golden Age of British painting and architecture lay between the years 1760 and 1830, a time in which British national power gradually increased and the Industrial Revolution began. The great age of Dutch painting, the seventeenth century, was also the age in which the Netherlands reached its zenith as a commercial, naval, and political power. Likewise, Poland's civilization shone brightest in the sixteenth century when the country was relatively powerful, prosperous, and secure. It dimmed in the seventeenth century when Poland fell into ruinous wars, economic decline, and domestic anarchy.[18] In the Middle Ages, eleventh century Sicily experienced a brilliant cultural renaissance under its ablest ruler, Roger II, at a time when it was also at its political, diplomatic, and economic peak.[19]

Still other examples prove nothing at all. It is difficult to draw any meaningful lesson from the culture of the Middle Ages taken as a whole. No single state ever dominated medieval Europe and no one people ever possessed an obvious intellectual hegemony for any long period. Gothic architecture, the finest single cultural achievement of the age, was not confined to one country, though it was most prominent in France in the twelfth and thirteenth centuries. This was a time when the French monarchy was adding to its territories and growing more centralized, but much of the time it was still overshadowed by England or the Holy Roman Empire, or both. The states of Renaissance Italy were probably less prosperous economically in the fourteenth and fifteenth centuries than they had been earlier, but their political condition was much the same as it had been for generations. They had always been small, numerous, and weak compared to the major European powers north of the Alps, and so they still were at the height of the Renaissance. French cultural domination of Europe was achieved in the seventeenth century, particularly in the first half of the long reign of Louis XIV (1643–1715), a time when France was also the strongest political state on the Continent. It is difficult to maintain that one condition followed from the other, however, for French cultural preeminence lasted throughout the eighteenth and nineteenth centuries even though the political fortunes of the country ebbed dramatically during the eighteenth century, rose to flood tide during the revolutionary and Napoleonic eras

[18] O. Halecki, *op. cit.*, pp. 273–4; A. Bruckner, "Polish Cultural Life In the 17th Century," *Cambridge History of Poland, op. cit.*, pp. 557–569.

[19] John Julius Norwich, "The Normans In the South," *History Today*, October 1966, pp. 700–703.

(1792–1815), ebbed again from 1815 to 1852, rose once more under the Second Empire (1852–1870), and declined again under the Third Republic (1871–1940).

In fact, it is quite possible that French painters have persistently been among Europe's best for the last three centuries for an elementary reason totally unconnected with politics: e.g. they have had better training than those of other countries; they have been products of the academies established in the reign of Louis XIV for the specific purpose of encouraging and developing artists.[20]

Finally, modern Ireland and Scandinavia provide examples of societies that have been culturally productive without being either powerful or decadent politically. Late nineteenth century Scandinavia, a region of small but independent countries, produced Strindberg, Ibsen, and Kierkegaard. Early twentieth century Ireland, even smaller and still under English domination, was the homeland of Joyce, Yeats, Synge, and Shaw.

Forms of Government

If attempts to correlate cultural achievement and political power lead to nothing definite, how about forms of government? Are certain types of political organization more conducive to cultural excellence than others? Once more, speculation usually starts with the ancient Greeks. How was it possible for a few hundred thousand people divided into many jealous, quarrelsome little city states to produce within four or five generations a whole galaxy of philosophers, dramatists, sculptors, poets, painters, political thinkers, and intellectual luminaries of every sort? The phenomenon certainly defies the law of averages. Some have answered quite simply that we are not objective about the Greeks. Because we happen to know more about them than any other ancient people we have analyzed everything they said and did, loaded them with

[20] William Fleming, *Art and Ideas* (N.Y.: Holt, Rinehart and Winston, 1963), pp. 514–15.

praise, and imitated their ways. The point has merit. We *do* know more about ancient Greece than we do about ancient Egypt or Mesopotamia or China, and we feel a closer kinship with the Greeks. Still, on anyone's estimate the achievements of Aristotle, Plato, Socrates, Euripides, Sophocles, Anaxagoras, Euclid, Archimedes, Phidias, Herodotus, and Thucydides represent triumphs of the human mind and spirit of the highest order.

Modern people in democratic societies like to attribute the excellence of the Greeks to the open-mindedness with which they approached all problems, to their democratic political forms, and to the dynamic spirit of liberty which allegedly characterized their city-states. This is not false, but it is only part of the truth. The same Greeks were also keepers of slaves, imperialistic, commercially greedy, suffused with racist ideas, perpetually immersed in domestic strife, and sufficiently intolerant to eliminate Socrates. Moreover, their democratic governments were often corrupt and most of them eventually degenerated into despotisms.

Judgments about the influence of democracy on culture in recent centuries are no more certain. In the late Middle Ages one of the most culturally advanced parts of Europe was Flanders. It was a rich, bustling, urban area with democratic governments in many of its cities. Nineteenth century Russia, by contrast, was rural, poor, and autocratic—the home of the most socially and politically repressive regime in the Western world. Yet nineteenth century Russia produced Tolstoy, Chekhov, Pushkin, and Dostoevsky.

One would think industrialism and democracy *ought to* stimulate cultural achievement since the one produces vast material wealth and the other tends to distribute it more widely than in autocracies. Thus many people have the necessary leisure to devote to cultural pursuits. Unfortunately there is little evidence that many of them do so devote it. Worse, democracy tends to add prestige to majority views of any kind and most men have never had elevated intellectual or cultural tastes. Still, the industrial and democratic age is only about

150 years old, whereas monarchy and autocracy endured for thousands of years, so judgments about the products of democracy are still necessarily tentative.

An opposite theory holds that the arts flourish under despotisms; that when a single person possesses supreme power he can bestow munificent patronage, invite new artists to his realm, and experiment without regard for public taste or the desire of some parliamentary assembly to spend money in another way. Hence the despot is able to create an ideal environment for artistic achievement. History provides considerable evidence to bolster this thesis. All the artistry of ancient and medieval Asia was produced under political despotisms. Artists there worked under relentless compulsion and governmental pressure of a sort that many moderns would find intolerable—yet splendid things were produced. The rigid control exercised by authority over all other spheres of life in the Byzantine Empire and in medieval monasteries may have had the effect of channeling the creative energies of multitudes of the ruled into the rich elaboration of churches.[21] Many an autocrat of Renaissance Italy gained immortality as a patron of the arts. In Rome the absolute monarchs of the Vatican lavished money on scholars, builders, painters, sculptors, jewelers, poets, and goldsmiths. Such secular despots as Ludovico il Moro of Milan and Lorenzo the Magnificent of Florence were not only generous patrons but respectable scholars themselves. Such an autocrat as Cosimo d'Medici subsidized the first translations of the Greek authors he had brought to Florence, founded the Platonic Academy, and established the city's first public library. Even such a monster as Sigismondo Malatesta was a patron of the arts. Like the tyrants of seventh and sixth century Greece (B.C.), Renaissance despots probably were patrons mostly to curry favor with their subjects and to give the impression that their own presence added lustre and prosperity to their cities. Nonetheless, and whatever their motives, they were quicker than republics to found chairs of

---

[21] Fleming holds this. *Ibid.*, pp. 171, 212–13.

humanistic study in universities where no economic advantage was obvious. Florence, which had a sample of virtually every known type of government from the fourteenth through the sixteenth centuries, was until about 1500 far in advance of Venice artistically and intellectually—though Venice was prosperous and her republican government was one of the least despotic in Italy.[22]

While there is no question that an autocrat has an unexcelled opportunity to nourish cultural development, it is doubtful that absolutism as a system is necessarily advantageous. Such absolute monarchs as the kings of seventeenth century Spain might be discriminating connoisseurs of the arts, but the attitude of most of history's despots has been one of indifference. The arts flourished under the bloodthirsty Egyptian Mamelukes (1252–1517), but Arabic culture became ossified in that land immediately afterward when the equally bloodthirsty Turkish Sultan Selim I conquered Egypt and banned the Arabic language save in courts and mosques. Jacob Burckhardt, who probably knew more about the Italian Renaissance than any man who ever lived, attributed Florentine intellectual preeminence to the extreme intellectual freedom that prevailed there and thought the success of Lorenzo the Magnificent as a patron was due not to his absolute political control of the city but to his willingness to accord perfect freedom of action to all the varied natures around him.[23] An examination of other parts of Europe is no more enlightening. Kings and nobles were the primary patrons of the arts in sixteenth century Poland. Achievements there declined when the kings grew weaker and money was drained off increasingly for military defense.[24] In the seventeenth century Netherlands, by contrast, a highly advanced culture existed among people

[22] The "absolutist" thesis is urged strongly by C. M. Ady, *op. cit.*, pp. 155–56, 158.

[23] Burckhardt, *op. cit.*, pp. 42, 199. The contrast with modern dictators, who try to bend everyone to their will and doctrines, is striking.

[24] S. S. Kormornicki, "The Renaissance in Poland: The Fine Arts," *Cambridge History of Poland op. cit.*, p. 294.

who battled the centralizing ambitions of the Orange dynasty, clung tenaciously to claims of local autonomy, and resisted the very conception of the modern centralized state.

Comparisons between Renaissance Italy and ancient Greece raise further points of interest but lead to no compelling conclusion. Athens in the fifth century B.C. was a place of general social and economic equality in the sense that almost nobody had great wealth, everyone ate simple food and wore simple clothing, and average wages for all kinds of work varied little. Yet in both the Hellenistic Age (which succeeded that of fifth century Greece and which had a brilliant culture derived from the Greeks) and in Renaissance Italy, extremes of wealth existed. In the latter era great families like the Medici lived in lordly splendor while the mass of the population survived at the subsistence level.

One clear point of similarity that does emerge from a comparison of the two ages is that in both cases the political units were small. From this it is sometimes maintained that this particular form of political organization is especially conducive to cultural development. But again it is easy to cite an opposite example. In seventeenth and eighteenth century Germany hundreds of princelings gave patronage to artists and intellectuals of all types but the results were disappointing. An occasional Bach or Handel appeared but an appalling amount of human energy was spent turning out third-rate music, poetry, and painting merely to glorify the patrons. The patrons themselves often wasted the time and talents of their protégés by loading them with petty tasks and personally badgering them.[25]

In summation we can do no better than to conclude that there does not seem to be any direct relation between the artist's personal freedom and the aesthetic quality of his work. One scholar puts it thus:

The spiritual existence of the artist is always in danger;

---

[25] R. J. White, *Europe in the 18th Century* (N.Y.: St. Martin's Press, 1965), pp. 46–47.

neither an authoritarian nor a liberal order of society is entirely free from peril for him; the one gives him less freedom, the other less security. There are artists who only feel safe when they are free, but there are also such as can breathe freely only when they are secure.[26]

Ideology

The ideology of a particular society exercises a heavy influence on the character of its artistic production but hardly determines its quality. The gigantic pyramids and huge, monolithic stone figures of ancient Egypt exemplify the spirit of Egyptian despotism. The individuality of Greek statuary and of Renaissance statuary and painting exemplify the individualistic spirit of Greeks and Italians of those ages. The sameness of the human figures and the pervasiveness of religious themes in medieval painting and sculpture indicate both the religiosity of the age and its belief in the unimportance of the passage of time. Still, such considerations do not explain why one age excels and another does not.

A consideration of the personal ideological orientation of artists and intellectuals is equally unenlightening. In modern times most literati are liberal in their political and social outlook, many are strident nonconformists, and not a few are revolutionaries of one brand or other. Most of the intellectual luminaries of fifth century Athens, by contrast, were political and philosophical conservatives. Most of the plays of the dramatists among them supported government policies, views, and interests. The same was true of the intelligentsia of the Middle Ages, despite the occasional appearance of radicals like Arnold of Brescia, Marsiglio of Padua, and William of Ockham. Such men as Plato, Aristotle, Shakespeare, Cervantes, Goethe, and Kant are generally recognized as ranking with the greatest writers of all history. Most of their works have universal themes: they are concerned with the whole human condition. They are not ideological in the modern sense.

[26] Hauser, *op. cit.*, I, 473.

Since the French Revolution, however, much intellectual and cultural activity has had an obvious nationalist inspiration. The works of Schiller, Hegel, and Nietzsche, and the music of Wagner, all glorified a real or imaginary Teutonic spirit which, in practice, was identified with Germany. Rimsky-Korsakov, Moussorgsky, Verdi, Mazzini, Lamartine, Michelet, and Kipling are but a few names at random from a host of nineteenth century European musicians, poets, novelists, historians, and artists of a dozen nationalities whose works had a strong nationalist inspiration. The quality of their productions varied widely. Some of the music in particular was of an extremely high order. Much of the writing was little better than propaganda and patriotic bombast. The point about which there can be no question, however, is the powerful stimulus that nationalism provided.

When an ideology is imposed by the state the effect upon artists and literati seems clearly inhibitory. Most of the artists and writers of seventeenth century France did their best work in the years when they encountered relatively little direction or interference—in the two generations when the government was dominated by Cardinals Richelieu and Mazarin, and Louis XIV was still young (1624–1680). The king, however, regarded literature and art as instruments of government, devices to raise the prestige of the monarchy. Consequently, he organized art production, established rules of acceptability, and regimented the nations's artists. Within twenty years after he began to rule personally, creativity was generally declining.[27]

The cases of the totalitarian states of the twentieth century seem clearer still. Though some of these regimes have been powerful politically none of them have any impressive cultural triumphs to their credit that can be said to derive directly from their ideologies. In Communist Russia most artists and intellectuals have been mere state employees rendering routine

---

[27] *Ibid.*, pp. 441–45. Of course the system he established for training artists paid dividends for the next two centuries, though under other rulers and regimes that did not treat artists and literary men as bureaucrats hired to expound the government's message. Cf. *Supra.*, p. 263.

homage to the regime. Those who have not, have been consistently in trouble with the government, or else silent. The finest literary production to come from the Soviet Union has been Boris Pasternak's *Dr. Zhivago,* a work whose themes are universal: not distinctively Communist at all. It was first published abroad, and its author was drenched with abuse in his homeland when he was awarded a Nobel Prize. Most other Russian writers and artists whose abilities are recognized internationally, men like the composer Shostakovich, the poet Evtushenko, and the writer Sholokov, have been subjected to much criticism by their government—usually on the ground they were insufficiently Communist. A major factor inhibiting cultural achievement in a communist state is the Marxist doctrine that art is nothing but the expression of the ideological orientation of the artist; that the dominant art of a society is but a reflection of its economic and social structure. Thus differences between artistic creation and mere artistic production, between masterpieces and fourth-rate hack work, are unimportant—really nonexistent. What is crucial is the ideological content of the work.

The Mexican painters Orozco, Rivera, and Siquieros might seem exceptions to the discussion in the preceding paragraph. All were Communists, their work shows a strong Communist inspiration, and it is of high quality. None of them lived and worked in a Communist society, however. All lived abroad in countries where they were free to express themselves as they liked. Whether their works would have been better, worse, about the same, or nonexistent had they lived and worked under a Communist dictatorship is, of course, impossible to prove; but the experience of their Russian counterparts indicates that they would likely have done less work and that of smaller worth.

In the cases of the major Fascist regimes of our century an immediate difficulty is that they did not survive long enough to allow a conclusive judgment. Mussolini was in power in Italy for twenty-one years; the Nazi regime in Germany lasted but twelve. Neither produced any intellectual or cultural triumphs. Democratic ideologues have usually attributed this to their lack of "freedom." Perhaps so, but it is more likely that modern dictatorships fail to achieve cultural excellence because they attempt impossibilities. They try to win all their subjects to some integrated total world view. This at once raises serious difficulties in the arts, for in this realm the masses understand and respect only what is natural, logical, orderly, customary, and clear. They are hostile to such experiments as nonrepresentational art or the kind of poetry written by Gertrude Stein. Hence dictatorial regimes, who are interested in the arts primarily as a means of conveying propaganda, encourage only what the vast majority understands and approves. This insures that the level of taste and discernment remains low. It means that the mass culture of the regimes takes such forms as "Stalin modern" architecture and the "heroic nationalist" style of painting favored by the Nazis.[28]

Social Systems

That a certain class structure exists in a society seems less important than preoccupation with an official ideology. In the ancient world Cretan art was less restrained and stylized, more "modern" than that of Mesopotamia or Egypt, though the social systems of all three places were similar. Various explanations have been offered: that Crete was more commercialized, or that religion counted for less in Crete, but none are convincing.[29]

In modern times no "class" really dominated Fascist Italy or Nazi Germany unless one wants to call the party leaders

---

[28] For a good brief description of this phenomenon in Nazi Germany cf. George L. Mosse, ed., *Nazi Culture* (N.Y.: Grosset & Dunlap, 1966), especially p. 140. Mosse thinks that Nazi insistence on subordinating all knowledge to the philosophic world view of the regime not only stifled German culture but blighted all intellectual development—with disastrous results for the nation. In World War II, "it was no accident that the Allies, not Germany, developed the atomic bomb, the 'miracle weapon' for which Hitler waited in vain" p. 200.

[29] Hauser, *op. cit.*, I, 66–70.

a "class," but the bourgeoisie were the backbone of these movements. In Soviet Russia, however, the bourgeoisie were proscribed and destroyed.

Unhappily, any discussion of the "bourgeoisie" in this connection at once leads into a morass of prejudice. Among the self-conscious "intellectuals" of the modern world it is conventional to sneer at the bourgeoisie as "anti-intellectual," and to make patronizing remarks about their hopelessly uninformed, parochial preferences in the arts. Whether or not this is justified now, it certainly was not in times past. The bourgeoisie were a major market for the production of artists in the Hellenistic Age. Many patrons of Renaissance artists were wealthy bourgeois, and the art produced for them was neither better nor worse than that which sprang from princely or papal patronage. Seventeenth century Dutch art was the product of a society dominated by the bourgeoisie, was middle class in theme, and was purchased largely by middle class people. Most of the luminaries of the eighteenth century French Enlightenment came from bourgeois families. In that age, middle class people wrote the books, bought the books, read the books, painted the pictures, bought the pictures, and attended the plays in which members of their own class for the first time got sympathetic treatment. The bourgeoisie had become the cultured class par excellence.[30] Significantly, the Middle Ages, an era in which the aristocracy dominated society more completely than it ever has since, and in which the middle class was neither numerous nor influential, is generally regarded as culturally and intellectually inferior to Renaissance and post-Renaissance Europe.

Popular Attitudes

One factor that seems both important and relatively constant as a stimulus for artistic creation is acclaim and support

---

[30] *Ibid.*, I, 116, 307; II, 502–503, 509, 532. In the case of the plays, drama itself did not grow noticeably better or worse because it began to depict middle class people rather than nobles in a favorable light.

for the artist. This is not the same thing as public beliefs about the proper role of the artist, nor is it the artist's conception of his own role. Neither of the latter factors seem important.

The ancient world regarded physical labor as demeaning. Hence poets were esteemed more than sculptors and painters since the latter had to do hard work with dirty materials. Nonetheless, the difference was one of degree rather than kind. The *products* of painters and sculptors were highly prized, and the higher esteem in which poets were held did not mean that Greek poetry was generally superior to painting and sculpture. Greek artists chiefly produced public portraits, statues, monuments, and temples. Those of both Roman times and the Renaissance, by contrast, worked mostly for private patrons and frequently sought to serve private desires. Medieval artists and artisans often decorated cathedrals for the glory of God and did not sign their names. Their successors signed their names and sought personal fame. Before 1500 artistry and workmanship were inseparable. The artist was regarded merely as an especially skilled workman who made splendid things that would be *used* by particular people or institutions. As late as the Renaissance, patrons decided what they wanted, selected the artist, took a hand in devising the program or project, approved or criticized the execution, and then paid or did not pay the bill. Beginning perhaps with Michelangelo this conception of the artist and his role began to change. More and more he came to be regarded as a "genius," a unique being set apart from the rest of humanity. With the Industrial Revolution workmanship and artistry were divorced. Workmen became mere factory hands performing mechanical tasks that had nothing of "artistry" about them. "Artists" became gentleman-dilettantes who "expressed themselves" in paint or stone or something else, with no regard for whether anything they made was useful, of good quality, or even comprehensible. Where earlier artists strove to do a good job—even if this meant copying what was recognized to be the best existing model or technique—their modern descendants try above all to be distinctive, "original." Modern patrons do not presume to give orders to artists: they are expected to stand in awe of the artist's genius and then to "appreciate" anything tangible which emanates from his "spirit."[31] Yet what does all this prove? Superficially, that it is now easier to pass off nonsense as art than it used to be. More seriously, it does not prove anything. Great art is still produced in the modern world just as it was in the Renaissance, the Middle Ages, ancient Rome, and ancient Greece. Whether or not the artist is an artisan or a "genius," whether he is anonymous or an egotist, whether he works for public or private purposes, does not seem particularly important.

Where the artist gets his inspiration seems equally immaterial. The Romans copied from the Greeks; the Renaissance Italians were immensely stimulated by admiration for the world of classical antiquity and did their best to emulate it; such an artist as the German Albrecht Durer was inspired by what the Italians had done; and members of any "school" of art are heavily influenced by others in the same "movement." But what does this prove? Quite extensive knowledge of the triumphs of the ancient world had existed in many parts of Europe since the early thirteenth century, and lesser knowledge of the subject for a long time before that. In some ages and places many men were inspired by it; in others a few; in still others none. Anyway, artists and intellectuals may have a variety of sources of information and inspiration but this does not explain why *their own works* are of high or low quality.

Excursions into other branches of knowledge do not help much. The European ruling classes were generally more receptive to new ideas in the eighteenth century than they had been in the seventeenth, yet there were many more original thinkers (Locke, Hobbes, Newton, Descartes, Pascal, Galileo, Kepler, Leibniz, Spinoza) in the earlier century. Perhaps an age of digestion has to follow one of original thought: as the philosophes synthesized the ideas of Locke and Newton, or Charles Darwin synthesized the findings of Lamarck, Mon-

---

[31] The changing roles of the artist through history is a major theme of Eric Gill, *Art* (N.Y.: Devin-Adair, 1950).

boddo, Diderot, and Erasmus Darwin. But this does not explain why the original thinkers appeared at one time and not another. Anyway, though there is always a *need* for greater knowledge the production of either great ideas or great works has been by no means uniform.

One thing that does seem vital at all times, whether in Periclean Athens, the Hellenistic Age, medieval Europe, or the Renaissance, is that at least some of the worldly mighty: kings, wealthy merchants, ecclesiastical princes, or even parvenu adventurers must patronize the arts and go out of their way to accord respect to those who produce them. At no time did these types vie so avidly to support the arts as during the Renaissance, and never did artistic production have greater prestige.

The attitude of the public is also of considerable importance. Whenever a church, bridge, watchtower, or anything comparable was to be erected or decorated in a Renaissance Italian town, architects and artists were invited to submit plans in public for people to discuss and criticize. The winner got the job. Even guilds held similar competitions and hired leading artists to do fine work for them. Thus artists were constantly on display and civic pride was regularly at stake. Everyone's interest in the arts was stimulated, skill and achievement were obviously valued, competition was keen, nothing slovenly or second rate was overlooked, and each artist was impelled to do his best.[32]

Yet it is easy to push this thesis too far. As we have seen, seventeenth century Dutchmen provided a great deal of employment for artists, but certainly did not support them munificently or hold them in particularly high regard.[33] In the nineteenth and twentieth centuries the arts are unquestionably encouraged by the existence of hundreds of national and municipal galleries, frequent displays of artists' works, aca-

---

[32] Stefan Zweig, who grew up in late nineteenth century Vienna, considered that the same intense public intrest in the arts was responsible for the high level of performance that prevailed in his home city. Stefan Zweig, *The World of Yesterday* (Lincoln: U. of Nebraska Press, 1964), pp. 18–19.

[33] Cf. *Supra.*, p. 246.

demic courses in the arts taught at all educational levels, plus all the apparatus of publicity that exists in a literate and technologically advanced society. The patronage of the wealthy and mighty still exists too, though it is much less important now than during the Renaissance. Many rich men now become avid collectors of art not out of love for it or even an understanding of it. Rather, they relish the prestige of being collectors or else they simply regard an art collection as a good financial investment. There is no indication that the activity of such collectors has improved the quality of contemporary art. It may even have tended to debase it since dispute is endless about whether many of the products sold to wealthy, undiscriminating collectors ought to be regarded as "art" at all.

It has often been alleged that the spirit of the Renaissance was responsible for its intellectual and artistic triumphs. That spirit was buoyant, optimistic, individualistic, full of belief in the dignity and power of man, anxious to experience everything. It viewed the world as a field for action and conquest. In short, the Renaissance was a creative, iconoclastic age. Therefore it stimulated artists and intellectuals.

This confident generalization is superficially attractive, but dubious withal. Determining what is and what is not "creative" involves many subjective judgments. Likewise while it is incontestable that Valla, Cellini, Michelangelo, and many others were full of buoyant individualism, a majority of their contemporaries were not. Most Renaissance men still took a dim view of human nature and human prospects. More damaging still, the medieval class which best exemplified the "Renaissance spirit" was the feudal aristocracy, and they were notably uninterested in either art or intellectual attainment.[34] Finally, in the Middle Ages more art was inspired by the clergy than by any other class. Most ecclesiastics were neither Renaissance bravos nor congenital optimists.

---

[34] Burckhardt, *op. cit.*, regarded the spirit of individualism, optimism, and daring as distinctive characteristics of the Renaissance. The famous Dutch scholar Johan Huizinga, in *The Waning of the Middle Ages* and other works, points out that the aristocrats of the middle ages had a similar attitude towards life. They merely expressed it in a different way.

Some scholars have speculated that the brilliance of Greek civilization in the fifth century B.C. was due to old and new forces existing for a time in a balance: attachment to religious ideas, loyalty to the city, and an aristocratic social pattern coinciding with the growth of a greater sense of the importance of the individual and a rationalistic questioning spirit.[35] A similar tenuous balance existed during the Renaissance: individualism bursting through the crust of a hierarchic, tradition-minded society, and a mingling of religious and secular motifs in the arts indicating a dualism of interests among the artists. A major difficulty with such a generalization as this, however, is that there is no convincing way to measure "individualism." It exists in every age. Any consideration of the robber barons, the bankers, the leaders of the Crusades, Roger Bacon, such popes as Gregory VII and Innocent III, even such figures as Peter Abelard and St. Francis of Assisi, indicate that there was no shortage of "individualism" in the Middle Ages even though it did not necessarily express itself in the arts.

The influence of psychological factors is equally inconclusive. Even though the Renaissance was an age of revolution in religion, astronomy, geography, literature, painting, sculpture, and commercial development, men felt that the social order was stable. In the twentieth century, by contrast, a feeling of unease about the future is chronic—despite the fact that four or five centuries ago private murders were much more common than now and nobody was safe out of doors at night. This suggests that a *feeling* of social stability may be a more important stimulus to cultural efflorescence than actual greater stability that is not apprehended.

The influence of technical developments is likewise unclear. There is no question that the Renaissance as a whole was stimulated and its influence increased by the historical accident that printing happened to be invented in the midst of it. Writers in particular were now able to address a vastly

[35] Chester G. Starr, *A History of the Ancient World* (N.Y.: Oxford Press, 1965), p. 319.

increased audience. Still, such developments are not *auto-matically* influential. An age has to be psychologically pre-pared to appreciate them. If Renaissance men appreciated movable type and the wondrous achievements being wrought in the fine arts, remarkably few of them were interested in the equally amazing machines sketched by Leonardo da Vinci and others. Even among the educated, only a handful of mathematicians and intellectual radicals paid much attention to the Copernican hypothesis for seventy-five years after Copernicus' death.[36]

Conclusions

It is extremely difficult to discover any formula which ac-counts for intellectual and artistic excellence. At least moder-ate economic prosperity seems essential, though vast wealth does not. Allegiance to a certain set of religious or philosophi-cal doctrines is sometimes an aid, but an excess seems clearly to stifle. Rigid adherence to prescribed standards seems inhibi-tory, but there is no evidence that complete freedom is neces-sarily stimulating. Public interest in the arts and acclaim for the artist, and patronage of the arts by the worldly prominent, seems definitely beneficial. Absolutist governments dedicated to a particular ideology and determined to impose it on their subjects seem unlikely to produce much of enduring cultural worth, though this does not appear to be true of simple, nonideological despotisms.

Beyond this one is reduced to guessing. Neither patrons nor a sympathetic public can *create* great art or give birth to artists. They can only encourage and develop such raw talent as already exists. The deeper reasons why a people, an area, or an age suddenly bring forth an abnormal number of outstand-ing thinkers, artists, and writers remain unknown. It is difficult even to imagine what *conditions* could produce an Aristotle,

---

[36] These points are discussed by Myron Gilmore, *The World of Human-ism, 1453–1517* (N.Y.: Harper & Bros., 1953), pp. 184, 230.

Dante, Da Vinci, Michelangelo, Shakespeare, Rembrandt, or Goethe. Interestingly, Renaissance Italians lived in one of history's most splendid eras culturally, and they knew it; but none of them could account for the phenomenon.

It is no easier to explain selective excellence. Why should English writers and architects have been consistently superior to English painters and sculptors for the past three or four centuries?

And how about cultural decline? In occasional particular cases, of course, the reason may be obvious. Byzantine culture suffered a mortal blow when the Byzantine Empire itself was destroyed by the barbarous Turks in 1453. The modest cultural achievements of the Carolingian Empire (751–888) were extinguished along with that empire by Viking raiders. Spanish and French wars in sixteenth century Italy and, perhaps, the Counter-Reformation as well, eventually depressed all aspects of Italian life. The Thirty Years War intensified an existing blight in Germany. But why did the brilliance of the ancient Greeks wane? Their Macedonian conquerors did not destroy their culture, but sought to spread it over most of the known world. Why did Spanish culture shine brightly at the onset of a political decline in the early seventeenth century and then fade when the decline deepened half a century later? Why did French culture dominate Europe for two and a half centuries despite extreme fluctuations in the political fortunes of the French state? Nobody knows. If laws governing the appearance of geniuses in history do exist, they remain undiscovered.

Bibliography

A book dealing with subjects as general as those considered in this volume is really based on whatever knowledge the author has been able to acquire in his whole career of study and teaching. Hence the list of books and articles that follows is not a bibliography in the conventional sense. It indicates only the sources of the quotations, portions of the factual information, and some of the ideas dealt with in the text. Nonetheless, the student who wishes to broaden and deepen his historical understanding could read with profit almost any of the works listed below.

Books

ADY, CECILIA M. *Lorenzo de Medici and Renaissance Italy*. London: English Universities Press, 1960.

ALBERTINI, LUIGI. *The Origins of the War of 1914*. 3 vols. London: Oxford Press, 1967.

ALBRECHT-CARRIE, RENE. *The Meaning of the First World War*. Englewood Cliffs, N.J.: Prentice-Hall, 1965.

ANGELL, NORMAN. *The Great Illusion*. N.Y.: Putnam's, 1933.

ARENDT, HANNAH. *On Revolution*. N.Y.: Viking Press, 1963.

ARISTOTLE. *Politics*.

ARON, RAYMOND. *The Century of Total War*. Boston: Beacon Press, 1955.

BARZUN, JACQUES. *Race: A Study in Superstition*. N.Y.: Harper and Row, 1965.

BELOFF, MAX. *The Age of Absolutism, 1660–1815*. N.Y.: Harper and Row, 1962.

BERLIN, ISAIAH. *Historical Inevitability*. N.Y.: Oxford Press, 1954.

BOORSTIN, DANIEL. *The Genius of American Politics*. Chicago: University Press, 1964.

BRINTON, CRANE. *Anatomy of Revolution.* N.Y.: Prentice-Hall, 1952.

BRINTON, CRANE. *Ideas and Men.* N.Y.: Prentice-Hall, 1950.

BROGAN, DENIS W. *The Price of Revolution.* N.Y.: Grosset and Dunlap, 1966.

BURCKHARDT, JACOB. *The Civilization of the Renaissance In Italy.* London: Allen and Unwin, 1937.

BURNHAM, JAMES. *The Machiavellians.* N.Y.: John Day Co., 1943.

BURNS, EDWARD MCNALL. *Western Civilization.* 2 vols. 6th ed. N.Y.: Norton, 1963.

BUTTERFIELD, HERBERT. *Man on His Past.* Cambridge: University Press, 1955.

————. *The Origins of Modern Science.* London: G. Bell, 1957.

————. *The Whig Interpretation of History.* N.Y.: Scribners, 1951.

CARR, E. H. *Studies In Revolution.* N.Y.: Grosset and Dunlap, 1964.

CHAMBERS, F. W. *The War Behind the War.* N.Y.: Harcourt, Brace & Co., 1939.

CHAPMAN, GUY. *The Dreyfus Case.* N.Y.: Reynal and Co., 1955.

CHAUNAU, H. P. *Seville and the Atlantic, 1504–1650.* Paris: A. Colin, 1955–59.

CHORLEY, KATHERINE. *Arms and the Art of Revolution.* London: Faber and Faber, 1943.

CHUDOBA, BOHDAN. *Spain and the Empire, 1519–1643.* Chicago: University of Chicago Press, 1952.

COWELL, F. R. *History, Civilization and Culture: An Introduction to the Historical and Social Philosophy of Pitirim Sorokin.* Boston: Beacon Press, 1952.

DANGERFIELD, GEORGE. *The Strange Death of Liberal England, 1910–1914.* N.Y.: Capricorn Books, 1961.

DAWSON, CHRISTOPHER. *Religion and the Rise of Western Culture.* Garden City, N.Y.: Doubleday, 1958.

DEHIO, LUDWIG. *The Precarious Balance.* N.Y.: Random House, 1965.

DOBZHANSKY, THEODOSIUS. *Heredity and the Nature of Man.* N.Y.: Harcourt, Brace and World, 1964.

EHLER, SIDNEY. *Twenty Centuries of Church and State.* Westminster, Md.: Newman Press, 1957.

ELLIOTT, J. H. *Imperial Spain, 1469–1716.* N.Y.: St. Martin's Press, 1964.

ERGANG, ROBERT. *The Myth of the All-Destructive Fury of the Thirty Years War.* Pocono Pines, Pa., 1956.

FERRERO, GUGLIELMO. *The Reconstruction of Europe.* N.Y.: Norton, 1963.

FLEMING, WILLIAM. *Art and Ideas.* N.Y.: Holt, Rinehart and Winston, 1963.

FORD, FRANKLIN L. *Robe and Sword: The Regrouping of the French Aristocracy After Louis XIV.* N.Y.: Harper and Row, 1965.

GAY, PETER. *Voltaire's Politics.* N.Y.: Vintage Books, 1965.

GEORGE, CHARLES H. *Revolution.* N.Y.: Dell, 1962.

GEYL, PIETER. *Debates With Historians.* The Hague: Martinus Nijhof, 1955.

_____. *Encounters In History.* N.Y.: World Publishing Co., 1961.

_____. *The Netherlands Divided, 1609–1648.* London: Williams and Norgate, 1936.

_____. *The Revolt of the Netherlands, 1555–1609.* London: Williams and Norgate, 1932.

GILL, ERIC. *Art.* N.Y.: Devin—Adair, 1950.

GILMORE, MYRON. *The World of Humanism, 1453–1517.* N.Y.: Harper and Bros., 1952.

GOERLITZ, WALTER. *History of the German General Staff, 1657–1945.* N.Y.: Praeger, 1953.

GREEN, ROBERT W., ed. *Protestantism and Capitalism.* Boston: D. C. Heath and Co., 1959.

GREENBERG, CLEMENT. *Art and Culture.* Boston: Beacon Press, 1961.

GUERARD, ALBERT. *France: A Modern History.* Ann Arbor, Michigan: University Press, 1959.

HARDACRE, PAUL. *The Royalists During the Puritan Revolution.* The Hague: Martinus Nijhof, 1956.

HAUSER, ARNOLD. *The Social History of Art*. Translated by Stanley Godman. 2 vols. N.Y.: Knopf, 1951.

HEIBER, HELMUT. *Adolf Hitler*. London: Oswald Wolff, 1961.

HELDMANN, KARL. *Das Kaisertum Karls der Grossen*. Weimar: Hermann Bohlaus Nochfolger, 1928.

HEXTER, J. H. *Reappraisals In History*. N.Y.: Harper and Row, 1963.

HINSLEY, F. H. *Power and the Pursuit of Peace*. Cambridge: University Press, 1963.

HOFFER, ERIC. *The True Believer*. N.Y.: Harper and Bros., 1951.

HOLLISTER, C. WARREN. *Roots of the Western Tradition*. N.Y.: John Wiley and Sons, 1966.

HOOK, SIDNEY. *The Hero In History*. N.Y.: Humanities Press, 1950.

HUGHES, PHILIP. *A Popular History of the Reformation*. Garden City, N.Y.: Hanover House, 1957.

HUMPHREYS, A. R. *The Augustan Age*. N.Y.: Harper and Row, 1963.

HUXLEY, ALDOUS. *The Devils of Loudun*. N.Y.: Harper and Row, 1959.

JASZI, OSKAR. *The Dissolution of the Hapsburg Monarchy*. Chicago: University Press, 1961.

JOUVENEL, BERTRAND DE. *On Power*. N.Y.: Viking Press, 1949.

KAHLER, ERIC. *The Meaning of History*. N.Y.: Meridian Books, 1968.

KANTOROWICZ, HERMANN. *The Spirit of British Policy*. London: Allen and Unwin, 1931.

KENNAN, GEORGE. *American Diplomacy, 1900–1950*. Chicago: University Press, 1951.

————. *Memoirs, 1925–1950*. Boston: Little, Brown and Co., 1967.

KLUCKHOHN, CLYDE. *Mirror for Man: The Relationship of Anthropology to Modern Life*. N.Y.: McGraw Hill, 1949.

LANGDON-DAVIES, JOHN. *Carlos: The King Who Would Not Die*. Englewood Cliffs, N.J.: Prentice-Hall, 1963.

LANGER, WILLIAM L. *European Alliances and Alignments.* N.Y.: Knopf, 1956.

LE BON, GUSTAVE. *The Psychology of Revolution.* N.Y.: Putnam's, 1913.

LUKACS, JOHN. *Historical Consciousness, or the Remembered Past.* N.Y.: Harper and Row, 1968.

———. *A New History of the Cold War.* N.Y.: Doubleday, 1966.

LYNCH, JOHN. *Spain Under the Hapsburgs.* Oxford: Blackwells, 1964.

MADARIAGA, SALVADOR DE. *Spain: A Modern History.* N.Y.: Creative Age Press, 1943.

MAGUIRE, JAMES J. *The Philosophy of Modern Revolution.* Washington: Catholic University Press, 1943.

MAJOR, RALPH N. *Disease and Destiny.* N.Y.: D. Appleton Century, 1936.

MATTINGLY, GARRETT. *The Armada.* Boston: Houghton Mifflin Co., 1959.

———. *Renaissance Diplomacy.* Baltimore: Penguin Books, 1964.

MAYER, MILTON S. *They Thought They Were Free: The Germans 1933–1945.* Chicago: University Press, 1966.

MCNEILL, WILLIAM. *Past and Future.* Chicago: University Press, 1964.

MILLER, JOHN C. *Sam Adams: Pioneer in Propaganda.* Boston: Little, Brown and Co., 1936.

MOLNAR, THOMAS. *Utopia: The Perennial Heresy.* N.Y.: Sheed and Ward, 1967.

MORISON, S. E. *Oxford History of the American People.* N.Y.: Oxford Press, 1965.

MOSSE, G. L. *Nazi Culture.* N.Y.: Grosset and Dunlap, 1966.

MULLETT, CHARLES. *The Bubonic Plague and England.* Lexington, Ky: University of Kentucky Press, 1956.

MURPHY, ROBERT. *Diplomat Among Warriors.* N.Y.: Pyramid Books, 1965.

MYRDAL, GUNNAR. *Asian Drama: An Inquiry Into the Poverty of Nations.* 3 vols. N.Y.: Pantheon, 1968.

NAMIER, LEWIS B. *Facing East.* N.Y.: Harper and Row, 1966.

NEF, JOHN U. *The Cultural Foundations of Industrial Civilization.* Cambridge: University Press, 1958.

————. *Western Civilization Since the Renaissance.* N.Y.: Harper and Row, 1963.

NEWMAN, BERTRAM. *Lord Melbourne.* London: Macmillan, 1930.

PALMER, R. R. *The Age of the Democratic Revolutions.* 2 vols. Princeton, N.J.: Princeton University Press, 1964.

————. *Twelve Who Ruled.* Princeton, N.J.: Princeton University Press, 1941.

PERKINS, J. B. *France Under the Regency.* Boston: Houghton Mifflin and Co., 1892.

PIRENNE, HENRI. *Mohammed and Charlemagne.* N.Y.: Norton, 1939.

PLATO. *Republic.*

QUIGLEY, CARROLL. *The World Since 1939: A History.* N.Y.: Collier Books, 1968.

REDDAWAY, W. F.; PENSON, J. H.; HALECKI, O.; AND DYBOSKI, R., EDS. *Cambridge History of Poland.* 2 vols. Cambridge: University Press, 1950.

REMAK, JOACHIM. *The Origins of World War I, 1871–1914.* N.Y.: Holt, Rinehart and Winston, 1967.

ROGGER, HANS, AND WEBER, EUGEN, EDS. *The European Right: A Historical Profile.* Berkeley: University of California Press, 1966.

ROSINSKI, HERBERT. *The German Army.* N.Y.: Praeger, 1966.

ROTH, CECIL. *The Spanish Inquisition.* N.Y.: Norton, 1964.

RUNCIMAN, STEVEN. *The Fall of Constantinople.* Cambridge: University Press, 1965.

SEAMAN, L. C. B. *From Vienna to Versailles.* N.Y.: Harper and Row, 1963.

SNYDER, LOUIS L. *The Idea of Racialism.* N.Y.: Van Nostrand, 1962.

SOREL, ALBERT. *Europe Under the Old Regime.* N.Y.: Harper and Row, 1964.

STARR, CHESTER G. *A History of the Ancient World.* N.Y.: Oxford Press, 1965.

SULLIVAN, MARK. *Our Times,* vol. 5. 6 vols. N.Y.: Scribners',
    1926–1935.

TAYLOR, A. J. P. *The Course of German History.* N.Y.: Coward-
    McCann, 1946.

————. *From Napoleon to Lenin.* N.Y.: Harper and Row, 1966.

TERRAINE, JOHN. *Ordeal of Victory.* N.Y.: Lippincott, 1963.

THOREAU, HENRY DAVID. *Walden.* N.Y.: J. M. Dent, Everyman's
    Library ed., 1962.

THUCYDIDES. *History of the Peloponnesia War.*

TIMASHEFF, NICHOLAS S. *War and Revolution.* N.Y.: Sheed and
    Ward, 1965.

TOCQUEVILLE, ALEXIS DE. *The Old Regime and the French Rev-
    olution.* Garden City, N.Y.: Doubleday, 1955.

TOYNBEE, ARNOLD. *A Study of History.* 12 vols. London: Oxford
    Press, 1934–1961.

TREVOR-DAVIES, R. *The Golden Century of Spain.* N.Y.: Harper
    and Row, 1965.

VAN TYNE, CLAUDE. *The Loyalists In the American Revolution.*
    Gloucester, Mass.: Peter Smith, 1959.

VIERECK, PETER. *Metapolitics: From the Romantics to Hitler.*
    N.Y.: Knopf, 1941.

WALTER, HANS-ALBERT. "Leopold Schwartzchild and the *Neue
    Tage Buch.*" *The Left Wing Intellectuals Between the Wars.*
    Edited by Walter Lacquer and George L. Mosse. N.Y.: Har-
    per Torchbooks, 1966.

WEDGWOOD, C. V. *The Thirty Years War.* N.Y.: Doubleday, 1961.

WEINBERG, ALBERT. *Manifest Destiny.* Baltimore: Johns Hopkins
    Press, 1935.

WELLS, H. G. *Experiment in Autobiography.* N.Y.: Macmillan,
    1934.

WHITE, R. J. *Europe in the 18th Century.* N.Y.: St. Martin's Press,
    1965.

WILSON, ARTHUR M. *Diderot: The Testing Years.* N.Y.: Oxford
    Press, 1957.

WILSON, FRANCESCA M. *Strange Island: Britain Through Foreign
    Eyes: 1395–1940.* N.Y.: Longmans, Green and Co., 1955.

WINGFIELD-STRATFORD, ESME. *Truth in Masquerade.* London:
    Williams and Norgate, 1951.

WOLFENSTEIN, E. VICTOR. *The Revolutionary Personality.* Princeton, N.J.: Princeton University Press, 1967.

WORDSWORTH, WILLIAM. *The Prelude or Growth of a Poet's Mind.* Oxford: Clarendon Press, 1959.

ZWEIG, STEFAN. *The World of Yesterday.* Lincoln: University of Nebraska Press, 1964.

Articles

BECKER, CARL. "What Are Historical Facts?" *Western Political Quarterly*, September, 1955.

BULLOCK, ALAN. "The Historian's Purposes: History and Metahistory." *History Today*, February, 1951.

COHEN, MORRIS R. "Causation and Its Application to History." *Journal of the History of Ideas* III, (1942).

GAGE, JOHN. "England In the Italian Renaissance." *History Today*, October, 1960.

GOODMAN, PAUL. "The Psychology of Being Powerless." *New York Review of Books*, November 3, 1966.

MCCARTHY, DENNIS J. "The Kalabalik." *History Today*, June, 1965.

NORWICH, JOHN JULIUS. "The Normans In the South." *History Today*, October, 1966.

PHILLIPS, W. A. P. "Chance and History: Nelson's Pursuit of Bonaparte, May–June, 1798." *History Today*, March, 1965.

WOODWARD, DAVID. "The Escape of the *Goeben* and *Breslau*, August, 1914." *History Today*, April, 1960.

Index